Conversations in the Abbey

Senior monks of Saint Meinrad reflect on their lives

Ruth Clifford Engs, Editor

Conversations in the Abbey

Ruth Clifford Engs, Editor

Table of Contents

Dedication

"Above all, the Abbot must not ignore or minimize the spiritual welfare of the lives entrusted to him."

Rule of St. Benedict 2:33

This work is dedicated to the seven abbots of Saint Meinrad under whom the various monks in this publication were formed or served:

Justin DuVall, OSB: 2004-present *2016*
Lambert Reilly, OSB: 1995-2004
Timothy Sweeney, OSB: 1978-1995
Gabriel Verkamp, OSB: 1966-1978
Bonaventure Knaebel, OSB: 1955-1966
Ignatius Esser, OSB: 1930-1955
Athanasius Schmitt, OSB: 1898-1932

Foreword

Reminiscing is a faculty proper to human beings. Dogs do not write histories. And history, it has been said, is not simply what happened; it is the way what happened is remembered. When we look back to recount the past, we therefore disclose something of who we are in the present.

This collection of remembrances by some of the senior monks of Saint Meinrad Archabbey offers the reader a slice of our history as well as a peek at our present. The monks interviewed form part of the living history, if you will, of the Archabbey and their individual recollections are colored by their particular experiences before entering the community and after they vowed themselves to remain here as monks of this house.

Needless to say, they did not found the community into which they professed themselves, and the community will continue after they themselves become the subject of recollections for monks currently too young to have known much more about this "greatest generation" and its times. The gaze backward must inevitably turn to the road that lies ahead.

But the recollections in this book are more than history, more even than the way what happened is remembered. The monks whose memories are recorded here are men of faith. They believe that God reveals himself in the circumstances of our lives, whether favorable or antagonistic. Faith is a condition of the way what happened is remembered, and while it does not necessarily alter the past, it does enlighten how we come to understand it in the present. For this reason memory has been key in the Judaeo-Christian tradition. The remembrances here are serious and humorous, profound and fleeting, joyous and sorrowful—in other words, they are the stuff of everyday life. They are also the witness to the continuous faithful search for God to which the monks who remembered have dedicated themselves.

In the course of her interviews with the monks, Professor Ruth Clifford Engs solicited the recollections that she subsequently shaped into the present volume. The three historical essays illustrate how the lives of each monk are interwoven with the history of Abbey Press, finance and development, and agricultural ventures of Saint Meinrad.

Her work preserves the memories of the past and gives a point of reference for the future. Though her perseverance and her professional skill, she has done us a great service.

To all who will read these pages and find your own memories stirred: may God enlighten you with faith to trace the lines of his hand at work throughout all the days of your lives.

Archabbot Justin DuVall, O.S.B.
Saint Meinrad Archabbey
July 11, 2007
Feast of St. Benedict

Preface

Introduction

This collection of interview profiles includes the reflections of men who have lived through much of the 20th century. They have experienced vast changes in society and the upheaval that has characterized much of the modern history of the Roman Catholic Church. The conversation profiles in this publication are from interviews with monks at Saint Meinrad Archabbey, a Benedictine monastery in southern Indiana. All monks in this publication were born in 1930 or before. In military history, this age group would be called the "greatest generation." At the beginning of 2007, the oldest of those interviewed was 106 years of age, the youngest, 76.

The Benedictine monastic tradition and way of life were begun by St. Benedict in what is now Nursia, Italy, in the early sixth century. The community has a tradition of hospitality and living a humble life. Many recent publications concerning monks and nuns have focused upon their spiritual and prayer life. However, the Benedictine lifestyle is a balance of both prayer and work with the motto, *ora et labora*. Both prayer and work are considered essential to the spiritual life, sustenance of the community and growth of the individual.

Therefore, this publication, in addition to spiritual reflections of each monk, will spend some pages on the *labora* of each monk and the community. Three historical essays focus on the work of the monastery: "Finances and Fund Raising," "Abbey Press" and "Land." These serve as a backdrop for the work of most of the monks interviewed for this publication.

Within the personal interviews of each monk, observations concerning his childhood, early life in the monastic community, career, spiritual life, and reflections on changes in the Church and monastic community, pre- and post-Vatican II, are discussed. Within these comments, little homilies and words of wisdom are found. All speak of the triumphs and crises that have marked Church history in the past six or more decades.

The History and Process of this Project

The oral history of "senior monks" was originally conceived by the late Edward L. Shaughnessy, a former seminarian at Saint Meinrad College and retired professor from Butler University. After obtaining permission to interview senior monks from Abbot Lambert Reilly, OSB, Shaughnessy began the interviewing process during the summer and fall of 2004. However, he died unexpectedly in January 2005. In the summer of 2005, the editor, Ruth Clifford Engs, a semi-retired Indiana University professor and an oblate (lay member and volunteer) of the Saint Meinrad community, was given permission by the new abbot, Rt. Rev. Justin DuVall, OSB, to continue the project.

Shaughnessy interviewed three monks in this publication before his death. The editor also interviewed these monks to ask additional questions not on Shaughnessy's original questionnaire. For these monks, the interview transcriptions by both Shaughnessy and Engs were used as the resources for the monks' comments. Although all monks were asked the same questions, some chose not to answer some of them. In other cases, they diverged from the questions but added interesting historical material that was included in their interview profiles.

The interviews were recorded on audiotape and then transcribed by the editor and other individuals. The transcription was condensed for this publication. In a few cases, material from essays concerning memoirs of an individual monk was used as part of the interview profile. References to these are found at the bottom of the interview. The complete raw transcriptions and essays written by the monks are found in the Saint Meinrad archives. In these complete transcriptions, details concerning printing operations, the history of the library, composing chant in English, the Civil Rights Movement, Rome in Pope John XXIII's era, and other material can be found.

The editor distilled the essence of various conversations and comments of each monk from the much longer transcription. This condensed and edited version was given to the individual for his review, comments and changes. Copyediting was then accomplished by Mary Jeanne Schumacher, the director of communications for Saint Meinrad Archabbey.

Personal Reflections from the Editor

I first went to Saint Meinrad Archabbey on a retreat around 1997. Needless to say, my stereotype of the monks spending much of their day isolated in their cells praying was quickly shattered. In fact, most of the monks with whom I have had a chance to interact with, or interview, lead—even in retirement—active, fulfilling and productive lives. Yes, they have dedicated their lives to God and the Church, and have taken vows of stability, obedience and *conversatio* (the monastic way of life), but this does not mean that they are not fun-loving, vibrant individuals.

The monks of Saint Meinrad are extremely talented in their chosen fields and avocations. Many have advanced academic degrees and are internationally known in their fields as artists, academics, musicians, scholars, writers and lecturers. They live life with a purpose and daily strive for balance between work and prayer. Because they do not have to take time out to pay the bills, cook their dinners or wash their clothes, they have time to pursue their careers and individual talents to the maximum. Although they take a vow of stability—remaining with this particular monastic community for their whole lives—many have traveled widely or lived in other countries or communities for years before their retirement, when they then come home.

In the life stories of most of the monks interviewed, doubt, uncertainty, disappointments, struggle and the "dark night of the soul" have been experienced, just as they have been experienced by most of us; this is the human condition. On the other hand, perseverance, accomplishments, peak experiences, lessons learned from failures, resolution of conflicts, and the telling of a life filled with challenges and continued striving for humility, the love of God and the Church, and peace emerge from these most inspiring and talented men. It has been a privilege and a great honor to be able to interview, and interact with, the senior monks of Saint Meinrad.

Ruth Clifford Engs, Editor
February 10, 2007
Feast of St. Scholastica

$\mathcal{A}$cknowledgements

Like most books, this publication could not have been accomplished without the help of many individuals. First of all, I would like to thank Abbot Justin DuVall; his secretary, Fr. Julian Peters; and the prior, Fr. Tobias Colgan; for their support and encouragement of the continuation of the project. I am also grateful to all the monks profiled in this publication for engaging in the interviews.

Invaluable advice and comments have come from my advisory committee. They include Fathers Meinrad Brune, oblate director; Simeon Daly, the former librarian; Cyprian Davis, the archivist; and Harry Hagan, who translated from Latin the quotations from the *Rule of St. Benedict*. I would also like to thank other monks at Saint Meinrad who have been most helpful and hospitable in the development of this project, including Brothers Maurus Zoeller, Terence Griffin and Dominic Warnecke and Fathers Louis Mulcahy, Joseph Cox, Gabriel Hodges and Augustine Davis. A special thanks to Abbot Bonaventure Knaebel, who reviewed the manuscript.

Various co-workers at Saint Meinrad have been very helpful, including Monica Corcoran, Ruth Denning, Mary Ellen Seifrig and Daniel Kolb of the Archabbey Library; John Wilson of the Business Office; Daniel Schipp, Mary Jeanne Schumacher, Janet Werne, Jo Bishop and John Farless of the Development Office; Brenda Ubelhor of the Oblate Office; and Pat Clark and Janet Braunecker of Physical Facilities. I am especially indebted to Gerald Wilhite of Abbey Press and his staff, including Norma Schipp, and Human Resources Director Mike Gramelspacher for information concerning Abbey Press. Thanks, also, to Gary Guy for his assistance.

In addition, I appreciate the support of the Reference Library at Indiana University, and the Department of Applied Health Sciences and

School of Health, Physical Education and Recreation for its continued support of my research. I am appreciative of Jain Liu, who took the current photographs of the monks, and Father Anthony Vinson for the cover photograph. Lastly, I would like to thank my husband, Jeffery Franz, for just being there.

Chapter One

Fr. Cyprian Davis, OSB

As a Benedictine monk of Saint Meinrad, Fr. Cyprian has several major responsibilities: professor of Church history in the School of Theology (1982-present), and the archivist for the Archabbey (1963-present), the Swiss-American Congregation of Benedictines (1978-present), and the National Black Catholic Clergy Caucus.

Born September 9, 1930, in Washington, D.C., Fr. Cyprian made his first profession as a monk August 1, 1951, his solemn profession August 1, 1954, and was ordained May 3, 1956. He graduated from Saint Meinrad College (1954) and completed theological training at the School of Theology. Fr. Cyprian received his STL in theology (1957) from Catholic University of America, Washington, D.C., and the licentiate in historical studies (1963) and doctorate in historical sciences (1977) from Catholic University, Louvain, Belgium. He served as assistant spiritual director at Saint Meinrad College (1965-67).

Fr. Cyprian has been awarded several honorary doctoral degrees for his research and writings concerning black Catholics. He has numerous publications including the popular *History of Black Catholics in the United States* (1990) and was editor for *To Prefer Nothing to Christ: Saint Meinrad Archabbey, 1854-2004* (2004). During the Civil Rights era, he participated in the March on Washington and the March in Selma, and was a founding member of the National Black Catholic Clergy Caucus.

Fr. Cyprian was interviewed by Prof. Ruth C. Engs on November 14, 2005.

Childhood and Early Years as a Monk

Tell me about your family.

I was born Clarence William Davis, Jr. in Washington, D.C. in 1930. My father was Clarence W. Davis, Sr. He was born in Hartford, Connecticut, and was a professor, first at Howard University in Washington, D.C., and then at the University of District of Columbia. My father was a professor of health and physical education. My mother originally was from Washington, D.C.; her name was Evelyn Jackson Davis. She was a school teacher and taught physical education in the elementary schools.

I had one sister; she is now deceased. Both my parents are deceased. My sister's name was Evelyn R. Davis Gardiner, then Evelyn Beckford. Most of her life, she lived in California and was a school teacher in Richmond, California, which is in the Bay Area.

How important was religion in your family as a child?

I am a convert to Catholicism; I became a Catholic when I was 15. One of the reasons why I became a Catholic was that I was very much impressed by the fact that the Catholic Church was the oldest Church, and I loved to read history. I read all about the Middle Ages and Catholicism, so I became a Catholic. My parents were not at all happy about it in the beginning.

Why?

My mother was a Presbyterian, although her father had been born a Catholic. One of the areas where blacks are traditionally Catholic is southern Maryland, because of the Jesuits' slave holding. His family was originally from southern Maryland, and so my mother was baptized a Catholic, but when my grandfather left the Church, my mother grew up as a Presbyterian. My uncle, her brother, was about 11 years old when they broke with the Catholic Church, but he remained a Catholic. He was the one who took me to Mass for the first time.

My father considered himself to be what, at that time, was called a Congregationalist. He became a Baptist at the behest of his mother. When I was growing up, my parents hardly ever went to church. My mother became a Catholic when I entered the monastery, and she became a very, very devout Catholic.

Tell me about your early schooling.

It was a time of racial segregation. All the schools I went to were public schools in Washington, D.C., and they were schools of all black students. I graduated from high school in 1948 and during that summer came out here for a visit. After I graduated from high school, I went one year to Catholic University in Washington, D.C.

What influenced you to become a monk?

I had read about monks in history and I was very much interested in becoming a monk. I used to go out to the English Benedictine monastery, which at that time was St. Anselm's Priory. A friend of mine said, "Why don't you write to various religious orders? They will send you all kinds of material." I thought that would be a good idea, so I did. One of the places I sent for information was to a Benedictine abbey. My friend said, "Well, you'd better explain to them that you are black." This was in the 1940s, and it was still a period of racial segregation. Many religious orders did not accept blacks, just like many of the dioceses didn't accept black priests.

I did explain in my letter that I was a Negro—in those days we were Negroes—but that I very much wanted to be Benedictine. I got an answer back and it said, "That's a very nice idea." But at that time, I was not yet baptized. They encouraged me to be baptized, but said, "The best thing to do is to join the Josephites." The Josephites were a religious community that worked for the evangelization of blacks. It was obvious they did not want to accept someone who was black. This was very ironic, in one sense, because I knew that, historically, this community had had some Negroes as monks. Their response made me so angry and I said, "I will never be Benedictine."

Then why did you come to Saint Meinrad, a Benedictine community?

At home in Washington, I had gotten to know a woman quite well who was a professor at Catholic University. She had a student who was from Saint Meinrad. He was always telling her what a wonderful place it was. One day she asked him, "Would they accept a Negro at Saint Meinrad?" He wasn't sure, but said he wanted to meet me. I met him and he began to talk to me about going to Saint Meinrad. He spoke about the fact that, if you wanted liturgy, this was the place to come for it. Later, when I started to talk about coming to Saint Meinrad, I was told by one friend that I shouldn't even think about it because Saint Meinrad is in southern Indiana and they would never accept blacks.

The monk who had invited me out here was Fr. Gerard Ellspermann, who was a doctoral candidate at Catholic University. I persuaded my parents to let me come here for a visit. I think my father was very leery about this, as southern Indiana was the South. It had its Jim Crow laws, except that they were never publicized. They didn't have signs; you had to know where you could go and where you couldn't go. But it was decided that I could come out here for a visit. I came by train to Louisville. It was one of the first places I ever saw "colored" and "white" reading rooms.

Fr. Kiefer, whom I knew as a seminarian at Theological College at Catholic University, met me in Louisville. He said he would need to make a retreat at West Baden, which at that time was a Jesuit seminary. He was going to bring me to Saint Meinrad on Sunday evening and then pick me up at the end of the week. I got here, but I was very unhappy. The atmosphere of the place just weighed me down; I wanted to leave. I really wanted to leave, but it wasn't possible because he was gone for the week.

However, by the end of the week, I had made many friends. The monks had been so kind; it was really wonderful and I was determined to come back here. What was interesting was that there were already two black brothers here. Neither one of them stayed, but they were here at that time. When I was ready to leave, the abbot, Ignatius Esser, came over and said to me, "Are we going to see you again?" I said, "I would like to come back." By doing that, of course, the abbot was indicating that this place was not closed to someone coming in who was black.

What was your family's reaction when you told them you were considering becoming a monk?

My folks were not happy about me coming here, as they thought that I should finish college. They wanted me to, at least, get a bachelor's degree because I'd gotten a scholarship. I did enter as a freshman at Catholic University in the fall of 1948. But this was also the time of the Korean War. My parents were very conscious of the fact that, although I would probably get a deferment, nevertheless, it was the Korean War. Most people don't realize that it was a very terrible war. Because of the war, I think they probably felt they might as well just let me come here. I stayed one year at Catholic University and then I entered what was then called the Minor Seminary in the fall of 1949; the following year, I entered the monastery.

Did your parents visit?

My mother came for my novitiate investiture and she was very, very happy. She really liked Saint Meinrad; and my father actually did, too. Abbot Ignatius was extremely kind to my parents. It's thanks to him, I'm sure, that I was accepted at Saint Meinrad. As I have mentioned, other religious orders and other Benedictine houses did not accept blacks at that time. That says a lot about him, which people don't always recognize. When the two black men who came before me did not stay, and then I did stay, I think I was a phenomenon, as many people probably thought I would not stay.

At that time, Saint Meinrad was in a Southern culture. There were certainly a lot of interesting ideas people had about blacks. African-Americans today would say that it was slightly racist. I would say, however, "There's no need to go into all that." It was nothing official and it was certainly not on the part of the superiors.

Who was your novice master?

Meinrad Hoffman. He was a dear man, but he was very austere and certainly believed in humility. The only way you are going to have humility is to have humiliations. He kept insisting that I did not have the kind of spirit I should have, that I didn't like to work and things like that. But in the end, I did persevere and he was very happy. We certainly parted friends. He was very much impressed by my mother and was extremely kind to her. I graduated from the college in 1954. Interestingly enough, when the time came for me to be ordained, it was decided that I would prepare to teach.

How did you feel about that?

I was very, very happy. I was to go into history and this is what I wanted to do. In 1956, I was the first black ever to be ordained a monk here at Saint Meinrad. I was sent to Catholic University in Washington, D.C., in the fall to get an STL [Licentiate in Sacred Theology]. At that time, the Theology Department here was affiliated with Catholic

University. We spent our last two semesters there. I passed the examinations—which was an oral and a written examination—and received an STL. I was very happy at Catholic University; it worked out very well. I came home in 1957 and I taught Western Civilization for one year in the college.

Discuss the earlier organization of daily life, the horarium. How did it differ compared to today?

When I entered the monastery in 1950, we were still under the old horarium. We would have the full office with Matins and Lauds, which were always said together, at four o'clock in the morning. Then Prime, Terce, Sext, None, Vespers and Compline, plus the conventual Mass. Of course, if you were a priest, you said your own private Mass. If you were a cleric, you might be called to serve a private Mass. It was a very busy day from a liturgical point of view.

These things changed. First of all, there was a change in the daily Office at the time of the Second Vatican Council. In fact, before

Fr. Cyprian, as a young monk.

Vatican II, the office of Prime had been suppressed. After Vatican II, we only had one midday office and not the three hours of Terce, Sext and None. Compline [in the evening] was said privately.

What expectations did you have of being a monk and have they, by and large, been fulfilled?

In terms of my life, looking back on it, my own concept of being a Benedictine monk is that a Benedictine should be a scholar. I don't think

I'm a scholar; I don't know if I belong in their league. But when you talk about what a monk does, there is the Benedictine tradition of scholarship. Part of *ora et labora* [prayer and work] for the scholar is just that. Scholarship is toil and it is of value and I think I'm part of that tradition. I'm very happy that I had that opportunity at Saint Meinrad and I also think that I have made a contribution to the history of the Catholic Church in this country.

Work

Tell me more about your work career.

I was assigned to go to Europe, to Louvain, and it was exactly what I wanted and had hoped for. I was the first monk from Saint Meinrad who went to Louvain. Up to that time, if monks were sent abroad, most of the time they went to Rome. When I went to Louvain, I stayed in the Abbey, which at that time was the Abbey of Mont-César. The Flemish form of the monastery is Keizersberg, but at that time, this monastery was French-speaking. My going to Louvain was, of course, a turning point in my life.

At that time, the University of Louvain was well known for the study of history. They trained you to be a scholar and to teach. You were not taught what to teach, but how to become a historian. It gave an orientation to my whole life, in a sense, and I appreciated that.

Describe your experiences there.

I was at the University of Louvain just at the time when all the changes in the Church occurred. I was there when John XXIII was elected Pope. I arrived in the fall of 1958 just after the death of Pope Pius XII. I think I was pretty naïve for the first year I was there. I never realized what an extraordinary thing was going to happen. I learned a lot at the University of Louvain. I learned how to speak French. I learned to be a scholar and how to do research. I think the students with whom I studied were, in many ways, extraordinary, too, because we worked together.

That was the best thing for me. Other classes were not that cooperative with each other; but with these fellow students, I was able to accomplish a lot because they were willing to sit down and explain to me what the assignments were and how to do them.

I learned an immense amount, more than I even realized now looking back at it, about an attitude toward scholarship. The man under whom I wrote was one of the international scholars in medieval history. That was my field, Medieval Church History. Now the extraordinary thing is that, ultimately, it took me ten years to get the doctorate. I did not get it in one fell swoop. I entered in 1958; by 1963, five years later, I had finished the work for the licentiate in history. I got started with what was to be my dissertation, which was to look at the *familia* at the Abbey of Cluny, beginning 909 to about 1350. My whole idea was to look at all the members of the community of Cluny who were not monks.

Who were not monks?

That's right. In other words, "Who were the non-monks, the *familia*, who belonged to the household?" At that time, I was interested in the origin of the lay brothers. We realized that if one tried to find out how the lay brothers originated in the evolution of monastic history, we would need to look for members of the household who evolved into the modern lay brothers.

I had a lot of help. The thing that impressed me so very much was that these Benedictine scholars were willing to sit down and talk to you. I met the men who were perhaps the last generation of real Benedictine monastic scholars. I lived in the monastery where the abbot was Bernard Capelle, a great liturgical historian, and also Bernard Botte, who was certainly one of the great liturgical scholars—he wound up acting as one of the *periti* [experts] at the Second Vatican Council. These were people who were willing to talk with you. I learned a lot from them, very simple men, you know, but really great scholars. That was good training for me, just seeing how these men lived and talked, and how open they were. They were not at all pompous in any way at all.

9

After you had finished your course work, what happened then?

I came back after five years without a doctorate, but with a licentiate, back to Washington, D.C., in the summer of 1963. I was able to have some vacation at home with my parents before I came out here to Saint Meinrad. I came back in the full throes of the Civil Rights Movement. I arrived in August at the time Martin Luther King had organized the March on Washington. I took part in that march. That was certainly a historic moment. I realize what a great opportunity it was for me to have been present for that event.

What were some of your remembrances of the march?

I had always remained good friends with the monks of St. Anselm. Years later, when I was a monk of Saint Meinrad, they would ask me if I had been refused admission to their community. I told them I never got to the point where I felt free enough to ask them if they would accept me, a black man. They ran a school, which was very well known, very good and definitely all white.

I felt they would probably say, "No, they would love to have me as a member of the community, but, you know, things being what they are." So I never got to the point of asking them. Also, because I thought if they refused me, I would feel that I couldn't go back there and I still wanted to go there for Vespers. So, at any rate, an interesting thing happened. During the morning of the march, I went to Mass at St. Patrick's Church in downtown Washington. The abbot of St. Anselm was there with a lot of monks. By that time, it was an abbey.

I remember also seeing Senator Ed Muskie. He ran for president. He was from Maine and was Catholic. He was outside with the group of people who were forming for the march at St. Patrick's Church. It was interesting. It was extraordinary. All kinds of people were there, people whom I thought were never at all interested in the question of racial segregation. So it was an extraordinary moment, an extraordinary moment. When I got back here to Saint Meinrad, I began to teach.

Tell me about your teaching experience.

That first year was hard. I taught for almost 14 hours. I taught in the college and in the theology school. I taught French because, at that time, they needed a French teacher to replace Fr. Hilary [Ottensmeyer, OSB], who had become president-rector of the college. I also started to teach, perhaps not the first year, Church history and then theology. Later on, they began to hire lay teachers. When this happened, our teaching load became like other graduate-level schools. We had a class load of six or eight hours at the most. This was taken for granted. Also, we had a sabbatical of one semester off every four years.

From 1963 until 1968, when I was teaching here, all kinds of things were happening, as this was the '60s. These were the turmoil years. What so many of us didn't realize is that we were living through very momentous times, not only for the country and the whole world, but also with the Church and with the Vatican Council; it was a fascinating time. Fr. Adrian [Fuerst, OSB] became president-rector of the School of Theology and we shifted in the way we taught. We changed to team teaching. We did a great deal of experimentation. It was done well, although it was very, very confusing. We were almost in the forefront of seminary education at that time.

At this time, a lot of problems began here. The death of key people, including Kieran Conley and Barnabas Harrington, resulted in problems. There was a division in the community based on where one stood on theological positions. We had a shift in our way of looking at monasticism. It was decided that we should stop having private Mass. But a whole group of young monks, like myself, thought we should have private Masses in addition to the conventual Mass where all the monks, including priests, would receive communion. This created quite a rift, even to the point of a *monitum* [warning] coming from the Apostolic Delegate.

What else?

Many other things were happening in the '60s. Martin Luther King, Jr. was continuing nonviolent demonstrations in Selma [Alabama]. In '65, he made a rather historic call for all clergy to come down to Selma and put their lives on the line for the cause of civil rights. Fr. Camillus Ellspermann, who was the brother of Gerard, said to me, "We're going down to Selma." Abbot Bonaventure had given permission for this. I said, "I was surprised that Abbot Bonaventure would ever do that." But he had given his permission to go to Selma. He said that any of the monks who wished could go. Fr. Camillus said, "Do you want to go?" And at first, I said, "No, I can't go. I have all these commitments. I can't go to Selma." That was the time when things were getting very, very dangerous.

Then I realized that I had to go. I couldn't very well let Fr. Camillus, a white man, go down and I stay back, so I decided that I was also going to go, so I said, "Yes." Camillus also asked Fr. Terence Girkin and Fr. Lawrence Ward—both of whom left the monastery later on. He asked a black minister from Evansville, IN, whose name was King, but no relation to Martin Luther King. So all of us went down together. We started at about five o'clock and drove all night and got to Selma the next morning. The day we arrived was the day in which the Unitarian minister was shot and killed.

We stayed at the parish run by the Edmundite Fathers that was for black Catholics. That was another extraordinary experience. There's no question that my experience in Selma was a basic, fundamental turning point in my life. We were kind of heroes. All of what was going on in Selma at that time was front-page news. Of course, it wasn't just political; it was also for social religious justice. The sisters who were there demonstrated in full habit. Archbishop Toolen, the archbishop of Mobile, said that clergy should not come down, but everybody ignored him and they came by the carloads. I was there when President Johnson announced that he was introducing legislation with regard to civil rights for voting rights and other things we were marching for. He gave his famous talk to Congress where he said, "We shall overcome." I was there!

We were on the line [clergy were on the front line between the marchers and police] when he made that announcement. We were also the foreign correspondents for *The Evansville Courier*. We would get on the telephone and tell them in Evansville what was happening. So we were in the newspaper. We arrived back about the middle of March. When we drove back, we spent overnight in Memphis. I called my folks, and my sister—who was always making remarks—said, "I'm proud of you." It was extraordinary. When we came back here, we had Mass with the whole student body. We talked and it was like a spiritual revival.

Everyone who went down there and who stayed at the parish—all the Catholic priests and nuns—saw this as a retreat, more than a retreat, it was a revival. People knew what they were doing and they knew why they were doing it. There was an element of heroism and danger because Mrs. Viola Liuzzo was also shot and killed after we left. So that whole experience was a turning point historically, especially in the history of the Catholic Church in this country.

Was this the experience that led you to focus on black Catholics?

People kept asking me about being black and Catholic and about the history of black Catholics. What was their story? My field was the Medieval Church in the Middle Ages. Having a professor who was one of the leading scholars in that area was what I wanted. I did not want to study American history. I didn't want to study about slavery stuff and all that.

However, I'd been at the American Catholic Historical Association meeting and I was chatting with John Tracy Ellis, the dean of American Catholic historians. I had never studied under Ellis; we just exchanged pleasantries. He was a very nice man. He said, "You know, the sad thing is that we just don't have any facts, any documentation in terms of history of black Catholics; it's not there. It's tragic." The thing about being a student at Louvain was that you've always got records. You were taught that there were always records. You have to look for them; you have to dig them out, but they are there. That was certainly the way you were trained to do research there—search out and find the sources.

I wanted desperately to get the doctorate. I wanted to write the dissertation I was writing. However, I had come to realize how important the history of black Catholics was and I had become very interested in this whole issue. Because it's true; very little had been written about black Catholic history. There were two volumes that had appeared in the 1930s by John T. Gillard, SSJ, and that was practically all you had. However, some things happened. Martin Luther King was assassinated in April of 1968. Riots took place after the assassination of King and they were burning places down everywhere.

That spring, a meeting of the Midwest Catholic Clergy Conference for Interracial Justice was slated to take place in Detroit, where they had just had a very serious riot. This group had been founded for white Catholic priests working in African-American neighborhoods. About a year or two before, they began to invite black priests. A call was sent out to all black priests by a guy named Herman Porter, with the Diocese of Joliet, who was a black diocesan priest. Porter said that Mayor Daley had insisted that they were going to stop the rioting and they were going to shoot to kill. Porter said that black priests had a duty to make a protest and to do something about this shooting of black youths.

He wanted us to come a day early to the Midwest Catholic Clergy Conference meeting. So we had this meeting and called it the Black Catholic Clergy Caucus, to decide what we were going to do as black priests. This was the first time black priests in the United States had ever come together as a body and had ever sat down and talked about their lives. It was a historic moment. The guy who chaired it was Herman Porter. An oblate of this monastery from the Chicago archdiocese, Rollins Lambert, was more or less the moderator.

As I listened to people, I discovered that many of these men had real grievances. They had a lot of bitterness and felt they had been treated very badly by their community and their superiors. They felt that racism was rampant, and they were angry. It was really consciousness-building. So many were angry. One of the guys kept saying, "Cyprian, Cyprian, get up and say something." I told him that I was not getting up and saying anything, because the people who were getting up were making the atmosphere very, very tense.

One guy who stood up was an elderly man who, in fact, was the oldest black Catholic priest there. His name was Fr. Norman DuKette. The family was from the Washington area and he had known my grandfather. It was an old black Catholic family. He was, at the time, from the Flint-Lansing Diocese, but was originally from the Diocese of Detroit. He had some words of wisdom. He was trying to tell us to calm down, even though he had been treated very badly and had gone through really hard times. The group should have stood up and given him an ovation and recognized who he was. He was the dean of us all. But everyone was so angry; every one of us were Malcolm Xs. They were practically calling him an Uncle Tom, and it really was wrong. Because this man, from a historical point of view, this man was one of the great ones.

Harold Perry, a bishop, was also calling for moderation, peace, reconciliation and so forth. Larry Lucas, a firebrand, a priest of the Diocese of New York, said the ideal had to be, not Martin Luther King, but Malcolm X. That's where we had to make our stand. Perry was saying that Martin Luther King was against violence and Lucas was saying, "He's dead, isn't he? Dead. That's what nonviolence got for him. It's over! Nonviolence is over!" They were screaming at each other, so Perry left. It was decided that we draw up a manifesto—a statement to the bishops—which we had to sign.

I began to think, what am I going to do? The abbot knew that I was supposed to go to the Midwest Catholic Clergy Conference for Interracial Justice. He didn't know about this other meeting, and here I was supposed to sign this manifesto that had ten points. One was that the Roman Catholic Church in the United States is a white racist institution. And I remember thinking, "How can we say that the Catholic Church is a white racist institution? The Church is the Bride of Christ." I remember that I was glad to use an example from history. I said to myself—I was also rehearsing what I was going to say to the abbot—"That historically we know that the Catholic Church, in some places and in some moments of her history, has been corrupt."

So I would be able to simply say to the abbot, "Well, in this branch of the Roman Catholic Church, we can say it's racist." The Church as a whole is not racist. The Church is the Bride of Christ. So I went up and signed with a clear conscience, figuring that's what I could tell him. Well, when I got back home, Abbot Bonaventure never asked me anything about it. I don't even think he knew. Other people knew that I had signed this manifesto.

At the caucus meeting, a decision was made to make the caucus a permanent body called the Black Catholic Clergy Caucus. I'm still a member of it and I'm one of the founding members. It's had its ups and downs, but it is interesting that it came out of the Civil Rights Movement in the context of the Catholic Church. In September, I went back to Louvain to work on my dissertation.

What happened when you went back to Louvain?

At Louvain, for a doctorate in history, you have to be prepared to defend your thesis and then you had to be prepared to defend a supplementary thesis. It didn't have to be written out, but it was supposed to be in an area totally divorced from the written dissertation. Now, I suddenly realized that I had my supplementary thesis. There was a weekly newspaper called the *American Catholic Tribune* begun by Daniel Rudd of Cincinnati in 1889. It was the first, and really the only, long-lived black Catholic newspaper. It had sponsored several National Catholic Colored Congresses for black Catholics. Names and a synopsis of the various congresses were there. This was the beginning, even if I didn't realize it, for my life work.

What I learned at Louvain is that once you've got names, then you can begin the trail. And that's what I did. At least I had a supplementary thesis. I got to go back to Louvain in '75, '76 and then July of '77, I submitted my thesis and defended it. I defended it in French. It passed; it was not stellar, but it passed. The highest ranking that you can get is *une grande distinctione avec l'applaudissement de jury*. That's when everyone stands up and claps. The jury came out and gave me a grand distinction, but they clapped anyway!

They didn't ask me any questions about the supplementary thesis, although it was on their program. When I came back to the United States, I realized that the supplementary thesis on black Catholics is what I was going to have to publish, because people were asking, "What is the history of black Catholics?"

I began working on it. I got a telephone call around 1983 from a guy named Lawrence Mamiya, a Japanese, who was an assistant to C. Eric Lincoln, a black professor of religion and culture at Duke University. He called me on behalf of Lincoln and wanted to know if I would be willing to do something in terms of the black Catholic Church. He said that Lilly [Foundation] was funding a whole program on black Church history. Abbot Timothy and the superiors were in open support of any kind of scholarship we did. I was up for sabbatical and the abbot said that they would give me, in addition, a leave of one semester off. So, I got the time off to publish this book.

Where did you go to collect the data?

I knew I would have to go to St. Augustine, FL. That's where the first Catholics arrived. In the archives, they've got baptismal registers going back to the 16th century. In these, the Spanish always indicated race. If a person was black and they were a slave, it was in the margin. If they were black and were free, it was in the margin. So everyone was identified. As soon as you've got people, you've got relationships, you've got society, and that's a fact to this day. The other thing is, obviously, I was going to go to Europe. If you're going to do the history of black Catholics, where do you go? You go to Rome.

Rome?

The Catholic Church is about the oldest bureaucracy in the world. Every bureaucracy has archives and perhaps the oldest archives in the world are the Vatican archives. I had received access. It's not easy to just walk off the street and enter the Vatican archives. I can't remember who it was, but someone had to write a letter for you to get a request for access. I arrived in Rome and met one of the assistant archivists, a Scot, and told him what I was doing. I was told that I would have to look through the finding aids. Those covered a whole wall! Well, the fact of the matter was, I didn't have that much time.

The next day I came back and this priest told me, "You're in luck, the Apostolic Delegation in Washington, D.C., has finally sent over all its archives to be deposited here. But they're in the process of going through and inventorying them." He then said, "There's a young Italian assistant archivist who was drawing up the inventory. I'll introduce you to him and, whatever he has completed, you can see."

The young man was very kind. He said, "You can look at whatever I have up to the point of 1922." So he gave me the inventory list and said, "All you have to do is ask for an entire box." He told the employees to bring the boxes down. There was plenty in the folders to study. The papers were extraordinary. I discovered at least two thick folders that talked about the condition of black Catholics. I was the first person to use these files since they had been created. It was brand new territory and it was enough. I realized I had my book. I then went to Paris to the Bibliothèque nationale de France. It's very important because of a collection of Modernist documents. Among these records is the journal of John R. Slattery, the first general of the Josephites. Then I returned home.

One of the things we were reminded at Louvain was that the time would come when you've just got to stop the research and begin writing. So I did. I wrote the book. It was published by Crossroad and it got an award. Here was a book on black Catholics. It was the only thing available and it's still in print.

I've met blacks and they'll say to me how grateful they are because of this book. They now know the answer to, "Where do we come from? What is our story?" They never had this before. The history of the Catholic Church in the United States wouldn't be what it is without black

Catholics. It is extraordinary. We are as much a community as the Irish community or the Italian or Hungarian communities. It's a community that has made its imprint on who we are as a Church.

Prayer

What do you think is important in terms of Benedictine spirituality to convey to younger monks, or even the laity?

I want to say right off, I am a historian. I am very, very happy that, in the period of uncertainty and in the period of confusion and anger [the 1960s], I was able to bring the background of Church history. It seems to me that understanding the history of the Church helps one understand why we have had changes and that we have always had changes. If we change, what did we change in keeping with our traditions? Church historians are able to point to the long, long history of the Church—a history which at times has been very colorful and at times has been rather tragic. Nevertheless, we bring to it a knowledge of the Church's passage through the centuries.

In terms of being a monk, a Benedictine monk, who traditionally have been the historians of the Church, I think I was able to bring an understanding of what really is the charism of the monk in his or her own time—who we are as a Church, where we come from, what our traditions are and, therefore, a better understanding of where we are going. That's what I always convey to my students—the importance of history. That means the total history, not just a snippet here and there, but as much as possible an understanding of the whole history of the Church.

What is your most favorite part of the Rule*?*

I don't think about it in that way. The *Rule of Benedict* is an extraordinary document. Here, again, it's a question of knowing the historical background of the *Rule*. This includes how it was composed and the many things that we've learned in more recent times regarding its development—for example, the influence of the *Rule of the Master* on the *Rule* composed by St. Benedict himself.

The chapters of the *Rule of Benedict* that mean a whole lot to me are Chapter Seven on humility and the next-to-the-last chapter, Chapter 72 on fraternity. I also find Chapter 64, on the qualities to look for in the abbot, of importance to point out, not because I intend to become abbot, but because St. Benedict describes what the abbot should be. This includes the fact that he shouldn't be turbulent, he shouldn't be jealous and he shouldn't be suspicious. These also are principles for all of us to live by.

What is your key to living the Benedictine spirituality?

If we are going to live a monastic life, we need to be persons who are patient, who are kind, who have a breadth of mind and are tolerant. I consider these things as being part of the hallmarks of Benedictine spirituality. The key to living a Benedictine spirituality is to have the breadth of soul, a love for history, a love for tradition, a love for beauty and an understanding that liturgy should always be beautiful. Other things include a love for the Church herself and a love for, and an understanding of, prayer. All of this is part of Benedictine spirituality. Our approach to prayer is a continuation of, and a practice, begun with the early desert monks.

What have been your most difficult times?

I would say the most difficult time would be that period when I had to work very hard to finish my dissertation. I felt myself continually under the gun until it was finally finished and I could defend it. I think another difficult time was the '60s because it was not just a question of civil rights, it was also a question of the Vietnam War. These were life-and-death issues and there was a great deal of disagreement. I felt at times very much alone during this period. In fact, I have often felt alone. I don't usually talk about my own concerns or my own political stances, unless I know that someone else has more or less the same kind of feelings that I have. I don't see myself as fitting into an extreme right-wing kind of political stance, partly because I'm a Roman Catholic and I believe in the teaching of the Catholic Church on social justice.

What have been some of your most joyful or happy times?

I'm very happy about having had the opportunity to live through the times that I've lived through, but I must admit that I have enjoyed most of the times. Some of the happiest moments in my life were when I was living in monasteries in Africa. This changed my life and changed my ideas about a lot of things. For me, it was a life-giving experience and for that, I am very, very grateful. All these experiences have played a large part of who I am now in the twilight of my years.

Vatican II: Its Effect on the Church and Saint Meinrad Archabbey

Some observers are of the opinion that society is falling again into a general disregard for spirituality. What do you think of this?

I think that we live in difficult times. We live in a period in which we talk about a general decline, even as a nation. Every nation, historically, has known its period of reaching the zenith—a high point—and then there's a decline. That is one rule that you see again and again throughout history.

Is there a lack of spirituality? I think in many ways there is, yet there's a growth spiritually. There are a lot of things that we don't do, perhaps, as well as before, but I also think that there are other things that we are doing very well. Just looking at the monastic life, as we live it here at Saint Meinrad. There is no question that we should always realize we can do better, we should do better, and we also should thank God that we are able to do what we are able to accomplish. I think that the problems we face are problems that have been faced before and we will survive, as before, if we are faithful to God.

21

Some Catholics think Pope John XXIII was overly optimistic and that, ever since Vatican Council II, the Church has been paying a heavy price for his initiatives. Still others applaud his gestures. What is your opinion of this?

I think that the Catholic Church is now going through a very difficult time. This is a time when our vocations are less than they were before. Some think that the clergy was never corrupt, or that bad things never happened in the Church. In every generation in the history of the Church, there have been difficulties of this kind. The Church has constantly needed to be reformed because parts of the Church are human, therefore, we shouldn't be surprised at problems.

All we have to do is look at the Church in the period of the Renaissance. We also need to remember that there have always been those who emerged from the Church and brought about reform and change. This has occurred in every period in Church history. We shouldn't forget that. Nor should we think that we have all the answers now, in our own time. The Catholic Church is catholic and it is ancient. We should always be conscious of the totality of our understanding of the Church and not just zero in on a recent past or very recent devotions. What I try to do with my students is to teach them to love the Church in all of her glory and example throughout history, and not just get hung up on 19th-century ideas and notions of the Church.

Compare the morale in the monastery today with that of 30 to 50 years ago.

I think the morale in our monastery right now is very good. Yes, a decline in vocations has happened, but I think there have been some very active things done to have more vocations and I think that's a very healthy sign.

Even if the Mass were to be celebrated in English, was eliminating Latin from the academic curriculum a good idea?

It would be absurd to go back to the kind of emphasis on Latin that existed when I came into the seminary in 1949. First of all, liturgy is no longer in Latin. The other thing is that when people learned Latin back in those times, it was only a certain percentage that really learned how to read and work in Latin. Most American seminarians in my day took Latin and never really understood it very well. It's a blessing that we have the liturgy in the vernacular. I think that I knew Latin as well as, or even better, than many other people. This was partly because it had been a part of my training as a historian to be able to read Medieval Latin. But I don't want to go back to the time when we celebrated Mass in Latin and the celebrant swallowed half the words and people rushed through the text. We don't want to go back to that.

Yes, there is need for Latin, but for people who are going to be working in certain areas. If you're going to be a canonist or if you're going to be engaging in other parts of the administration of the Catholic Church, it's good to learn Latin. If you're going be a historian, you should learn Latin. We should learn Latin in the seminary to the extent that we might desire to specialize in certain areas. Then we should learn Latin the way we learn any other language. We should not only be able to understand it, but also to know how it hangs together and how it is a part of literature.

Comment on the positive or negative changes in the liturgy that have been undertaken in the recent history of the Church.

The changes that took place after the Second Vatican Council, especially in terms of celebration of liturgy, were much more reasonable. We did a very good job here at Saint Meinrad in adapting the liturgy and adapting the chant to English. I think one of our great contributions, especially to the monastic order here in the States, was our liturgical reform. This included the translations, the choice of readings and the music itself. It was a great improvement and it was very beautifully done. I think we kept in mind, as a community, some real principles that are part of the Benedictine charism.

The changes that we have, I think, have been very good. There has been a movement among some of the clergy today to go back. I think that, in doing so, they are trying to recapture something that never existed. For example, Pope John Paul II wanted us to have a better idea of the meaning of the Eucharist. Of course, for the Eucharist that is absolutely true, as we should have devotions to the Eucharist. We should have a better understanding of the Eucharist because it is important that the laity understand the doctrinal teaching of the Church regarding the Eucharist, which is certainly very important.

Assuming that you agree that there is no going back to pre-Conciliar days, what has been lost? What has been gained?

There's always something lost when there is a change. Everyone who reaches the age of 75, like I have, can look back and say, "Yes, we did this thing when I was young, and these are experiences that young people today will never have." All that is true. I think I find it very difficult to say what has been lost. But in the '60s, students really did study and I think this has been lost. We studied precisely because of what was happening in the Church. People wanted to know about the problems and difficulties, so they were reading and studying. That kind of reading and studying is not as evident today in the seminaries. I think we have to go back and try to rekindle a deeper desire to learn more fully theology, Church history and the other sacred sciences. What has been gained? I think a lot of good things have been gained.

Is it correct to speak of the Catholic Church today as different from what it was in the mid-20th century?

Of course, it's different because the Church doesn't stand still any more than any other institution or reality stands still. Only God is eternal. Things always change; things are always different.

Yes, there's a difference. You realize the marvelous things that have happened. I'm now 75 years old and, when I look back on the time of Blessed John XXIII, I realize that he was one of the really great pontiffs of the 20th century. Most of the popes in the 20th century were remarkable, there's no question about it. But in so many, many ways, John XXIII and what he did were most remarkable. I think the next man who did so much, and for whom I still have the highest regard, is Pope Paul VI. Now that isn't putting down everybody else, but I put these two men in the context of the times. I think that God was present in guiding the Church during the pontificates of these special two men. That's the way I look at it.

Comment on your hopes for the future of the Archabbey and the Roman Catholic Church.

I think that, even though we're going through a difficult period, that doesn't mean that we are in a decline. What it does mean is that we have to keep rethinking our ideals. I think we are doing that right now under the present abbot. We are rethinking what is important in our monastic way of life and how we should deal with a community that, in some ways, is aging. We should be very grateful that we have young people entering into our community, which is not the case in some other houses.

In a certain sense, we should remember that a Catholic Christian is always optimistic, partly because Christ will always prevail and we believe that we are followers of Christ. Therefore, in the good times and the bad times, we need to remember that He, Himself, will always prevail.

Profile based upon: Fr. Cyprian Davis to Prof. Ruth C. Engs, November 14, 2005, Interview Transcription, Saint Meinrad Archives.

Chapter Two

Fr. Columba Kelly, OSB

Fr. Columba's lifework as a Benedictine monk has been music. He was professor of music at Saint Meinrad College (1964-98) and choirmaster (1964-78). He helped develop liturgical Latin-style chants in English in the wake of the changes resulting from Vatican II.

Born in Williamsburg, IA, on October 30, 1930, Fr. Columba graduated from Parnell High School (1948), attended St. Ambrose College, Davenport, IA (1948-51), and received a BA in philosophy at Saint Meinrad Seminary (1956). He made his first profession as a monk July 31, 1953, his solemn profession August 6, 1956, and was ordained a priest at Einsiedeln Abbey in Switzerland, July 5, 1958. In Rome, Fr. Columba received the Licentiate in Sacred Theology from Sant Anselmo (1959) and a doctoral degree in sacred music from the Pontifical Institute of Sacred Music (1963).

At Saint Meinrad, he served as prior (1978-84), and since 1978 has been a visiting professor of church music in the School of Theology. He has been an adjunct professor at several colleges and has given numerous lectures over his career. Fr. Columba has composed thousands of English-language chants based upon the principles used to create the original Gregorian chants. His compositions have included antiphons, responsories, psalm tones and other material including "The Passion According to St. John," which has recently been released on CD.

Fr. Columba was interviewed by Prof. Ruth C. Engs on November 14, 2005.

Childhood and Early Years as a Monk

Tell me about your childhood and early schooling.

My mother and father were farmers. In fact, my father was farming the family farm that had been bought in 1856 by my great-grandfather, who made money in the Gold Rush. It's in eastern Iowa near the English River. It had become a 360-acre family farm when I was born in 1930. My dad, who had been out husking corn, said my birth was almost "trick or treat." This was because it was 7 o'clock at night on October the 30th. I was named John.

My mother had a ruptured appendix when she was a teenager—this would have been the early 1900s. Because it was too late to get her to the hospital, they used the car lights through the kitchen windows and operated on the kitchen table. For the rest of her life, her legs would swell and the doctor told her, when I finally arrived, "Don't you dare have any more kids." She lived to be 102. So I was the only child. They didn't get married until they were 35 years old. She was 36 when I was born.

However, I had first cousins and I went to a one-room school for eight years. The school was only about three-quarters of a mile from the house. I walked down the road to school and my companions were all the neighbor kids. The closest relative I had was a first cousin who was one year older than I. She was always one year ahead of me in school and was kind of like a big sister. That was the closest I would have to a family relationship. So you learn to entertain yourself and take care of yourself very early. Of course, being around adults, my vocabulary really expanded. I was known for big words at an early age.

Describe your experiences at the one-room school.

It was out in the country on one square acre that had been donated by a local farmer. They built a schoolhouse on it and it took care of the kids in that area. I was one of them. It was one room, and we had a stove in the center to heat in the wintertime. Kids could come in with frostbite, practically, from walking to school. All the grades were taught in this one room. So when you finished your recitation, you either went back to your seat, or if you were good, you might get to go to the sandbox in the back of the room and play.

We did all these creative things, like building towns in the sand while other kids were being interviewed. And you eavesdropped on kids that were ahead of you, so you got an inkling of what you were going to get next year. You also heard what the kids last year said, "Oh those dummies." I didn't think of it at the time, but I look back at it now with the educational problems we have today and realize we got the best possible education because the teacher knew every single one of us.

In fact, when I got to about the fifth grade, I was sloughing off on math. The teacher lived in the farmhouse beyond ours. One day she stopped at our house and talked to my mother. That evening, Mom and Dad sat me down and we had a discussion about what I should do about my math lessons. Those were the days when the teacher's word was gospel and whatever she said, the folks believed. There was no way I could defend myself against that. So they didn't defend me; they defended the teacher.

Every day the teacher would line us up from grade one on up to eighth grade. You all had to read something from a book. We all did this public reading, so that was all part of my background. Today this is all coming back to haunt me. This is because I'm finding text that people are translating from the original languages into English. It's obvious they don't read them out loud. This is not good for oral communication, as these texts are intended to be used as public readings or to be read by a lector. I just did "St. John's Passion" and we read a couple of sections. I had to fuss around with the rhythm and the wordplay to get it to make some sense. If you looked at it, you'd see the whole sentence. But if you're listening, the thing didn't make much sense.

Describe your religious upbringing.

My parents were very religious. They saw to it that we went to Mass and my dad made sure that night prayers were done. You didn't go to bed without doing night prayers. They were good solid—not off-the-wall religious—but just solid, pious people.

Were you brought up in a Catholic community?

The only Catholic neighbors we had were these first cousins; they lived a mile north of us. To the west were good Protestants. To the east were Protestants. To the south were excellent Methodists. He was also a high degree Mason. So we had Masonic Lodge people, Methodists, Lutherans, etc. Ecumenism was just part of the community. We all got along. In fact, when I was helping bring water for the threshing machine one summer, the neighbor, Dick Owens, who was a Mason and a good Methodist, was talking to my dad. He looked up at my father, Joe, and said, "You know, Joe, you're a pretty good guy for being a Catholic." There was that thing about Catholics being terrible people, then. Yet, because of the relationships, because we knew each other and helped each other, this was obviously not the case all the time.

Ecumenism was already there. I had no problem with relating to non-Catholics, because we lived and we worked with them. They were part of our threshing community. They were part of our hay crop. These farmers would get together and help each other. In the summers, you would help with harvesting of the hay. As a kid, I had enough strength to guide the horses and the farmers would pitch the hay into the barn. For oats thrashing, you had what they called a "ring of farmers." Almost a dozen farm households, including the women, would come together. They cooked this huge thrashing meal. Then 24 or 30 men would help you thrash your oats. Then you'd go to their farm, so it was a constant ring. Once the combine came, all these thrashing rings broke up. We're talking about the late '30s before the Second World War. So that's the kind of background I had growing up.

How did you get into music?

They're two stories. I don't know what grade it was, but the teacher learned in teacher training in normal school that you're not supposed to let kids write with their left hand. Make them write with their right hand. I had started to write with the left hand, but she came behind me, pulled the pencil out of my hand, put it in the other hand and forced me into writing with the right hand. So I can't write well, but I'm ambidextrous.

The creamery in the local town of North English sponsored the summer fair called the Creamery Picnic. They would hire local kids and a local talent band. When I was maybe about four years old, I remember the folks took me there. They put me up on the railing fence. I was watching the band and I started directing it. Everybody was watching me direct the band, so this became a big joke about the Kelly kid who was into directing bands at about the age of four.

My mother had studied art and my parents saw to it that I had piano lessons at the very earliest age. When I took lessons, the teacher noticed that I was strong in the left hand so she gave me pieces that had good left-hand parts, including Chopin. She said, "I can't give these pieces to the other kids. Their left hand isn't strong enough." So I would be learning things that had strong left-hand parts. My parents got this second-hand player piano for almost nothing that had a nice stiff action. This turned out to be good training. It also played rolls and I would cheat by playing those darn rolls. Finally, the teacher said, "You know, he's probably wasting practice time. Why don't you take that out?" They took out the guts of the piano so that I had to make my own music. I had piano lessons all through grade school.

What kind of high school did you go to?

It was a public school; however, the town is Catholic. The board of directors were all Catholics. They hired sisters to teach and they hired a principal who was a Catholic. It was run like a Catholic school. They didn't teach religion there, but the Catholic faith undergirded everything. It was five miles or something east of us in a little town called Parnell, Iowa.

I had Sister Mary Ignatius. I'll never forget it because, as a freshman, she taught us English. On Monday morning, she figured all the kids had all weekend to do homework so you had to have lots of sentences ready to be put on the board and diagrammed. There was no excuse. Today, kids have every kind of excuse. But you had no excuses in those days, even if you had basketball practice or whatever; you have time to do it. She was very strict on this. So today I get very upset with people who have poor grammatical constructions. I'm working with liturgy text and I'm just tearing my hair out at the awkward constructions they're winding up with and the inability to communicate orally.

In high school, I continued piano lessons with a sister who taught me all kind of things. In fact, I started picking up flute and violin. I went to state contests and won prizes. I won the state contest in piano one year. In fact, I did Chopin's *Fantasy Impromptu* and all those tough pieces. I played them for state contest as well as a couple of Bach inventions.

Did you do other activities in high school?

Well now, basketball was a disaster. As a freshman, I went out for basketball, but I was already beginning to get nearsighted. I didn't know it, and my parents didn't know it either. The coach figured it out. I'd be shooting the basket and it was obvious that I was not seeing things clearly at a distance. So he went to my folks and told them to get my eyes checked. Sure enough, I was nearsighted. Of course, that was awful. Here's a high school kid who has to wear glasses. Ugh.

Another thing I did was to take typing. This would have been the fall of '44. I think we were freshmen. Three of us boys decided we'd like to learn typing. But boys don't take typing; that's for girls. In fact, the class was all girls because they were being trained to be secretaries and typists for companies. They all could type at 120 words a minute without any mistakes. We just wanted to learn to type. The sister said, "Fine, sign up." She let us have a lower standard as long as we were able to do touch typing. She gave us good grades. For the girls, that was different. She would tell them they made too many mistakes. Boy, she'd be all over them. "No, do that again." She didn't do that with us. So we learned to type.

Now that we have computers, I look back and say, "Thank God we did that." There's a monk here who's not much older than I, but he never learned to type. Therefore, he's locked out of using a computer. What a shame, because all my life's work is on the computer now. Everything's through computers—writing music, making text, whatever. Anyway, those are the things that happened in high school; they kind of set me up rather nicely. Then I went to college.

Where did you go to college?

I graduated from high school in '48 and went to St. Ambrose College in Davenport, Iowa, that fall. It was a diocesan college started by the bishop. Now it's called St. Ambrose University. I started the year Harry Truman won the election. In the early morning after the election, several of us freshmen went downtown to pick up the Chicago *Herald-Tribune*. On its front page it said, "Dewey wins by a landslide." But we had been listening to the radio all night and knew better. We wanted a copy of that paper, so all of us bought a copy. When we went back an hour later, they had taken them off the shelves. But we were down there early enough before the guy in the newsstand realized he had better not keep that paper out any longer, so it was one of those historic moments.

In college, I'd been toying with a vocation. It was either that or go to Korea. That was the time when, in a sense like many of the kids in the Vietnam period, I didn't see any sense to that damn war. So I said, "This is the time to make the move." I had already visited here during a Thanksgiving vacation and had sized up the place. I thought, "Yeah, this is where I would like to come." Then as the draft began I said, "Okay, I better make the decision now. Otherwise I'm going to wind up in Korea." At St. Ambrose, they wanted me to join the diocese and I said, "No, I don't feel called to be a diocesan priest. I want to be a monk instead." So halfway through the junior year, I transferred to Saint Meinrad Seminary to finish my college work.

What were the influences that led to your decision to become a monk?
You know, being the only child, I had my own room in the farmhouse and my own space. I would kind of play "Mass" or "setting up the Mass." So already I was going that way in grade school and high school. When I was in high school, I went to a music institute at Loras College in Dubuque. There I met the famous Harry Seitz, who had been head of music for all the public schools in Detroit. He was one of those dynamic characters and would do a one-week church music workshop. My parents sent me to that, because I used to play the reed organ in the local parish church. Well, he helped me train my voice and he knew Saint Meinrad. He'd been down to Saint Meinrad helping out Father Eric. Harry helped me to breathe properly and project. I took private lessons from him and, of course, we'd end up discussing monasticism and Saint Meinrad. He said, "Check the place out."

Did you meet priests who were good role models?
Yes, especially once I got to college. There was a Father Madsen in the diocese who was music director and everything else. In high school,

we had contests and I got to know some really fine priests who obviously were talented. They weren't dumb. They were highly talented. They were priests and were leading people. They were good role models and we had several of those in college. And, of course, I met some of the people here.

I came down here for Thanksgiving vacation and that's when I decided, "Yes, I must come here." It's one of those things where God speaks to you. If you're a good fundamentalist, you'd say, "I was struck by the Holy Spirit and God spoke to me." Well, yeah, okay. Hear voices? But you get the point. The message gets through to you somehow. "This is where you should be." I did it in order to beat the draft, if you wish. I transferred so that I would have seminary status, because I was just a lay student at Ambrose. I thought since I'm going to join a monastery at some point, I might as well make that move now.

Then what happened?

Well, they didn't know what to do with this guy who's almost finished college but hasn't had an awful lot of Latin, and besides he's not been in the seminary high school. In those days, you started your seminary's four-year high school in the minor seminary and then went into the major seminary. I had none of this. I'd been dating girls, running around and doing Joe College stuff, you know. Friday night, you'd have a beer and pay a dollar to the guy that plays the right tune and have a date. Gee whiz, this is all part of college.

They took me for a year and a half in the school here. Since I didn't fit into any of their curriculum, I was called a special student. Now you know what that term means. So I always say to people, "I was a special student, but they ordained me anyway." That's what they called me, because I didn't fit the mold. I took Latin, other languages and philosophy courses. They get to see you and understand who you are, and you get the lay of the place. The next stage was the novitiate in '52. The following year on July 31st—Abbot Ignatius' feast day—I made first profession.

How did your family feel about you becoming a monk seeing that you were an only child?

You know, that's the worst of it. They were definitely against it. Of course, mother was very upset because I'm not going to have any grandchildren. She said, "Gee whiz, why do you want to become a priest in the first place, and then be a monk?" And my dad would say, "Oh, you've got good brains. You wouldn't have to do that. You wouldn't have to become a monk." There was the idea that monks were second rate. If you couldn't do anything else, at least you could become a monk. That's a big problem today. If somebody has all kinds of talent and brains and looks like they'll go places, they say don't waste it by becoming a religious.

What was the tone and nature of the discipline under which your vocation was formed?

Oh gosh, everything was done very precisely and you had the usual jobs. You clean toilets; you clean wards and rooms. That's what novices do. They still do it today, "Start at the bottom, guys, and learn what it's like. Here are the household chores." You also had meditation, spiritual reading and so forth, so your day is completely scheduled. And there's recreation, always with the same people. It's kind of like a family, you know. These are the people you're going to live with. And they all come with different personalities.

The abbot of that time, Ignatius Esser, believed very much in making sure to test the humility of a monk. He would always see to it that, at some point in your novitiate, you would be confronted with some kind of mistake you made. He would then literally have your back to the wall and would say, "You've done this. Are you stupid or don't you care?" There would be a dramatic pause. Should I answer that? If you've got any sense at all, you won't. This was done to almost everybody. At least you learned pretty quickly that you weren't singled out. This is not bias; this is part of policy. We're going to test your humility. When you set up Ignatius' books for Mass, you had to have the ribbons exactly in order. If they weren't, he would take the time, while you were standing there, to rearrange the ribbons correctly.

There's another wonderful illustration. We took turns cleaning the abbot's choir stall. Somebody did it one week and then somebody else next week. In this particular case, there had been a white spot on his choir stall. Well, birds had gotten into the church. The windows were open and this spot was a bird dropping. Well, Ignatius knew darn well what it was and he didn't touch it. So the novice master came to us one day and said, "Ignatius wants to see you in church." So we all filed out single file and got ourselves in a semicircle around his choir stall. He stood there and said, "Who cleaned my choir stall last week?"—the spot had been there awhile. So one of them said, "I did." "Who cleaned it this week?"

Fr. Columba, as a young monk

And one of the other ones, who was very shaky because he realized something was coming up said, "I did."

Then the abbot said to this person, "Come here. What is that?" Now this novice knew darn well what it was, but said, "White paint." "No," the abbot answered. "No, it is bird excrement." He couldn't quite use the word "shit." "Now how do you remove that?" And Ignatius took out his white handkerchief, very carefully, and unfolded it, moistened it, and cleaned off the spot. Of course, then we all had to do penance. But I describe this because these were the kind of things that were done to make sure that you were of solid character. We look back now and laugh our heads off, but at the time we were quaking in our boots!

Do you have anything to say about making your profession?

I made solemn profession in '56. One warm night in July, I'm called to the abbot's office. This time it's not Ignatius Esser; it's Abbot Bonaventure. He has a little slip of paper on his desk. I'm standing in front of his desk and he says, "You will be going to Rome this fall to San Anselmo to get your licentiate. While you're there, study Italian so that you can go to the music school to get your degree in music. When you get your degree in music, you're to come home and be choirmaster."

There was no discussion about this. It was simply laid out for you. This was how you dialogued about your future with the superiors in those days. All this took less than six minutes. In five or six minutes, your whole future was mapped out for you. I went over to Rome in the fall of '56 and in '59 got my STL. I then started music school that fall and went on and did the master's and doctorate in musicology.

Work

Tell me about your career.

I came home from Rome the third of January 1964. On my desk, Abbot Bonaventure had placed a letter. I put my suitcase down and opened the letter. It said, "When you read this, you are choirmaster." So, it seemed, it was just like what he'd said would happen.

Since your time in Rome was during the early period of Vatican II, can you give any details about your time there?

Dennis Dougherty, a classmate, and I were sent to Rome together in 1956. He made solemn vows with me. Later, he left Saint Meinrad and wound up teaching at Marquette in Milwaukee; he died there. We had visited relatives in Ireland, went on to Einsiedeln and then took the train down to Rome.

Our Fr. Guy Ferrari met us. If he hadn't died of diabetic shock [1965], he would have been Saint Meinrad's first cardinal. He had a heart of gold. Guy met us in his car. We were in the back seat and he leans over from the driver's seat and says, "Welcome to Rome, you two. If you don't lose your faith in the first year, you never will. Because you're going to see all the scandalous behavior that goes on in Rome. You see, this is the holy city of Rome, and by that you mean the shenanigans of the clergy, the weakness, the politics and everything else that goes on; that will test your faith. The Holy Spirit guides the Church, anyway, in spite of all this." By golly, it's absolutely true!

Amazingly, we found that there was a priest shortage in Rome and Italy. Italians don't want to become parish priests in some poor, neglected, forgotten parish in southern Italy that has no income. You get chickens and eggs and barter, but your future is poverty. We Americans think the priest shortage first happened over here. Oh, no. Rome has had a shortage of clergy since at least the '40s and '50s. What they did was to bring in religious from Spain. What Italian vocations they got were people who scrambled to get into the curia and become part of the bureaucracy. It's hardly the best motive in the world for being a priest, but they do it to become part of the bureaucracy and have a safe job. They may be pretty honest, otherwise, but it's such a narrow focusing of a lifestyle. When we were at San Anselmo, it was the golden age of the Church, because it looked like it would go on forever and that Latin would be the language.

Then I left San Anselmo to live at San Gregario on the Capitoline Hill, because it was closer to classes. Because of my schedule of classes and music assignments, I had to cross town twice a day. What traffic! I had a Vespa and that's the only way to get around Rome, because you could park it anywhere. I have a doctorate in driving, because I never had a serious accident with it. With classes and rehearsals, I went until about eight in the evening. Dinner was served at 8 o'clock. So that was my time from 1959 to 1962. The last year, I spent the morning and afternoon writing the dissertation.

Because these were the years leading to the Council, were you aware of the politics?

Politics were already pretty strong when I was there in '56, '58. Giovanni Battista Montini, who became Pope Paul VI, was at the Secretary of State with a man named Domenico Tardini. Pius XII was playing politics because he just didn't want to take either side. Tardini was ultraconservative. Montini believed that the Church had to make some changes and move. He was more open-minded than Tardini. Today we call it progressive.

So Pius XII set both of them up as head of the Secretary of State representing the Holy See. This was a very important position in Rome. Tardini did internal affairs and Montini external affairs. Well, it was like when the Roman Empire had two people ruling the empire; eventually, one of them had to go. Montini was shipped to Milan and made archbishop of Milan in 1954 to keep him out of Rome. It's called lateral arabesque. He arrived not with great glory in Milan, and had to kind of work his way back up. He stayed in exile until 1958 when he was made cardinal by another person in exile, Angelo Roncalli, who became Pope John XXIII.

I was in the piazza when Roncalli was elected Pope John XXIII in 1958. The Italians were shocked. As soon as the announcement *Habamus Papam* [we have a pope] and his name, Angelo Roncalli, was announced, the Italians turned to me and said, "Who's he? Who's he? Who's this big fat guy?" So Roncalli becomes pope and we all know what very quickly happened.

He started all kinds of things. He began the visitation in Lent of all the parish churches in Rome. This was the first time the Pope had done that for centuries. On January 25, 1960, he's at St. Paul Outside the Walls. I'm in the schola and we're singing chants for the Mass. It's the feast of the Conversion of St. Paul, and the cardinals were invited. Right after Mass, all of the cardinals filed into the chapter room of the Benedictine monastery attached to the church so the Pope can talk to them. We figured Mass was over, even though we had not done the Recessional.

Meanwhile, one of the Americans has a little Sony radio. The Vatican Radio was announcing that there would be an ecumenical council. The problem was that the timing was off, as the radio station thought the Mass was over. The cardinals were now being told what was already being announced over Italian radio. We waited in the church for the cardinals to come out. We expected them to come out with smiling faces, like good cardinals should. But their expressions were all something like, "Oh, no!" We knew they didn't want it. Only the Pope was happy.

What happened next?

Fr. Guy Ferrari, who at that time was curator of the Borgia Apartment in the Vatican, was working under Tisserant [Eugène Gabriel Gervais-Laurent], dean of the College of Cardinals and part of the Vatican entourage. Guy would come back in the evening for our 8 o'clock supper and tell us what had happened that day at the Vatican. He and Tisserant would have coffee in the morning together. One day Tisserant said, "Yeah, this pope is really something. You're negotiating with him across the dinner table and by the end of the meal, before you know what's happened—because he's smiling all the time—he gets his Council going!"

The cardinals try to roadblock it. They said, "Well, you know we really think it's too much work to get this thing done." They figure they can stop him because they know that, at his age, he can't last very long. He knows it, too. He made a famous remark soon after his election, "Well, here I am at the top of the heap and the end of my rope." All they want him to do is make some cardinals for the next time. So they say to him, "Oh, we can't have this Council because we've first got to have a Roman Senate. We haven't had that for 400, 500 years." So, a Senate was the compromise.

But he got them on board. We'll have the Senate first; then maybe we can have the Council. The cardinals agreed because they figured he wasn't going to live long enough for this. Sure enough it starts; 700 and some canons are presented in the Senate and it goes on week after week, month after month. Guy described to me that one day the Pope was flipping the pages of the many canons. Finally, he got up and addressed them. He said, "I want to thank you for all this wonderful work you've done on this. Now, I propose that we vote, in one vote, for all the rest of these canons. All those in favor of these canons, please vote…. Fine, thank you for this wonderful Senate. Now we will all proceed to have the Council." And they went on then and prepared for the Council. But the Senate was extremely conservative. Let me give you a couple of examples of their canons [decrees].

One of the decrees declared that clergy were not allowed to frequent bars. Well, a bar in Italy is a coffee bar. It's where all the clergy go to get their coffee and talk. You can also get a drink, too, in the sense of an American bar. The clergy said, "You've got to be kidding." They paid no attention to that canon whatsoever. The clergy continued going to coffee bars. But it's still forbidden, according to the Roman Senate.

Another one was that all clergy who had automobiles had to have them registered at the vicariate or Roman chancery office. Two Americans who were doing graduate studies had cars. These American priests went to the office with the canon in front of them. They said, "According to this canon, we're to register automobiles here, aren't we?" This monsignor looks up at them and said, "Oh, get out of here. We have no intention of doing this thing whatsoever." He shooed them out of the office. So, when you get these edicts from Rome, you want to listen carefully as to what they mean. Is this really workable or not? That was all part of the politics, you see.

You can see why I kind of just grin about new things that come up. For example, "You're now going to kneel for this. Get people up and down now in Mass." I preside in Tell City [2005] and the ruckus and disturbance is incredible. It's all supposed to be more reverent, but it's actually destroying all sense of reverence. People getting up and down, up and down, and not sure when they should be getting up and down. With that noise, you can't continue the Eucharistic prayer, or if you do, you have got to shout it out over the bedlam. Is that supposed to be more reverent? Having been in Rome all that time, you realize in Rome they would have just said, "Duh," you know? "Besides we can't kneel anyway; we don't have any kneelers. We've got moveable chairs in St. Peter's." So the Romans look at us and think, "What's wrong with you guys? Don't you have any common sense?"

How about the Council?

This business with the Senate is what led up to the Council. The guys who were running the Church lost control of the Council. John XXIII put worship first, rather than doctrine. He said, "I want the bishops, all of them, to get up and talk. Since they all think they know something about liturgy, then we'll have the liturgy document first to get them talking. They all said something about liturgy because they all thought they knew something about it, whether they did or not. If he had started with doctrinal issues—this sin and that—a lot of bishops would be scared to say anything.

In the spring of 1963, Hannibal Bugnini, the principal architect of liturgical changes during Vatican II, who later becomes head of the Post-Councilor Commission for Implementing the Document on the Liturgy, gave a music seminar. In this seminar, we discussed what was going on in the Council with the liturgical document. He said it could go either way. However, he forecasted that, "Although Gregorian chants are the models for the normal music of the Church, for pastoral reasons we will promote the vernacular." This document got approved in the fall of '63. I came home and the monks asked me about changes. I said, "Oh, I know exactly what's going to happen...."

My former novice master, Placidus Kempf, who went out and did weekend work occasionally, came to me and said, "The Prayer of the Faithful, how will we do that?" I explained it to him. Or someone would ask me, "Are you sure that this is what the Church wants?" I said, "Trust me, this is where it's going." And sure enough, there was a decree from the Councilor Congregation of Worship, from Bugnini, about what's going to be. There goes the Latin chant!

Having done a doctorate in chant, I understood how they wrote it in the first place. The original is Hebrew or Greek and then they translated it into Latin. Latin is the first vernacular of the Western Church. English now is simply the second vernacular. The official language of the Latin Church up to the fifth century was Greek. It's only about the time of Leo the Great [pope 440-461] when it switches to Latin.

What was the reaction to this?

Some didn't want to hear that, because Latin is the language of the Church. Oh, come off it, guys. It's already vernacular. So from '64 until now, we're still at it. It's been just a constant battle of musicologists against each other saying, "You can't sing chant in English." And I say, "You can't sing Latin chant in English, but you can sing chant in English." In fact, we do it here every day. There was also a lot of experimentation, but the conservatives didn't like it.

In '74, I had a sabbatical and visited Bugnini, but in 1975 they moved him out of Rome and sent him to Iran. He died shortly after; I'm sure of a broken heart. The Congregation for Beatification was joined with the Congregation of Worship and the head of Beatification was made the head of Worship. However, he knew nothing about worship. He was a conservative and he was going to hold the line, and he did. In the meantime, I had reworked the Good Friday liturgy, which if Bugnini had stayed on, I think we'd have gotten permission to do it. 1975 was a crucial year. It was like a steel door closed. Since then, you fight for everything in terms of liturgy.

How did you rework Latin into English so it made liturgical sense?

I took my doctoral dissertation under the direction of Eugene Cardine, who is the one who discovered that the ways of writing chant in ancient manuscripts also told us how you sing it. They give you performance practice indications. It would be like looking at Leonard Bernstein's score of the *Fifth Symphony*. On it he says, "Move it here, slow it down there, crescendo there." These notations give directions for doing all kind of things. In other words, how do I perform these notes and phrases?

On the ancient manuscripts, we found that what looked like squiggles were the conductor's gestures on how to sing it. Some people said this is primitive stuff and decoration. Like heck, it is! It's the real rhythm of the chant. Look at the early notation and follow it. In other words, redraw it as you sing it. This was my doctoral dissertation. It's called semiology, the study of signs. The notations are found in the earliest manuscripts that date from around 900. If you draw it with your hands, you've got the exact rhythm. They really knew how to bring out the meaning of a text as it's orally proclaimed. In other words, how would you say something effectively and convince people with effective speech? Chant is doing all that, and so you take those rules and principles from the Latin and you apply them to what English demands.

What happened here at Saint Meinrad?

I came back in January 1964 and we started an experimental Divine Office that included both priests and brothers. The first problem was to write things in English for that group. All they did was recite the psalms, but they wanted to sing some things. So I composed some simple responsorial settings, a couple of antiphons, a couple of hymn settings. Once we got that going, my plan was to add the proper antiphons for feast days and everything else, but at that time we were still divided into three choirs—experimental choir in Chapter Room, the main one in Abbey Church, and the brothers' oratory had its own.

We had three choirs going at the same time. In order to have unity, we first had to have division. We broke into three to get to one. During the spring of '64, I was writing new things. Fr. Cyprian [Davis], who knew his Latin, had an altercation with me. He said, "Father, these things are too simple and we're losing all that rich variety we had with the Latin Office. There's not enough written to sing." All that I could say to him at that time was, "Patience, Fr. Cyprian, we'll get there someday."

We had all this wonderful Christmas, Lent and Easter music, and we had to create this all in English bit by bit. Now we've got all these things!

The difference between the liturgy in Latin and the liturgy in English, structurally, was what we did in the experimental Office in the Chapter Room. We reduced it to the primary four elements, so we could build it from its core base. This included a hymn, psalmody, reading and prayer. Abbot Primate Rembert Weakland, who later became Archbishop in Milwaukee, was able to get permission for the Benedictines to develop their own Office if they did two things. They had to have the basic premise from the *Thesaurus*, which is a collection of texts to use for the Liturgy of the Hours—antiphons, responsories, hymn text, psalm tones and so forth. The other guiding rule was you were to have common prayer three times a day: Morning Prayer, Noon Prayer and Evening Prayer/Vespers.

We did the first official English Office for the feast of the Ascension in 1967. Rome finally broke down. We had already been creating stuff and doing it. It was decided that if you have non-clerics and lay people attending, then you're allowed to use the vernacular. But if you didn't, if you were a closed community, you were to stick with Latin. Some communities even sent letters saying that it was beneath the dignity of Benedictines to be using the vernacular instead of their own sacred language.

How do you feel about what you have done for the liturgy here over the years?

I consider everything I've said is coming out of the context that I consider myself a true traditionalist, not a reactionary. That tradition is the handing on of something living. The word *traditio* means to hand on, to hand over. All those studies of ancient manuscripts for chant made it possible to do something brand new in English. That's tradition. It's the same thing as the structural liturgy. The basic elements for what was there in the beginning, such as the prayer of the Church and the Eucharist, are now restored.

Prayer

In terms of Benedictine spirituality, what would you wish to convey to your younger confreres and, maybe, to the laity?

Benedictine spirituality is creating a viable working family of faith. I use the term family because I think it's the closest image I can get. It's a community, you know.

What is your favorite part of the Holy Rule?

It's hard to say there's a favorite part, because it depends upon my needs at any particular time or what's going on in the life of the monastery or my personal life. But I guess I've used a lot of the chapter on the tools of good works. I've often given talks about this, as if it were like a modern mechanic's toolbox. The mechanic has special tools that he can pull out on a given occasion; that's precisely what Benedict's talking about. The mechanic would have different kinds of screwdrivers and wrenches, depending on the job he's doing. We've got these various tools and good works. They're all lined up and they're not necessarily used in consecutive order. It depends upon the job. So that's one of my favorite chapters, because it's so flexible.

Other parts of the *Rule* I like concern eating, drinking and clothes. Benedict says, in general, "Don't go out of bounds or over the edge. Don't eat too much, don't drink too much and don't waste money on clothes, but they should be nice." He said, "Anytime a monk goes out, he should look good." He should not show up in shabby clothes just because he's poor. Balance is what runs through the whole *Rule*.

What is your key to living the Benedictine spirituality?

Doing it! It's like any art and craft; you've got to practice it. And so the important thing is going to choir, doing the prayers together, keeping yourself focused on these things day after day, and letting it begin to shape you just as any good craft does. My favorite example is Art Rubenstein's advice to a young Midwest visitor to New York, who asked,

"How do you get to Carnegie Hall?" You practice, practice, practice. What do you do to implement the *Rule*? You practice, practice, practice!

Over your lifetime, what has been your most difficult time?

I guess the most difficult time was when the atmosphere changed from being open to creativity to a fear of change being disruptive of good order and beauty. This happened in 1975 when they started cracking down on experimentation. For example, Father Harry Hagen set up the structure of the St. John Passion for me to use on Good Friday. I began to see that this ought to be in the framework for the entire service.

We worked the readings, the Prayer of the Faithful and the communion rite all within that Passion setting. You ended with the burial when they were stripping the altar. The congregation, in the opening and closing of this, sang a hymn, *Wondrous Love is This*. This is from American tradition. The American tradition came into the Latin traditions. The setting of the solo parts was done in the tradition of Roman chant style. The choral parts were done in a contemporary harmony and the organ was done ultramodern. All of these traditions came together on Good Friday to represent the Passion.

We used it for about two years, in '76, in '77. Then Abbot Timothy said, "I'm just not comfortable with doing this now," because he probably was under pressure as it was not traditional. So we stopped doing it and we haven't used it since. That was a rather crushing thing because we knew it worked.

This thing may be published now, it's ironic, from Catholic Press as a special project. They've heard parts of it and are excited about it, so I know it's worth something. It probably could not be done as the official liturgy, unfortunately. I would like to see it as the Good Friday service, because it has all the material of it. So that was one of the things that was depressing.

How about your happiest or most joyful times?

I guess one of the most joyful times was when we had First Vespers of Advent in English for the first time around '67. I had written the antiphons in chant style based upon hymns. I'd re-improvised those melodies that go for the antiphons, the responsory and so on for this Vespers. They sang those not in Latin, but in English. I went back to the choirmaster's office and one of the monks, who's not a musician, comes stomping in. And I wondered, what's he going to say? And he says, "By God that was Advent." And I thought, "Wow, that's wonderful. It succeeded. It worked!" In other words, it's transferable from the Latin experience. He had experienced the material in English and it worked. As a non-musician, he found it did not break his spiritual tradition.

Vatican II: Its Effect on the Church and Saint Meinrad Archabbey

Some observers feel that today as a society we are falling into indifference in regard to spirituality. What do you think of this?

I was in college from '48 to '52, after the Second World War—we were called the "silent generation." But things were percolating and they exploded in the '60s to almost a free-for-all. Then came a reaction to the free-for-all in the '70s and '80s, especially in the Church. The culture is in disarray because, all of a sudden, "Hey, you guys, we need some discipline. We need some order. We need to get rid of this chaos, and that's still going on." The sad part is—and I don't know how long this retrenchment will go on—that it's killing any kind of creative work. Not only the irresponsible, but also the responsible. I guess once we begin to wake up from that, maybe the next phase will be saying, "Hey, maybe we need to relax." So maybe in 2010, 2020, things may loosen up again. My problem with this whole culture is that the psychology of the people right now is into fundamentalism. Hopefully, we can ride through that, because it's not going to produce anything of great value…no way.

Some Catholics think that Pope John XXIII was overly optimistic and that, ever since the Vatican Council, the Church has been paying a heavy price for his initiatives. Still others applaud his gestures. What's your view of this?

Overly optimistic? Well, I still say he was a realist. I think, in a sense, he wanted to restore some of the things that we lost, and that meant change. How's that for an irony? We're going to have to change in order to restore. John XXIII certainly was a realist. He knew exactly how weak humans were. A few days after he was elected, he made a famous remark to journalists. When asked, "How many people work in the Vatican?" He said with a twinkle in his eyes, "Oh, about half." He didn't give a number, because he had inspected various places and had to wait in the reception area for people to get back from their long coffee breaks.

Has the Church paid a heavy price?

Well, emotionally, for some people it's a heavy price, but for the rest of us, it has been a glorious opening. Thank God for that at the monastery. For example, we would be in terrible shape here if we still had to keep absolute separation between ordained priests and the rest of the community. That's what we had back then. You couldn't speak to brothers without permission. They couldn't speak to you. We had no common Chapter. Then, all of a sudden, the brothers are treated with dignity and equality. There is now inter-communication and they share responsibility.

Assuming that you agree there's no going back to pre-Conciliar days, what has been lost? What has been gained?

What's been lost, I think, is a broad perspective that included the Latin tradition and all that flows out of this tradition. Until we have greater respect for where everything has come from, we're still going to have problems. What we've gained, though, is a greater understanding of the content, because most Catholics didn't really know Latin. Many priests, also, didn't know Latin that well, you know. There were only a handful who could read and maybe speak Latin in this house. So, yes, we have greatly benefited from Vatican II, in spite of these people who want to go back to the Latin. If you go back to the Latin, you will be cutting people off from knowledge of the faith. Literally cutting them off. And then the faith will really suffer because it will not be based on solid content. It will be based on personal feelings, which is not Catholic.

Even if the Mass is to be celebrated in English, was eliminating Latin from the academic curriculum a good idea?

No! It would be like eliminating Latin and Greek from medical school. Because if you don't know your terminology, then you're going to be in serious trouble, because practically all the terminology in medicine comes from either Latin or Greek. The more you know of both those languages, the better off you are. You can limp along, I guess, as a doctor without them. You can get by, but I think that for a solid basis you need a little bit of Latin and Greek. The two sacred languages of the Church are Hebrew and Greek. I believe that Fr. Harry [Hagan, OSB] still teaches these languages. I think that Hebrew, Greek and Latin should be available and every seminarian should at least be introduced to those. Ironically, that ought to occur at the college and not the theology level. By the time they are in theology, it's almost too late.

Pastors need a good old-fashioned liberal arts background. They should study philosophy, not just in history, but as a practice, because they need to think logically and use the rules of reason. Any leader, especially spiritual leaders and pastors, needs to have that kind of training. If they don't, it will be the blind leading the blind.

Striking changes have been made in the liturgy and parish organizations since the days of the Council. Please comment on positive or negative changes that have occurred in recent years.

My problem is that many parishes are still not adequately using the resources of the members of the community, the laity who are not ordained. We have yet to reclaim the traditions, such as all those wonderful ministries like porter and lector. These ministries of the Church got subsumed into the preparation of priests. They were called minor orders and the Church simply dropped them. I would like to see them re-established. It's not something new, but it's going to be a change because we haven't done this for several centuries. But it's going back to one of the very valid traditions of the Church.

We ought to have the ministry of financial officer. The father in a parish shouldn't have to be tied down with all the bookwork concerning budget and finances. That's where you need an accountant, somebody trained in accounting who knows the rules of the game. Most priests don't have any business experience. I think Peter would have said, "No, that's for somebody else. These are things for deacons to do. Let them also distribute to the poor." That's going back to tradition. That's being a real traditionalist.

The number of religious vocations declines every year through death and retirement. What's the meaning of these changing patterns to the monastery and the Church at large?

The culture's changing. Becoming a cleric or religious is no longer a step up the social ladder. In older days, when there were big families and people were poor, if you had a son who was a priest or a daughter who joined the convent, you could proudly say, "We've got a religious in the family." Today many parents say, "Oh, don't squander all that intelligence. You can become a doctor or lawyer. You don't have to become a priest." That's an argument that's actually used to discourage a young person from becoming a religious. Women who want to become a nun are told, "Why do that when you can have a career?" Because of changes in our culture, it means fewer vocations. But in the long run, it might mean a purification of and strengthening of those vocations, because a person chooses it for the right reasons.

Compare the morale of the monastery today with that of 30, 40 or 50 years ago.

Well it's a whole different ethos. I use that word because it's the environment or ethos that's different because the culture's different. I would say there's less tension now than there was 40 or 50 years ago. The regulations were such then that one didn't know when the ax might fall. It was just, "Do what I tell you. Don't ask questions." The superiors kept a tight lip on information, which was basically on a need-to-know basis. Today, there's more open communication, and it's encouraged. Now, instead of the abbot putting up a sign saying that silence will be enforced, there's a discussion about why we need to keep silence. The morale today is much calmer. Of course, one gets discouraged about what's going on in the world and the negative reaction to the Church. That does affect people, but within the house I think there is very positive energy.

Is the decline in vocations affecting the house?

Yes. But in the last few years, we have been getting vocations. We're happy with the quality of these young people. They're coming for the right reasons and are solid. They're not misfits who can't do anything else, like we used to get. We screen nowadays. We used to get requests from parents who would like to send their son to a monastery because they can't handle him. Sorry. This is not the place. Go send him to some other institution, but not to a monastery. That was part of the mentality then. If a kid can't make it in the world, ship him off to a monastery. We laugh about this now.

When did vocations start to increase here?

About three or four years ago, we began gradually increasing because of Fr. Anthony [Vinson, OSB]. He's now working with vocations and is using the Internet. We used to rely on the schools. We called them the feeder schools. We closed the high school and then closed the college, so we have no feeders from the schools. We had to do some advertising and let ourselves be known. There was a resistance to that for several years. Today, because of the culture, you have to, at least, get your name and who you are out there, so that people can make a choice. We're making ourselves available as a choice. That is producing some vocations and it will probably continue. So I'm hopeful.

Comment on your hope for the future of the Archabbey and the Church.
 I just hope that we get around to really implementing what's really there in the Vatican II documents. One of the dangers we have is not reading the documents and studying them. Therefore, we are not putting into practice what the documents are suggesting, whether it be on the liturgy or the constitution of the Church. I think the Archabbey and the Church have a great future but, like any other prophecy, let's wait until it occurs and then we can go back and we have 20/20 hindsight. But I have great hope that we'll continue.

Profile based upon: Fr. Columba Kelly to Prof. Ruth C. Engs, November 14, 2005, Interview Transcription, Saint Meinrad Archives. The complete transcription includes further details about recollections of the Vatican Council and its personalities, and more details of composing chant in English.

Chapter Three

Br. Jerome Croteau, OSB

At Saint Meinrad Archabbey, Br. Jerome's major work for most of his career was in landscaping (1954-2001), where he drove a variety of tractors. He also worked in the vineyard and wine cellar (1952-85) helping to cultivate the vines and make wine.

Br. Jerome was born April 8, 1929, in Belcourt, ND, a community in a Native American Indian reservation. He graduated from St. Ann's Indian Mission Grade School (1945), St. Ann, ND, and attended St. Paul's Indian Mission High School in Marty, SD (1946-47). In 1947, he became a candidate in the brothers program at Saint Meinrad, made his first profession as a monk on May 10, 1949, and solemn profession on May 10, 1952.

Br. Jerome's other services to the Benedictine community include being assigned for a year (1949) to the building crew, where he helped construct St. Bede Hall, serving on the St. Meinrad Volunteer Fire Department (1955-88), and being assigned (1950-52) to Blue Cloud Abbey, where he did masonry work.

Br. Jerome was interviewed by Prof. Ruth C. Engs on July 13, 2005.

Childhood and Early Years as a Monk

Tell me about your childhood.

The name of the town I grew up in was Belcourt, North Dakota. I was born April 8, 1929, and was called Adolph. I had six brothers and sisters. One sister became a nun. The town was on the Turtle Mountain Reservation, the smallest reservation in the United States. The town was also small, although there are a lot of people on the reservation. People just seemed to build where they wanted to, so there was no order to where the houses were built. When I was growing up, there were two general stores, one grocery store, two gas stations and one café. There was also a pool hall, where they served snacks. The Indian mission and parish church were called St. Ann, the patron saint of the mission.

Tell me more about your family.

My dad was French and my mother was Indian [Chippewa] and French. They were both Canadian French. My grandfather came from Canada. He was a squatter next to the reservation. That's how he got interested in the reservation people and how he got in contact with the Indians.

During most of my childhood, my father worked at the mission. He was a jack of all trades. He also liked to fish and hunt. My father started as a mechanic, but this was during the Depression, so he got a job where he could find it—the WPA, the CCC and other work the government started during the Depression. He then started a gas station and other things.

When he couldn't buy gas during the war [World War II], he started his long career at the mission. He was a handyman for the mission, but did not get paid much. Because the mission did not have a retirement benefit program, during the last ten years of his working career he was a night watchman in a new jewelry plant that started in the next town. When somebody asked him why he had worked so long at the mission, he said it was because we were able to go to a Catholic school. I know he would have done better if he would have gotten work somewhere else instead of staying on the reservation. My father was 80 when he died and was greatly loved by his family and all the people who knew him.

The memory of my mother is not as clear. Although I do remember that she was a good wife and mother, and a good housewife. She was a good cook and was able to keep most of the recipes in her head. She was also in charge of our big garden. The first couple of homes that we lived in were not all that great, but she made an effort to keep them clean and neat, even with all of us running around in the house. This was especially true in the wintertime when we were not able to get outside.

Are there other memories of your childhood?

Where we lived, just about everyone had a backyard where we had a few cows and pigs. We always had a big garden. The biggest crop was potatoes and then some sweet corn. We also raised a lot of peas and green beans and carrots. In the spring of the year, we hauled manure for the garden and plowed it under. When we started Blue Cloud Abbey, I started their first garden.

I think my childhood was in a healthy atmosphere. Because of this, I was able to appreciate God and his reaction and also the people of God. I thank God that I was born at that particular time and place and that I was not 40 years earlier or 40 years later.

How about your schooling?

I graduated from grade school at St. Ann's Mission in December 1945. I was always slow in school. I stayed two years in a couple of grades, but I don't remember which ones they were. There was not such a thing, then, as a special teacher for slow students. I know I was not ready for high school. Then I went to St. Paul's Mission, Marty, South Dakota, in January 1946. The school year was half over, but it did not take long for them to see that I was slow in learning. I was given a special teacher to help me along with my studies, but it did not help much because I did not do well in my classes. So after a year and a half, I quit school and came here [to Saint Meinrad].

What was it like living at the mission school?

When I went to Marty, there were 500 students from grammar school through high school. We all lived in dormitories like when I first came here. Marty was founded by Fr. Sylvester [Eisenman, OSB] on the Yankton Reservation. [The boarding school was opened in 1922 with the help of the Sisters of the Blessed Sacrament from Philadelphia, who taught in the school. Fr. Sylvester, a monk of Saint Meinrad, died in 1948.]

The Yankton Reservation was not a Catholic reservation and there were not many Catholic children there. Children were bused or trucked in to the school from other reservations. Fr. Sylvester built one of the biggest Indian missions around by asking for small donations. Marty was a school for both boys and girls, but there was strict separation. Although we went to school, church and had meals together, the rest of the time we were kept apart. We did have parties, dances and picnics, and we used to go roller skating on Sundays. But it was well scrutinized by the nuns.

We did not go home for Christmas or Easter, although we had off from school. Most of the time, this was when Fr. Sylvester would have his big work drives on the building. But there was not too much to do on holidays anyway. We from St. Ann's were lucky, as I had a cousin living at Marty. He taught mechanics in the trade school. His place was our second home, and his family was very good to us. Before the mission school was built, they used to go to the government school.

Besides the regular courses in school, Marty was also a trade school, and we were able to choose what we thought we would like to do when we would get a job outside. I took carpentry and painting. Besides the trade school, Marty had a big farm. A lot of boys worked there to learn farming. I was not interested in tractors then. I learned that here at Saint Meinrad.

At the time I was there, they were building the new grade school and trade school. I helped with the building and did a lot of truck driving. It was ten miles to the next town, where there was a railroad station. Everything for the building came on the railroad cars. We had to carry the cement, bricks, and tile and load them onto the trucks. Fr. Sylvester had the habit of saying, "I want volunteers to do something," and then he would say, "You, and you, and you," pointing to certain ones. Charles McCloud, who was from home and my best friend, and I were always among those he asked.

Did you have any fun or recreation at Marty?

We had sports. The biggest thing was basketball. And Marty had one of the best teams around. We played the towns in the area, but we were not allowed to play in the state tournament, so the Catholic schools had their own state tournament. Fr. Sylvester did not like this, as he did not think the Catholic schools should play against each other. However, he let us play anyway. I was on the team, but most of the time for real games, I kept the bench warm. Marty had one of the best church choirs around and, believe it or not, I was in the choir and schola [music group]. And that was when it was in Latin.

Did anyone else in your family go to Marty?

When my older brother wanted to go to Marty, Fr. Sylvester did not want to accept him because he did not have enough Indian blood in him. But Fr. Hildebrand [Elliot], the one who built St. Ann's Mission, persuaded him to take my brother. So, all seven of us went to Marty. I don't think Marty did me any harm. However, when I came here, I was a little shocked because of the way they made us toe the line at Marty. I don't think there are too many kids these days who would have lasted at

Marty. I do think they were overly strict, but I don't think it did me any harm.

I was at Marty [in the late '80s] for a visit and was disappointed in how poorly the place was kept up. When Fr. Sylvester was in charge, it was always in good condition. The Indian agency was running it. There were not very many students there and not many Catholics for that big church.

When you were in school, did you learn anything about your native Indian culture or language?

No, they didn't believe in any of that at that time. We were supposed to get away from that sort of thing. Now, they are going overboard the other way. My nieces and nephews are all involved in this stuff. I have some nieces in Denver and some in Arizona. I have a brother and family in Arizona and one in Colorado. I don't know if they are learning the language, but they are learning the cultural part. But in my days, we weren't supposed to get involved in this.

Tell me about your religious upbringing.

My father was a man who loved God and his family, his church and country. He only had a grade school education, but his knowledge of how to live and raise a family was far better than some people with a higher education. He was well respected and left a distinct impression of himself on the minds of his family, his church friends and the people in surrounding towns.

At St. Ann's, we had a lot of picnics with Fr. Stanislaus [Maudlin, OSB], the scout master. [Fr. Stanislaus, a monk of Saint Meinrad and cofounder of Blue Cloud Abbey, died in 2006.] There was a special group of us, including my sister Lois, who is now Sister Mary Claude, that Fr. Stanislaus used to take on special outings for sightseeing, picnics and movies. Fr. Stan also took us up in the Turtle Mountains. One of the biggest hills was a monument dedicated to Fr. Belcourt, the founder of our town.

Why did you come to Saint Meinrad, how did your parents feel about it and what expectations did you have?

I was around religious [nuns and priests] all my life and got know what it was all about. You know, it just came to my mind to do it. Nobody suggested going to a religious community. I went to one of the priests at the mission on my own and said something about it. Of course, there were monasteries in the Dakotas, but he was from Saint Meinrad. My mother was not happy, because she didn't know there were monasteries close by. But he told them that I was interested and they sent me literature. I came here at age 17. I really didn't have any expectations. I didn't know what I was getting into.

Were you the first person to come to Saint Meinrad from your hometown?

There was one who was in the fratery [priesthood training]. He then went to Benet Lake and became a prior in one of the Benet Lake foundations.

How did you arrive here?

On the train. There were two of us who came. He went to the oblate house. What they called the oblate house at that time was a good high school to go on to the brotherhood. I was with the junior brothers.

Did you know any of the German brothers?

Yes, I got along with all of them. I didn't have any problems with any of them. There was one of them who didn't speak English. I think he could understand, but he couldn't speak it. The Germans had a separate [Divine] Office. They were under the same superior, but they didn't come to our Office; they had their own Mass.

Tell me about your novitiate.

You started as a candidate for six months, but I was a candidate for nine months because I missed a class that I was supposed to be in. When they asked me to come, they didn't tell me that I was supposed to be here in August. I came here in September. Someone coming from the reservation wasn't that common.

When I first came for my novitiate, I had two novice masters, Fr. Gualbert [Brunsman, OSB], who went out to South Dakota to the Blue Cloud mission. He was our novice master when I came. In the middle of my novitiate, Fr. Claude [Ehringer, OSB] was the superior. They were two different men altogether, so I always joke that, "I've got a split personality because of that."

What was your daily routine during the first years you were here?
In those days, we got up earlier. I think we got up at 3:20 when I first came here. I still get up at 3 o'clock in the morning. We had Office and Mass at the same time. In the novitiate, they gave you an assignment every day. I worked in the kitchen to make coffee in the morning and in the evening. And then I worked in the vineyard. I'd say we came back about 11 o'clock. We went back to work about 1 o'clock. After lunch, we'd go back to wherever we were assigned. We came back here about 4:30 for Vespers at 5.

You weren't allowed to take a shower then, after work. I remember when I was a novice, we just took a shower once a week. But because we worked outside on the building and stuff, the five of us who worked outside could take a shower every day, because we worked harder than some of the other people. The showers were downstairs in the basement, where the Development Office is. In the '60s, this changed and everyone could shower every day. But we didn't have our own showers until we got the new monastery [built in 1982, where each monk has a private bathroom in his cell].

What did you eat when you first came here and what were the seating arrangements?
One of the things we had was "nonsense." It was cornbread all chopped up. We put molasses on that. A lot of the time we had meat, except on Friday and Wednesday. We didn't have meat those days. When I first came, we had to sit together. The brothers sat in one place, the fraters sat in one place and the fathers sat in another place. Now we sit in order of seniority of profession.

Meals were family-style. But even a year or two after we moved over to the new monastery, the food was brought over here in bulk. Then we decided just to keep the cafeteria.

In the early years here, did you have visits from friends and family?

Yes, but not as many as today, as they lived far away. When I first came here, the only time you could go home was after you had made solemn vows. You couldn't even go home for weddings then.

When did you start taking vacations?

Br. Jerome, as a young monk

Under Abbot Bonaventure [Knaebel, OSB]. If your folks were still living, every five years you could go home for a visit. I was one of the first ones to take it. This must have been in the last part of the '60s. The only vacation you had in the early days was to go to Camp Benedict for just a week once a year. The German brothers went together, the junior brothers went together, the fraters went together and so did the fathers. There was a list you signed up on and the same group usually went at the same time with the same people.

At the camp, you got a group of people together and did different things. You got up later and had Mass. I don't remember what time it was. Before a meal, we had some prayers to do. It was a different routine. Since there were a lot of caves out there, a lot of people liked to go caving. There were some people who had equipment. We had a river right there for swimming. They had dug it out and dammed it, so it was bigger right near the camp.

What changes have you seen in the Abbey in terms of recreation?

You're more free to do your own thing now. You still have to be a community person, but recreation now isn't a strict thing. You're on your own as long as you behave yourself. I usually stay up in my room and watch some TV, do some reading or go out for a walk. In 1999, at my 50th anniversary of profession, I was allowed to have a TV in my room.

We used to go down to play volleyball or some other games at the Placidium. We would play handball and some other games. Since we didn't have radios, you had to entertain yourself. Of course, we didn't have that much time after supper because we had Compline, night prayer, at 7 o'clock. You went to your room after that. You were on your own after Compline, and you didn't have to go to bed until 9 o'clock.

What is different today?

I like to get up early now, because I like to take my walk in the morning. When I was younger, after Compline I used to walk around, but back then we had a shorter recreation. Under Gabriel [Abbot Gabriel Verkamp, OSB], we had recreation until 9 o'clock. I go to bed before that now and I get up at 3 o'clock and take a walk.

What were other changes?

I remember when I went out to Blue Cloud; we had a radio out there. But I think when I came back we still couldn't have one in our room. I would say we didn't have one until the late '50s, once Bonaventure became abbot. Everything started to come in after Bonaventure became abbot, but even more so after Gabriel. He also made other changes. We had the junior brothers, the senior brothers, the fraters and two novice masters. He changed that. One novice master was over all the novices and the subprior was made the brother instructor. Fr. Claude still stayed as novice and junior master.

Did you have phones or air conditioning in your cell in the old monastery?
No. The whole community had to use the phone in the porter's office. That was the only phone that we had. They finally put a phone booth in the corridor. It was more private, but you had the porter there while you talked. We didn't get air conditioning until we moved into the new monastery.

When you came here, did you wear the night scapular [a small piece of cloth worn over the shoulders at night]?
Yeah.

When did that stop?
I don't remember. Probably about 1960 under Abbot Bonaventure, because I don't think Ignatius [Abbot Ignatius Esser] would have stopped that custom.

Was there a difference in personalities between the abbots?
Yes, between all six of them. It always seems to be a contrast. They're all different. Ignatius was something else. He was aloof in the monastery. He was in charge and you knew he was in charge. He never went to recreation; he never associated with people at all. Now Abbot Bonaventure did. You know he started many things. Gabriel was a saint; they say our second abbot [Fintan Mundwiler] was a saint. I think we've had two saintly abbots.

Looking back on your formation, how different was it back then compared to now?
There were a lot of differences. We had a half hour conference about once a day. The novice master, Fr. Gualbert at that time, would talk to you. You then would do your work and went to church when you were supposed to. Nowadays, it's just like going to school. The novices are

having instructions all the time. That's a big difference. We had a half hour of what life was about and that was it.

Has your life as a monk been fulfilled?

Well, I think I've got my hundredfold. It was not all roses, but I still think I got my hundredfold, and I hope to get it everlastingly.

Work

Tell me about your work experience after your novice years.

I went up to Blue Cloud Priory [South Dakota] a year after I made vows. I was there for two years, where I was a mason putting up concrete blocks. Br. Vincent [Brunette, OSB] was putting up the sandstone, and I was in the back putting up the other wall.

In January '52, I returned from Blue Cloud. I had to return here to prepare for my perpetual profession of vows, which was to take place in May of that year. Abbot Ignatius told me that, following my profession, I was to return to Blue Cloud, which I wanted to do. At this time, Fr. Claude was brother novice master and superior of all the brothers. He went around Abbot Ignatius' plans, so I stayed here.

When I was at Blue Cloud, the health of Br. Bartholomew [Enright, OSB], who was in change of the vineyard, got worse. So Fr. Claude assigned me to help Br. Bartholomew, and I began to work part-time in the vineyard, which was behind the carpenter shop. Along with this assignment, I also helped make coffee for all three dining rooms. When Br. Bartholomew died in December 1952, I was told to remain in the vineyard until another monk could be found to take his place. Well, you know how that goes.

You wanted to go back to Blue Cloud?

Yes, it was just about like my home place, and I was used to that. It was exciting. I'm glad I stayed here now, but at that time I thought the end of the world was coming. I had to fill out a slip of paper when they were looking for people to go there. I wrote on it, "Whatever Ignatius wanted for me to do." Ignatius had told me when he went out for a visitation to Blue Cloud, when I was up there, that "I want you to go back out to Blue Cloud." It was alright with me. Once I got back here, there was a different tone. Fr. Claude, the junior master at that time, convinced me that I had to stay here.

How did you feel about that?

I'm better now, but at that time, I think I even said that I was ready to leave here and start all over at Blue Cloud. But Fr. Meinrad Hoffman, who had been appointed subprior, told me that Blue Cloud would not accept me if I made such a change. I found out afterward that he wasn't allowed to tell me that, as it was against canon law.

Describe your jobs here.

As part of my job in the vineyard, in 1953, I went to St. Louis to see a winery at St. Stanislaus, a Jesuit seminary. The community operated a 40-acre vineyard and produced Mass wine for sale to the public. We went to get information on how to operate a similar vineyard and winery here at Saint Meinrad. I realized that my hopes to return to Blue Cloud Priory were at an end. But I now realize it was for the better that things turned out that way. I can only say that God indeed works in strange ways!

The vines in our old vineyard were about 75 years old and each year were producing less and less grapes. This required us to buy about half of the grapes needed for winemaking. That's how the new vineyard on Monte Cassino Hill came about.

I became involved working in the wine cellar in 1954. It was under the supervision of Br. Herman [Zwerger, OSB]. I continued my part-time assignment in the kitchen, which worked out well since Br. Herman also worked there. But Br. Herman's health also began to fail and I became more and more involved in the wine cellar.

What did you do there?

We brought the grapes down to the wine cellar. It was down in the basement where the Development Office is now. We crushed the grapes in vats. We had a crusher to crush the grapes, we picked the pulp away and the juice would come; then we would put the juice in a barrel. I was involved in the whole thing.

Tell me more about the development of the vineyard.

In the fall of 1954, we prepared the ground for a new vineyard in back of Monte Cassino on five acres of land. Br. Charles [DeSutter, OSB] made his profession of vows and was assigned to the vineyard. Br. Ambrose [Kaschmitter, OSB], who was in charge of the orchard, also helped. Then I, in turn, would help him out in the orchard. These two areas, the orchard and vineyard, were both under the supervision of Fr. Dominic Metzler, who was the farm manager at the time.

In the spring of 1955, it rained and rained and rained. Although the vines should have been planted in May, it was well into June before we were able to plant them. The vines were all Concord grapes, which do not make the best type of wine, but they grow well in this area.

We used horses and tractors from the farm. I wanted a tractor, but Br. Ambrose wanted to make use of the horses. It was not until the fall of 1955 that we got a tractor. I was able to get a pickup truck through Army surplus. I think I must have been overexcited about this new equipment, for as we were unloading the pickup off the big truck, I fell off and landed on my head!

This accident put me in the Jasper hospital for three days. At the time of the accident, our doctor thought I had broken my nose when I fell. But Br. John Miller, who was the infirmarian, told the doctor that I had not broken my nose, rather that was its natural flat shape.

In 1958, the St. Stanislaus Winery stopped growing grapes and making wine, so a group of us went there to buy their equipment, which included some vats. We had better equipment after that. In 1961, Br. Ambrose was assigned to the dairy barn, so I also took care of the orchard. At the same time, I was becoming more and more involved in mowing as part of the landscape work.

In 1963, Br. David [Petry, OSB] was put in charge of the vineyard, orchard and landscaping. That was the origin of the landscaping crew, as we call it today. In 1985, when Br. David died, Abbot Timothy [Sweeney, OSB] appointed Br. Dominic to oversee the landscaping department as well as the vineyard and winemaking. It was at this time that Father Abbot told me he thought it would be good for me to slow down a bit, so my work was limited to the landscaping crew.

When did you start to do landscaping?

When I started mowing the golf course around 1954, this was when I more or less got started on landscaping. Fr. Michael Keene planned a golf course for the theologians of the seminary, which, of course, needed to be mowed. Fr. Dominic gave us one of the old farm tractors, provided that I would keep the course mowed. We then got a second tractor so we could do bigger areas and I kept getting more involved with it. The whole section down there at the bottom of the hill was the garden and the section nearer the town was all orchard, but it was old. We pulled the trees out because we didn't want the stumps and made a lawn. We built a new orchard near Monte Cassino, too.

At that time, there was not much work involved in the landscaping operation. Fr. Dominic assigned one of his workers to mow with a team of horses a few times a year, and Fr. John Thuis, with the assistance of some fraters and brother novices, did hand mowing on the north side of the Abbey Church.

Tell me more about the golf course.

The golf course was in back of the guest house. It had nine holes. The first hole was right on top of where the flagpole is now near the guest house. The first green was on the hill further to the west. The course went around the hill. The course opened when Fr. Michael [Keene, OSB] became prior under Abbot Bonaventure around 1955. It was open for about ten years and closed in the mid-'60s. It closed because Santa Claus [Indiana] opened and had a better arrangement. It had regular greens while we had sand greens.

When you were doing landscaping, was it all brothers or did you hire people?
It was in the middle '60s, when we started to get bigger after they put Br. David in charge of landscaping, we hired two people. There were also three brothers. Today it's all hired out. Last summer there were no brothers helping out. This is a summer job. When they are not in school, they find something else for them to do. The last full-time brother stopped in 2000.

Where there changes in equipment over the years?
They were using horses when I came in 1945. It wasn't very long after that when they just used tractors. When Fr. Dominic died [1957], we were already done with horses. They were real nice Belgian horses.

Did you have a sabbatical at any point?
I was on sabbatical at Mount Angel Abbey [St. Benedict, OR] in 1988. Abbot Timothy asked me to write about the Marty experience.

Did you have other jobs?
I was a volunteer fireman. About '56, we had a fire department with half the people from the town and half from the monastery. I think there were 12 people from each. We had horses for parades and show. We started with one truck and got the second one after I was here. The first one was a Chevrolet; the second was what we called a pumper. It had all kind of equipment for grass fires and forest fires. It had a big pump on it that supplied water for the other truck. We go to the whole township from Fulda to Dale. The forest fires were the worse ones. They were hard to work with.

Describe what would happen when you were called out for a fire.

We had a siren. It now goes off every Saturday at noontime from the big tower near the middle of the seminary. We would run to the fire-house and get on the phone and find out what's wrong. I was one of the drivers, so I was usually one of the first ones down there and would get into the truck. The firehouse was located at the bottom section of where The Valet is and had two firetrucks. The trucks are now located in the brick building at the bottom of the hill near the Abbey Press. Both the abbey and the town use it. The fire station was moved down there in the late '90s.

I left the fire department when I came back from my sabbatical around '88. There is only one monk from the monastery now, and that's Br. Benjamin [Brown].

Prayer

In the Rule of St. Benedict, *what is your favorite chapter?*

I can't really say that I have one.

Do you have a key to living Benedictine spirituality. In other words, what's important to you as a Benedictine monk?

Just to live decent every day, and to do what God wants you to do. That's a daily chore every day.

What has been your most difficult time?

When I couldn't go back to Blue Cloud. I was ready to quit then.

Why didn't you quit? Why did you stay?

I don't know. Something in the back of my brain said, "No, just keep going." I guess I talked to people. I can't say that I'm an overly spiritual person. The next time I was ready to quit was when I was retired from landscaping. I'm not ready to retire; I'm not used to that. Although I know that I can't do what I used to be able to do, I didn't care to be suddenly taken off.

So what are you doing now?

In the morning, I take care of the church and mop the corridors and a couple of the chapels. In the afternoon, I take off. I am free in the afternoon.

What has been your happiest time?

I can't pull up one big thing. I try to be happy every day by putting all it's worth into every day.

Vatican II: Its Effect on the Church and Saint Meinrad Archabbey

Compare the morale in the monastery today with 30 or 40 years ago.

I can't say it's any worse, or any better, than when I first came. We're still being human.

How do you feel about the Mass being in English rather than Latin?

Oh, I like the English Mass; when they put in a little bit of Latin, I don't like that. I don't see any reason why we would want to go back to Latin, you know. I can't see how we have kept our faith with all that Latin stuff, because you didn't know what you were doing.

As you know, the number of religious vocations has been declining every year. What has this meant to you in terms of the monastery?

When I first came, people kept coming here all the time. Now there is just too much outside to distract people. There is just too much outside to lure people away. We didn't have all the stuff we have now. We didn't have all these toys that people have now. You had to get your own toys. We had to make our own stuff; we had to play our own games. We didn't have all those luxuries that they have nowadays. Although I hear that younger people are now looking for something, which is good. I think we have gone from one extreme to the other.

What is the future of the Church?
    I really can't speculate on that too much. I don't know what it's going to do. I pray for the Church, but I don't have much expectation of where it's going.

    Profile based upon: Br. Jerome Croteau to Prof. Ruth Engs, July 13, 2005, Interview Transcription, Saint Meinrad Archives. Also:
    Croteau, Jerome, OSB, "The time I spent at Marty: A reminiscence." St. Meinrad Archives, 3 pp., ca. 1989.
    _____, "Growing up in North Dakota," Saint Meinrad Archives, 9 pp., ca. 1989.*
    _____, "The Vineyard Remembered," Saint Meinrad Archives, 9 pp., 1991.*

Chapter Four

Br. Terence Griffin, OSB

As a Benedictine monk of Saint Meinrad, Br. Terence Griffin spent much of his working career in the Business Office (1960-77), and in payroll and insurance (1977-84). He also served in the health service (1984-02). In 2001, he began working in a new business venture at Saint Meinrad, Abbey Caskets.

Born in Pittsburgh, PA, on February 15, 1930, Br. Terence attended Assumption Grade School and graduated from North Catholic High School (1947) in Pittsburgh. After high school, he attended Duquesne University and received a diploma in accounting at Robert Morris Business College (1952), both in Pittsburgh. He subsequently worked in the office of two steel-related businesses in Pittsburgh before coming to Saint Meinrad. Br. Terence made first profession May 7, 1960, and solemn profession, June 10, 1963.

Br. Terence serves as cantor for various religious services at the Archabbey, is a member of the schola [the monastic choir], acts as an assistant guest master leading tours of the Archabbey, and has been for many years assistant custodian (1984 to present) for the chapel at Monte Cassino Shrine.

Br. Terence was interviewed by Prof. Ruth C. Engs on September 19, 2005, and November 15, 2005.

Childhood and Early Years as a Monk

Tell me about your family and childhood.

I am from Pittsburgh, Pennsylvania. I was born February 15, 1930, and was named Daniel. Both my parents and my aunts and uncles were immigrants from Ireland. Dad was a bus and trolley driver. We had trolleys in those days. We were an Irish Catholic family and obeyed all the rules of the Church. I attended Catholic schools, Assumption Grade School and North Catholic High School, on the north side of the city.

This school was operated by the Society of Mary, the Marianist Brothers, who have their headquarters in Dayton, Ohio. We were taught by nuns [St. Joseph Sisters] in grade school. The nuns were very strict. When I graduated from high school in 1947, I was not sure of what to do, so I went to Duquesne University for one year. I dropped out and switched to Robert Morris Business School, because I wanted to get into bookkeeping and accounting.

Do you have any high school memories?

This sounds strange to me now, but all my socializing was with Catholic boys, as this is who I went to school with. I had no bad feelings toward anyone who was non-Catholic. When I think about it now, the public school kids probably thought, "What is wrong with you people? Aren't we good enough for you? How come you don't hang around with us?" In the summertime, we would play ball with them and swim. Still, I hung around with boys from my own school, but I would go to the games or to the dances at the public schools.

How about your religious upbringing? For example, did you serve as an altar boy?

I did serve as altar boy for Mass in grade school. I didn't think much about a religious vocation until my mid-20s, when I was already out of school working. I knew a lot of parish priests and got along well with them while in high school. It gradually occurred to me that maybe I would like the religious life. I wanted something simple. I didn't want to be a priest who would have to get up and preach from the pulpit on Sundays. I just thought that the monastic life might be down my alley. However, I didn't know much about it. The diocese's vocation director, fortunately, used to be at my parish, so I knew him well. I spoke to him about this possibility. He knew about Saint Meinrad, because Pittsburgh seminarians were attending here at the time. He was the one who suggested coming here.

I would imagine that a lot of people were probably surprised at my coming here. I did not tell many that I used to attend Benediction every Wednesday evening. This was the singing of certain hymns, or canticles, before the Blessed Sacrament. Usually, it was for a particular purpose, like devotions to the Blessed Virgin. Some of us would attend that after work. The point was that I was not fervently religious, but I did do that. Now that I think of it, it was a place to meet with your friends, both boys and girls. Afterward, we would talk and then we might go out somewhere. That was the extent of my religious life, other than Mass, of course. This was all before the Vatican Council.

How did you see the Church in those early years?

My view of the Church was probably like everybody else. We did what we were told and I didn't think much about it. I was not fervently religious. There were certain complaints, but nothing major.

Before you came here, what did you do in terms of work?

I did work in two different jobs and they were both clerical. I worked first at Pittsburgh Forging from 1952 to 1955, but I was laid off because business became slow. At Forging, I would order the steel. I would check and see how many pieces they were going to use on a particular job. When they were running low on supplies or I knew they were going to finish, I would order for the next job. That was a fairly responsible job, now that I think about it. I did like that job. The atmosphere was dirty and sooty, though, and I had to walk through it.

From 1955 to 1959, I worked at Pittsburgh Coke and Chemical. They were decent, lower- to middle-income people. I did minor clerical work. I had been to bookkeeping school and they needed someone with that background. So I got my first good break; they gave me a job in the business office. I was able to use my bookkeeping studies to good advantage. It was a decent job; I also worked with blueprints.

Where did you live?

I still lived with my mother and dad. Irish men are supposed to be slow at going out and socializing. There was an Irish joke about this. The priest said, "Christ was Irish, don't you know. He stayed home with his mother and father until he was 30 years old. He would go out drinking with his 12 friends every night." I have heard that Irish men don't think about marriage until they are 35 years old, and they stay at home. Today, people think that is unusual, because they want to leave home and board somewhere.

How did your parents and your friends feel when you told them you were coming here?

I am pretty sure most people who were my own age, or older, were surprised at my coming to a monastery. I had an active social life, but I didn't get serious with any one girl. Even my parents, who were pretty religious, didn't think I had any inclination at all for a religious vocation. I am sure they were surprised. They are both dead now, but they enjoyed it here when they visited and they could see I was happy here and that this was my lifestyle.

I think that I am a simple person and I like the simple life. That is what I used to tell young men about me, when I was hosting them as potential candidates. I would say to them, "As long as you are not looking for a lot of excitement and can follow a routine, this is the life for you. You are not tied down and nothing is real, real strict. You can talk, you can laugh, you can socialize. But it is still a simple life and if that is good enough for you, then this is the place for you."

When did you enter the monastery?

I came in 1959. I was 29. I thought about it for a while. I am great at delaying in making decisions. So I took a chance. I didn't really have much of an idea of what I was in for. "Of course," I thought, "you can always leave." I still did not have any idea in the world what to expect. I realized that there would be changes in my lifestyle. So I came. I never felt that it was overly burdensome. Fr. Claude [Ehringer, OSB] was novice and junior master for 20 or 30 years, I understand. He was old-fashioned in his way, but I think he was good for that time. He was strict. People would just expect that, and that was the way it was.

So how did you get here?

By train. Trains were more commonly used then than they are now. You could go to downtown Pittsburgh and get a train to downtown Louisville, Kentucky. This was a hub and you could take a bus from Louisville to Evansville, Indiana, and back again. Today it would be airlines and you would have someone pick you up at the airport.

As a novice, what happened on a typical day? How does it differ compared to today?

The brothers' and novices' Divine Office started at 4 o'clock in the morning. Fortunately, I guess you would say, less than a year after I came, they moved it to 5:15. I always joked, "I joined at the right time." The brothers had Office separately and in English. The priests would be in the church and they would recite it in Latin. Matins was very long and we were grateful we didn't have to say it. We were in the brothers' oratory. We would finish before they would and then would march into the church by twos. We would file into place behind them and wait for them to finish. We were supposed to be quiet while they were finishing. Then we had Mass together.

The novices and juniors did what I just described. However, the senior brothers did not do this. They attended Mass in their own oratory and didn't even come to conventual Mass, like they did on Sunday. They would eat breakfast and report for work. There were so many jobs to be done back then. After Mass, we had meditation. It was not spiritual reading either; it was just simply meditation. Right after Mass, each priest would say his individual private Mass and the brothers would serve them. The priests had a long chapel. It was called the Apostles Chapel. There were six altars on either side of the room and each one had a painting of an apostle on the wall. The priest would have to speak in a low voice, as there were many others close to him.

Then there were the "second row Masses." There were not enough altars for all the priests. So the younger ones, the ones with less seniority, would be assigned to wait—remember this was right after conventual Mass. The "first row" said Mass and went to breakfast. The "second row" had to wait until they were finished to say their Mass and so they would come very late to breakfast. Of course, you didn't want to be assigned as a server for those saying second Mass, as you couldn't eat your breakfast until they were finished.

Then everybody had a job to do. The brothers were working in the kitchen at that time or working at the farm. They were doing a lot more trades. Brothers would work on landscaping, plumbing, electrician work and regular maintenance. Some of them would get dirty, but they would have to come to Noon Office, no matter how dirty they were, and put their habit on. Maybe they changed shirts if they were really dirty, then eat, and take their habit off afterward. But this began to be too much trouble, so about 20 to 25 years ago, it was decided that we didn't have to wear our habits for Noon Office.

Over the years, supper and Vespers have alternated. You did one and then you did the other. Right now, Vespers is at 5 o'clock and then supper. Back then, it was supper, Vespers, evening recreation and then Compline [night prayers]. After Compline, the novices would set the table for breakfast. Your place was set with a napkin and a plate and silverware. Your napkin had your name on it.

Tell me about recreation during your earlier years here.

Br. Terence, as a young monk

Recreation was compulsory. It was separate for brothers, priests and fraters—clerics—those who were going to be priests. Nowadays, we are all bunched together. Those first eight or ten years after I came, there was still separation. But I was content. I was very, very happy. The happiest years in my life, I guess. There were a lot more brothers than there are now. So our recreation rooms were just filled and there was a roaring noise. We played cards, checkers and Scrabble. We would sit around and talk, play music—at that time it was records. But those recreations were just roaring and there is nothing like that now. The idea was you would have recreation until about 8 o'clock, then Compline, then silence. You did not have to go to bed. You could read a magazine, for example, or write letters. Just no talking.

The first eight or ten years when I was younger, we would play volleyball, handball and softball. Not every day, maybe two afternoons or weekends. Great camaraderie. I enjoyed that. I liked sports and I didn't mind it at all. But, of course, many did not like it because they weren't athletically inclined and weren't interested in this. Today, I don't think the superiors could get everybody to play volleyball or handball. But as I said, it was compulsory then, but I enjoyed it.

When the seminarians were away at Christmas time, we could use their gym. We could play pool, ping pong and even bowl. This was a big treat. In the summer, it was too hot to do that. Then we would use the seminarians' tennis courts or swim in their lake. Today the tennis courts are being removed; they are being torn up.

For many years, we had summer school—a six-week course. Mostly nuns attended. It just stopped about two or three years ago. There were a few priests and, of course, a few lay people. But it was mostly priests and nuns. They came to our daily Office and Mass and we became friends with them. On occasion, we would play volleyball and swim. The prior at that time, Fr. Gerard [Ellspermann, OSB], who is now dead, came up with a rule one summer. He said, "The use of the lake from 1 to 3 is for the monks, and from 3 to 5 is for the nuns." But that didn't last long. It was funny. People were complaining about that right off the bat.

Is there anything else about recreation that's different today?
As I mentioned, recreations were loud and rowdy back then. Nowadays, the recreation room is almost empty. Sometimes, five or six people watch TV. It sure isn't like it used to be.

Why isn't recreation rip-roaring today? What happened?
I don't know. A lot of us are older, of course. There was no television during that time either and there was no radio. You had magazines. Nowadays, people watch television and don't talk. In my opinion, people want to do their own thing today. In other words, "Why do I have to do this just because you want to do it? If I want to listen to Beethoven, then I'll listen to Beethoven. You can listen to country music or whatever

you please." Everybody does their own thing. Some of it is because we are older and we are not looking for excitement.

Now, we still have a morning coffee break and that is pretty good. Ten or twelve people show up there. The younger ones, for some reason, do not come. Perhaps they are at school or working. There is good camaraderie at the morning coffee break, and at lunch there is lots of talking and laughing among us. Abbot Lambert [1995-2004] would try some socials on occasion. Nothing major, just drinks and snacks, just to get the people together. Some people complained about it. I thought it was a good idea. It does not happen very often. I think he had a good purpose of wanting to get people together in a large group. I like to read a lot and so I am content with the reading.

What do the younger men do?

The juniors and novices have this building that is called the Placidium. They go down there; they have video and a refrigerator. They can make more noise down there. Some of them are going to school and they have to study in the evenings. I hear them once in a while saying, "Oh, I can't go down there; I have to study." However, some do go down and just hang around.

How about meals then and now?

For supper, we sit in seniority. The tables are set, there is silence and there is table reading. The reading now is the autobiography of our new pope [Benedict XVI]. In the past, we had reading at noon and supper. Now there is just one reading a day. Back then, when you were assigned as a table waiter for a week, the table waiters had to do two meals a day. Now they have to do just one meal a day—the evening meal. Now at lunch we can talk and there is no reading. We go through a buffet line. There are two lunch attendants to help out.

How many people sit at table now compared to the past?

Right now, there are six people to a table. Back then, there was one long table. If you were a table waiter, you would have a bowl of potatoes or meat and set it out on each table, family style, enough for four people. Nowadays, even for supper there is a buffet line. Now the table waiters set up the food in the buffet lines. They pour the coffee, milk and water. Back then, the table waiters would have to clean up afterward. The lunch is lighter today and it only takes two attendants. Some changes are for the better.

When did this change?

When we came over here to the new monastery [1982], we continued to have meals family style. Because of the renovation of the church, they couldn't get the carts through [from the kitchen in another building to the monastery]. They had to haul the food in a laundry truck and come around on the outside. To make it easier, they just put the food in big pans and we went through buffet lines. This was to be temporary while the renovations were going on. But it was so successful and more efficient that they just left it as it is. That was not their intention when they started. It was just done out of emergency. Now we still stick with that. We go through the line; however, the elderly do get a tray. I got a kick out of this; everybody was leery about it and wondered how it would work out. It turned out that it was much, much better than the original plan. We also have wine for supper.

Work

Tell me what kind of work you did as a novice.

First of all, a couple of us worked on the farm. We collected the eggs at the hen house. It was not heavy work, though. The hens would be on a nest and you had to pick up their eggs. This meant that you had to reach under her to get the eggs. She would snap at you, so you had to get her attention and then grab her by the head. Of course, we tried not to hurt her. We just held the head with one hand so you could grab the eggs with the other. She would give up and would not put up much of a fight, so we just took the eggs and left her alone. We collected the eggs in a basket.

At certain times of the year, we would put up hay. That was much heavier work. The baler would bale rectangular bundles. Now they are round. You can see them by the roadside. I guess they use a forklift or something. I do not know what the weight of the bales was then. You could lift them, but it was a struggle. Then the wagon would come and you would throw the bale on it. Someone up in the wagon would stack it, and then you would come back to the barn and unload the hay from the wagon up into the loft and then stack it in the loft.

You would stack the bales higher and higher. Sometimes your foot would slip in between the bales and you would sink in up to your knees. That was just one disadvantage. It took a lot of energy, but it was good for me. I had never done anything like that; I was a city boy. You would have a hard time getting novices to do that today.

My classmate, Br. Raban [Bivins, OSB], worked with the hogs. I never did that for some reason. He seemed to like it, so I guess they let him do it.

Tell me about the hog operation.

They raised the hogs, fattened them until they got a certain weight, and then they slaughtered them. They were for our consumption. They also had dairy cows, but we did not have anything to do with that. They milked the dairy cows twice a day, about 3 o'clock in the morning and 3 in the afternoon. There were a few monks who did that, but it was mostly employees. I admired the laymen and their wives. I think they worked in two four-hour shifts. They worked in the morning, went home about 9 o'clock, then went back again in the afternoon and did the same thing all over again. We would sometimes take the guests to watch them milk the cows.

Were there other novice jobs?

Yes, we picked grapes each autumn. It took a week. The novices and anyone else who volunteered would do this. I volunteered a few times. When I was working, we used a clipper that almost looks like a wire snipper. You would use those to clip off a bunch of grapes. You had to work on your side of a vine and another person worked on the other side. Presumably, the bunches would be sticking out so we wouldn't be getting in each other's way. We then put them in a bucket. As a novice a few times, we did work in the wine cellar crushing the grapes. That was interesting, but we didn't do that too often.

The crushing would produce juice. Then you added sugar and this, I understand, caused it to ferment. I don't remember anything more than the crushing. Then the mixture had to sit for a long time. Br. Benjamin [Brown, OSB] might know. He was our last wine crusher in the wine cellar.

How was the wine?

We only had dark wine. When Br. David [Petry, OSB] was here, he wanted to branch out, so he started planting green grapes. He traveled to upstate New York, where he could purchase green grape plants. It took a couple of years for them to get developed. But for the most part, it was all dark wine, which was fine with me. I was so disappointed when they closed the winery.

I was sorry when they closed down all these departments. We closed the chicken house. We closed the farm, the dairy and the hogs; then we closed the vineyard. Now we buy it. We get a variety, we get the dark, the rosé and the light wine. That's fine with me, but I was disappointed that they were closing the wine cellar. Ideally, a hundred years ago, the monks were supposed to be independent and do everything themselves. In this day and age, you buy from a company in large economy size.

Tell me about your jobs after your novitiate.

Once I was professed, I thought life was easier than when I was a novice, because as a novice you had a lot of odd jobs. And you kept busy all day from morning until almost bedtime. When you became professed, you had an ordinary workday job from 8 to 5 like everybody else. You worked during the day until supper and then you were free in the evening. So I found that easier. In 1960, I took first vows and then I went to the Business Office to do bookkeeping. This was the year Kennedy was elected president. I stayed there over 25 years. I was very fortunate, as it was something that I enjoyed. And it was a nice atmosphere. I liked that a lot more than the novitiate.

When I first started out in the Business Office, it was all monks. Fr. Rupert [Ostdick, OSB] was the boss. Then we hired one girl; then we hired another girl. When they left, usually to get married or to have children, they were replaced by another girl. So I made a lot of good friends over the years. Pretty soon, there was Fr. Rupert and me and three or four girls. So that became the trend in the Business Office. Right now, it's all employees.

So that was a change that took place gradually. I then went from the Business Office here on the Hill down to the Abbey Press. I was in payroll then. I was paymaster for departments on the Hill also, but the office was located at the Press. So I made a lot of new friends down there, too. I enjoyed that aspect of it. A nice part of the job is the friends you made.

Anyhow, I worked there about 10 years. From payroll in 1984, I went up here to the monastery infirmary helping the elderly as a nurse's aid. It was quite a drastic change.

There was one other brother, Br. Ivo [Staples, OSB], who died a couple of years ago, and me. Br. Daniel [Linskens, OSB] was the boss. He was over at our health service most of the time. He would come here when needed. Of course, there weren't as many patients. Nowadays, it's all women who work there. Br. Dominic [Warnecke, OSB] just left there within the last few weeks. He gave showers. He took the food carts back and forth and took out the trash and the laundry. Anyhow, they need more people now than they had. As I said earlier, they started out hiring one gal, then a second and then a third. Now it's all girls. Women are kinder and more patient with the patients, and not so brusque as a man.

Then I went from the infirmary on a sabbatical for two months in 2001. I don't know why I was chosen for a sabbatical. Maybe they really did think I was working hard and deserved it. When I came back from that, I started in the casket business.

What did you do on your sabbatical?

I lived at the Ferdinand convent. I didn't live in the main building. It was something like our guest house. I studied computers. I didn't know anything at all about computers, so I learned about computers and took piano lessons. Part of it was just relaxing. When I came back from that, I got into caskets.

Abbey Caskets features wooden caskets. They started with wooden caskets tapered toward the foot similar to what the monks are buried in. They had two of them, a light one and one with a dark stain. Now there are six models. Some are rectangular with a domed lid. The one used by the monks is flat on top. I help deliver them sometimes. I drive a van, do some bookkeeping, do the invoices and so on. I call the truckers in Evansville and arrange for their trucks to come. We advertise by way of brochures, which we mail out. We also have a Web site.* We get a lot of people calling us because they saw us on the Web site, which surprises me. We also do mailings to alumni, religious orders and so on.

Prayer

What is your favorite part or chapter of the Rule of St. Benedict?

What I like about the Benedictine *Rule* is that it is not specific. It adjusts to what climate you are in, and whatever work you're doing, I think that the *Rule* is adaptable to the times we live in and the work we're doing. We were teaching 12 years of school here, and that was our major work. We've had to adjust and find some different type of work for people to do, because we closed down eight years of school. Now, this didn't happen overnight. It was over a period of time.

St. Benedict allowed for imperfection in people. He realized that people were imperfect, were flawed. He gave them a second chance and a third chance. He realized that he was not dealing with saints. He was dealing with imperfect—I wouldn't want to say sinners—but with flawed human beings.

What's your key to living Benedictine spirituality?

I would say balance. We live a moderate life. Trappists and Cistercians are very strict; they don't talk or eat meat. We talk and joke and laugh and enjoy each other's company. We enjoy a good meal and we hold down a job. But to balance that, we have recreation. If you like to read and you're a monk, it's a big advantage. Naturally, you should include holy works by a saint or a Catholic intellectual. There is time to do this, even though you hold down a job. They allow time for this. These can be books, not necessarily by a St. Augustine or saint anybody, but a Benedictine or other Catholic authors. That's what's good about the life. You can have both. It's a balance.

In work among the laity, they may have children to raise, committee meetings to attend and travel that takes up their time. We don't have that. We have plenty of time to read. It helps a lot, I think, if a monk likes to read because he can take advantage of this. Of the others who don't like to read, they probably don't appreciate the free time and I don't know how they spend it.

What were your happiest times?

I sound like I'm writing a fictional story or Hollywood movie, but the happiest moments were the first ten years or so I was here. I was really happy then. I guess I had settled into a routine and it was calm and collected. I really didn't need to have a lot of excitement. Although we had some excitement, as I've told you, with recreation. I had a simple life and a job that I liked, the time to read and recreate and, fortunately, I got along with the vast majority of the monks, keeping in mind separation. As I mentioned, the brothers recreated in one room and the priests in another. At that time, it was simply done that way. I, of course, just recreated with the brothers.

What were your most difficult times?

When you're new and your superior is older than you are, there is a certain routine that you follow. You think, "This is the way it is done."

And you're happy to do it that way. Ten or 15 years later, new people come in behind you. When my old superior retired, they appointed someone younger who, in my opinion, was too lax with them. He didn't make them toe the line. I think that gave me more irritation than anything else. For example, in the early '70s, the Vatican Council changed things. Those coming here didn't go by the same standards as I did. They had different ideas, they had a different concept of discipline, and there was always a generation gap. Their superior, in my view, was not strict enough with them. Many times, I would say, "Oh, they can do anything they want; they can get away with murder!" It irritated me. Anyhow, this was what caused me more unhappiness that anything else.

However, I think any life gets like that. I think that happens to anybody, whether it's in religious life or not. A person, who has been working at a job for 20 or 30 years, sees that a new person who comes in is less disciplined. That irritates the older person because that's not the way he used to do it. It's not necessarily that you're wrong and they're right, but things were stricter then. At the present time, I guess I have adjusted to this, as I get along pretty well with the newcomers—the novices and the juniors.

Vatican II: Its Effect on the Church and Saint Meinrad Archabbey

The changes that have affected the contemporary Church may seem now to have been inevitable. Some think Pope John XXIII was overly optimistic and that, ever since Vatican Council II, the Church has been paying a heavy price for his initiatives; others applaud his efforts. What is your opinion about this?

I would say this is somewhat a two-edged sword. For the most part, the Vatican Council was beneficial. In other words, it was good for the Church. It was a good thing John XXIII had the Council at that time, because otherwise there would have been defections. But, naturally, some people are going to take advantage and go too far. That's not his fault. Everybody says, "Give me a little bit more freedom," and they take advantage. You go to church now and it's in English and, of course, the youngsters only know that. What if the Church decided to go back to Latin and have the priest face the other direction? They wouldn't put up with that! So I say it was a good thing he did come along and make the change, even allowing for some people abusing it.

How about at the monastery?

I would say that it affected the monastery in the same way it affected the world and the Church in general. Our liturgy changed like the Church's liturgy. My answer would be the same for the monastery as for the Church. And I say it is a good thing he came along and did it then, because there would have been more of a rebellion otherwise.

How about other changes?

It was an age of protest and questioning of authority, even defying authority; you didn't just accept it. You said, "Why?" Women spoke out. Many religious, both men and women, left their communities or the priesthood. This period also coincided with the Vietnam War. It was a bad time to be a superior for men's or women's communities.

Compare the morale of the monastery today with 40 to 50 years ago.

I don't think there is any grumbling going on now or unhappiness. People are generally happy and contented and they get along well, keeping in mind what I've often said, that recreations are not as lively and everybody doesn't recreate together. Overall, I think we are very lucky. There are no factions, such as liberal or conservative. So I think that the morale is good.

The number of religious vocations declines every year. What is the meaning of these changing patterns—to the monastery and to the Church at large?

As you know, there is a vocation problem. Not enough people are entering and those who do come are older. They may be well into their 30s and are usually well educated. This is typical for either monks or seminarians now. This is good because they know what life is all about, compared to somebody who came here right out of school. So it's good in that respect, as we are getting vocations from people who are older and experienced.

For example, Br. John Mark [Falkenhain, OSB], who is now a junior, which means he is in his three-year period before taking his solemn vows, is around 38. He's a psychologist and sometimes gives retreats. Last year, a group of priors from all over the country were here for a workshop. Br. John Mark was their retreat master. A year ago, as a novice, he was part of a panel discussion for the alumni on pedophilia. This year he's giving another talk to the alumni. This is unusual for a junior monk to be given all this responsibility.

Because we have fewer vocations, as compared to the past, we have to replace them by hiring employees. There are a lot more employees doing jobs today here than 30 or 40 years ago. Remember what I said earlier when I started in the Business Office? It wasn't a big staff, about three or four—all monks. Now it is all employees. That is how they are going to solve the problem of not enough monks. They are not going to have any choice in the matter. We are just one small sample of the Church in general.

How else is the loss of vocations affecting the Church?

You read about the loss of vocations all the time. But that's not my problem; that's the bishops' problem. In Rome, three or four months ago, the bishops around the world, including those from the U.S., discussed, "What should we do about vocations?" They decided at the time not to make any changes in the rules—just to go out of your way more to attract young men. Encourage someone whom you think would make a good priest. Talk to them and encourage them. The bishops will have to come up with some kind of a strategy.

As you know, they are merging parish churches. The pastor will be told, "Starting this week, you are getting a new assignment. You are pastor of this church plus that church." This is sort of mind-boggling. Somewhere in the Indianapolis archdiocese, Brownsburg, I think, a priest had a grade school. It was a fairly decent size, having 200 people. Now, in addition, he has been assigned another parish, which also has a grade school. That is a sign of the times. How he will manage and whether he can do a good job, I have no idea. There is going to be plenty more of that. Someone who is in a smaller area or in a smaller town often has three separate parishes. They just drive around to different parishes. That is just a fact of life that does not affect me as a monk so much.

Even if the Mass was to be celebrated in English, was the elimination of the Latin from the academic curriculum a good idea?
    You mean Latin in the schools? I don't have anything against that. Sister Clare [Smith, RSM] in the theological school faculty teaches Latin.

Should it be mandatory for all seminary students?
    No, you have to be practical and realistic. What is the language most useful today? Spanish, Spanish, Spanish. You know why? Because Hispanics are everywhere in the country and you have to be able to relate to them and communicate with them. So Ms. Nury Nuila-Stevens teaches Spanish. I think our seminarians have to take Spanish classes. If not, I think they should. I'm not begrudging anybody who wants to study Latin, but it's not something that is practical today.

Comment on what you think have been the positive or negative changes in the recent history of the Church.
    I think a positive change is the emergence of the laity in the actual running of the Church. There are complaints that there is a shortage of priests. The archbishop [Most Rev. Daniel Buechlein, OSB] is in Washington attending a meeting right now, talking about this question. What should we do about married priests or ordaining women? I do not want to get into that. The bishops realize that we have to do something. What should we do? Some say that women are being overlooked, are not appreciated and are not in positions of authority. What the bishops are saying is that they cannot be ordained priests. However, I think that

some women are teaching theology in seminaries or Catholic schools. We have a few here. Women really are, in fact, very much involved in the operation of a parish. Women, sometimes a nun, are chancellors of some dioceses. That is a most important position.

My sister, who is retired from bookkeeping, worked at a parish part-time, so I learn from her when I visit her. A large parish has a big staff of people and, to me, the priest is like chairman of the board. He is in charge of it all, but women are doing the actual work in instructing engaged couples, RCIA [instruction for those entering the Church] or whatever. Women are actively involved in the operation of a parish. Some people complain that women are not ordained; they don't ask for their opinion. But in the Indianapolis archdiocese, for example, the chancellor is a woman. Women are principals of Catholic grade schools and their teachers are mostly women. So they are actively involved. I certainly am in favor of that. I am saying that despite the decline of vocations. Maybe we can survive, despite the shortage of priests.

Assuming that you agree that there is no going back to pre-Conciliar days, what has been lost? What has been gained?

Between one nation and another nation, you could go to Mass and it would be the same language. That was a uniting force. When it was announced that we were going to start saying Mass in English, instead of the Latin, the one disadvantage was that you could not go to any country in Europe and attend Mass there and understand the language. I would say that's a minor loss. It is minor because it does not affect most people unless they are traveling in Europe or Latin America.

I would say the respect for authority is less. As mentioned before, as I got older and further along in seniority, the newcomers' discipline was different from mine and that sort of rubbed me the wrong way. Keeping in mind that, in the past, some parish pastors, as they got older, were dictators, "You do it my way." That was not favorable, but at least everybody knew where they stood. Summarizing it, I would say the respect for authority has been lost.

What has been gained?

The biggest gain is more involvement of the laity, including women, working in the parish. There are lay men, too. But the biggest change has been the involvement of women. In my sister's church, sometimes there is a husband and wife team instructing the engaged couples. This is a good idea. They work together as a couple. The biggest change has been the presence of women because they were not involved at all before.

Is it correct to speak of the Catholic Church today as different from what it was at mid-20th century?

Yes, it is different. The traditions today are different than 50 years ago. There are certainly a large number of Hispanics in the Church today in this country. I think people used to simply do what they were told. It was a case of "Father knows best." This was done on a smaller scale here. We did what we were told by the novice master. That's the way things were in a monastery. Nowadays, there is questioning of authority. You do not always run to the leader to ask what to do.

The parish priest realizes he is dealing with highly educated people. A good man takes advantage of this and says, "What do you suggest we do for this situation?" He won't begrudge this and won't make the final decision on his own. A good sensible, practical person will use the talent of the people in his parish. A good abbot might ask someone like Br. John Mark for his advice. Instead of the leader making the decision and everybody following, people speak out and people make their own decisions. In those days, a problem between me and my superior was a microcosm of the Church in general.

What are your hopes for the future for the Archabbey and the Church?

I think you have to look at the Archabbey in context of other religious orders, both male and female, in this country. I think we're doing well, relatively. Our vocations are pretty good compared to some. We had to change and we have to keep adapting, in order to recruit for our seminaries. They're working hard to convince young men to come here. So they're going to have to continue this. I would hope very much that our theology school continues into the far distant future.

We have to keep adjusting to what work we can do and what we're good at—similar to how we adjusted when the college closed down. One thing we have here, which I think we should expand on and advertise in some way, is the guest house. You see guests flocking to our church. They are always coming. Last weekend, teenagers filled the church and all those benches along the side. People seem to enjoy coming here, to get away from the hustle and bustle of their urban life. I think we should take advantage of that.

We need to hold more retreats for both young and old. We have a new guest house. I'm always so edified when I see the youngsters come here and join us in church and that they want to be here. We have to adapt and take advantage of our assets. We will be all right in the future and I would say the abbey will do well as long as we keep adjusting to the times.

Profile based upon: Br. Terence Griffin to Prof. Ruth C. Engs, September 19, 2005, and November 15, 2005, Interview Transcription, Saint Meinrad Archives.

*Abbey Caskets Web site: www.abbeycaskets.com

Chapter Five

Fr. Camillus Ellspermann, OSB

As a priest and monk of Saint Meinrad, Fr. Camillus has had a varied career that ranged from teaching at the seminary schools to full-time parish work.

He was born in Evansville, IN, on December 18, 1925, and came to Saint Meinrad in 1939 as a student. He graduated from Saint Meinrad High School, College and School of Theology, and was ordained May 13, 1950. He made his first profession as a monk on September 14, 1945, and his solemn profession September 15, 1949. Fr. Camillus received an STL (1951) and a master's degree in sociology (1955) from Catholic University, Washington, DC. During his first 25 years as a priest, he taught Latin (1951-59) in the high school and sociology at the college (1951-65). He was infirmarian (1951-61) and assistant spiritual director of the high school (1961-64). He served as instructor and novice master to the brothers (1964-67), spiritual coordinator in the School of Theology and head of the Deacon Internship Program (1967-75). During the Civil Rights era, he was part of the March on Selma.

For his next 25 years, Fr. Camillus was assigned to various parishes for pastoral work including St. Benedict (1975-1991) and St. Henry (1991-2001) in southern Indiana and two parishes in Wyoming (2001-2005), after which he retired, due to illness, and came back to the monastery. Over the past decade, he has been writing his memoirs concerning his varied experiences as a priest and monk over his long years of service. His brother, Fr. Gerard, was also a monk of Saint Meinrad.

Fr. Camillus was interviewed by Prof. Ruth C. Engs on September 23, 2005. [Fr. Camillus died on February 2, 2007, before this book was published.]

Childhood and Early Years as a Monk

Tell me about your childhood and family background.

I was born in Evansville, Indiana, on December 18, 1925. I'll be 80 in December. I came from a large family of ten children. The two youngest ones—boys—died in childhood. One died of pneumonia at one year of age and another one was killed by a car at three years of age. I have written about this in my *Memories*.[1] This booklet contains many incidents of my childhood. My other siblings were Fr. Gerard, who also was a monk here. He had his doctorate in the classics and died in 2000. Another brother, Charley, died of cancer. He has six boys. I have a sister, Helen, who's still living. She is 86 years of age and very lively. My brother Vince is 84; he lives in Florida.

My next oldest brother, George, is two years older than myself, and has early Alzheimer's, but he can still play bridge like crazy. Then myself, and then there was a seven-year interval after my two younger brothers died between my next sibling, Rose Marie, who is presently 72. My youngest sister, Yvonne, was a Sister of Providence. She traveled in various locations around the Midwest and left the convent after 18 years. She was married about 27 years ago. I had the wedding at St. John's Church in Indianapolis for her. She was really my confidante, my critic, and the best member of the family to share with.

My father was a florist. He died, very young, at the age of 52 of a stroke and heart attack and was diabetic. My mother lived to be 89. She was a widow for almost 40 years. She died a very quiet, holy death at the Little Sisters of the Poor in Evansville.

We lived in a working class neighborhood. Most people worked at the Servel plant that made gas refrigerators. In the 1930s, it was a very, very busy industry. We lived two blocks from the Catholic church and school—a short block and a long block. I was an altar boy. Sometimes at the last minute, I would be called to serve at the 6 o'clock Mass. It had a good influence on me. I was not a good student and didn't do any homework.

In fact, I was the meanest kid on Iowa Street, which is not an exaggeration. If you talk to any of my peers, they would agree. Lennie Ellspermann was the meanest kid around. I smoked a lot in grade school, "shot cigarette butts"—that means picking them up out of the gutter and smoking them. So it was really a miracle of God's grace how this mean little kid came to be a priest and join the monastery. Some of this I have written about.[2]

With this background, what led you to come to the Saint Meinrad high school?

I came here because of the environment of the seminary. I had graduated from St. Joseph Grade School, Evansville, in 1939. That was the year that my brother, Fr. Gerard, who was a monk here, was ordained a priest. At this time, he said, "What are you going to do, Len?" and I said offhandedly, without serious thought, "I thought I might go to Saint Meinrad." My brother enrolled me. I had not thought about it, as I had a little puppy love going during the summer in the eighth grade. Her name was Betty Ann Bayer. It was a wonderful experience for life and for priesthood. She was such an innocent, sweet little girl, not by today's standards, but by standards then. I never even kissed her. I went to the seminary in September. I was only 13 years old.

When I announced I was going to go to Saint Meinrad to my family, my older sister Helen said, "Huh!" Mind you, I was the meanest kid on Iowa Street. She said, "I'll give him two weeks." My father corrected her very severely and said, "Helen, give him at least two months." Neither said I'd make a good priest, but they did not discourage me from it.

During the summer and Christmastime of my high school years, I worked in the hospital. My father died suddenly in 1941 and I went to work when I was 15 years of age at St. Mary's Hospital in Evansville. The reason I bring that up is that about every year I fell in love with a different girl. And then, later, the nurses. I worked there until I entered the monastery. It was a very good experience for me. Later, I worked with the sick in our community and that's why I took the name Camillus. Those were good years.

When I came here, I learned to study and fell in love with study. From being "Peck's bad boy and the meanest kid on Iowa Street," I took to this regimented seminary life like a duck to water. I thoroughly, thoroughly enjoyed it. I grew to love to study, grew to love literature. At that time, if you had your homework done, you could ask for permission to read novels. About my junior year in high school, most of us fell in love with the classics—the Russian authors and Lorna Doone and Dickens. It was an experience that I don't think our peers in the high schools in the cities had. It was our love affair; we learned romance.

I also grew to love writing. That's my favorite pastime now. I had a couple of minor strokes two years ago and it affected my left side. I have a hereditary tremor, bad this morning you see, and I never could write by hand, so I learned to type, 55 to 60 years ago. I think with my fingers, and I'm presently hoping that the use of my fingers will come back, because, unlike most people, I wrote from brain to fingers. They just talk, you know—my fingers.

Why did you decide to become a priest and a monk?

There was no special sign from God to make me want to be a priest. The desire came gradually over a period of six years. I came to a decision, almost lock-step. I said to myself, "Well, why don't I become a priest?" I never gave it any real serious thought until it was time to enter the monastery when I was 20 years of age. There was accelerated course work during the war years [World War II]. We made up an extra year then. So I had to make a decision during Christmas of '44. I had just finished the sophomore year of college in the Minor Seminary. I was a prefect on the third floor of the dorm and I remember walking half the night, making this decision. I applied for admission to the monastery.

That was the beginning of the first decision, serious decision that I made about my future. I've talked and verified this with a lot of my classmates through e-mail correspondence and we all pretty much feel the same way. We were not exactly lock-step, but we didn't seriously question our future. Most of us thought, "We will never make it; we wouldn't be accepted," but we were. Our self-image was low.

I entered the monastery in February 1945. We were candidates until September because we were in the accelerated year. We entered the novitiate September 13th. After the novitiate followed three years of formation. Going through the eight-day retreat in preparation for solemn vows was hell. I was in the deepest, darkest depression I have ever known in my life. I went ahead and made my solemn vows with my classmates September 15, 1949.

That was the only time in my life I felt anything approximating the contemplation of the greatness of God. It was just a very unusual experience of feeling that my whole being was filled with God. I've never had it since, and never before. So that was a major, major decision. For monks, the final solemn vow is a more serious decision than ordination. I was ordained a priest in May 1950 by Bishop [Paul] Schulte.

What was the reaction of family and friends when you decided to become a monk?

That did not surprise them at all because Fr. Gerard was already in the monastery. They showed no reaction to it. It was early '45 and the war was still going on with Japan. It was just taken for granted.

Did you go on for additional education?

In the fall of '50, four of us went to Catholic University, Washington, D.C. The school administration had an arrangement with the university. If we took our final theology year at Catholic U and passed the test on the Hundred Theses, in addition to proper class work, we could get a licentiate in theology. So I got mine the cheap way. Now they have to spend two years getting it. The following five summers, I did graduate work in sociology and came back here for the winter. I should have stretched it out, as I enjoyed my experiences there. In '55, I received a master's degree.

How did you see the Church in your earlier years?

The Church was different then. It was legalistic, it was canonical, it was disciplinary. I say that, not so much theologically, but sociologically. As an institution, it was radically different; it was strict. We didn't question things at the time; we just went along. It was a Church of laws, but we didn't know that. We enjoyed the Church that we lived in and that we were subject to. We enjoyed the seminary training within this kind of atmosphere. However, over time, I have had some very serious questions about the Church.

In those early years, there was acclaim and high status for being a priest. A priest was a priest, you know. Families rejoiced in their children being ordained priests, especially working families like my own. It was a source of upward mobility for us. We didn't know it, my folks didn't know it, but it was. I would have never had a college education and graduate school if it hadn't been for my becoming a priest. And I'm thankful for that.

What expectations did you have and have they been fulfilled?

I didn't have any specific expectations. I entered the Minor Seminary with no expectations and went along with the program. I had no idea what a monk's life was like.

Reflect on your years in the novitiate. Describe something of the tone and nature of the discipline under which your vocation was formed.

Our formation was more rigid and disciplined. The contemporary monks in formation now have a lot more freedom than we had. This is good, very good for them and for the community. Recreation is no longer separate. We now have a fusion between those in formation to be brothers and those to be priests. In the old days, we were separate. Now we're all brothers until we're ordained. Although there were differences then in the process, the values were the same for both groups as a way of achieving the goals of monastic formation.

Fr. Camillus, as a young monk

Most monks that I've met and most religious, including Holy Cross brothers and Jesuits in Wyoming, say that their formation was basically the same. Once you have met one religious, you have met them all; poverty, chastity, obedience and, of course, we [Benedictines] have stability and conversion.

That gets us to the next question. Discuss your earlier life and the daily routine. Is there a difference today?

Yes, and it's gone through phases over the years. Abbot Lambert [Reilly, OSB], for example, was strict on silence. He reintroduced day silence as being important to the community. If you want to talk to some-one now, you pull them aside and talk to them quietly. Today we have two periods of *lectio divina* [sacred reading], one in the morning and one in the evening with strict silence. We have Morning Office, breakfast and then about 40 minutes of *lectio*. After Vespers, in the evening until sup-per, we have about a half hour of very strict silence. You're not supposed to be talking. We also have night silence. Instead of getting up at 3:40 with the summons of the wooden knocker by a junior, we get up at 5:00 now. Instead of Morning Office at 4:00, it's now at 5:30. The Mass time has varied from morning, which is good, until the evening over the years. The times for work are approximately the same.

The kind of work done by the German brothers, who were skilled craftsmen such as bakers, shoemakers or tailors for making habits, is now almost gone. Work is now more academic. One of the problems, not just in recruitment, but also for the community, is that the spirit of the original monks doing manual labor is gone. The men coming in now are more academic and are more trained. They have degrees and are older. The challenge we're facing now is trying to recruit working class people to be monks. Most come from a more academic background.

Are there other changes?

I would like to talk about recreation, which all of us older fathers had. In the old days here, after lunch and the evening meal, we would have reg-ular periods of recreation. The fraters [monks in training for the priesthood] and the priests and the brothers all recreated separately, so we had three different recreation groups. Now there is no distinction at all. I remember one day I was playing bridge after lunch with some other priests when the news was announced of President Kennedy's assassination.

Today our communal life has given way to contemporary culture. We don't have time to associate with one another as much as we did in the old days. Recreation then was part of the old system and was a very pos-itive part of that system. Today we have people who come from a differ-ent culture, so they don't miss it. In addition to recreation, the prayer schedule has changed, I think for the better. I've seen this in the daily Office, as a matter of fact. It's adapted to a more contemporary way of life. We haven't sacrificed praying, though.

Are the values of the community now different?

I don't think they're that different. The times are different; the culture is different. Someone has characterized the present as being a little more free. We still have the same service, the same application of the Holy *Rule,* the same consideration for the aged, along with openness and kindness.

Work

Tell me about your career.

I'm atypical as a monk. I was here the first 25 years and then I did parish work for 25 years. I don't know whether you've talked to many other monks like myself, but it's very critical I think. I say that I'm atypical because most of the monks, or ordained priests, do not have full-time parish work. We're a breed unto ourselves. My monastic formation here, from the novitiate, to being a junior, ordination, early priesthood, teaching here and being part of the community was a very important factor in my ministry to people.

I started here in the monastery in '45. Now I'm back for what I call my second novitiate. I came back here August 4th of this year [2005]. I've gotten to talk to candidates, novices and juniors. After having been gone for 30 years, I'm being reintroduced to monastic values. Since I've been home, I've had the same difficulty of being corrected for speaking in times of silence that I did when I was a novice here going on 65 years ago.

How about your early career?

Well, during the summer after I got the STL [license in sacred theology], I came home. I was supposed to go on for theology. But they decided that I should teach biology, so I started to monitor graduate courses and got some books from Fr. Fabian Frieders. He has since left and is married. He taught biology here. Then, at the last minute, two weeks before school started, I was told I would teach Latin in the fall of 1951. Then Fr. Abbot Ignatius Esser also asked me to be the infirmarian for the community. So for ten years, I was Fr. Infirmarian. It was fulltime. I was teaching 14 hours a week. This included eight hours of Latin and three or four hours of sociology.

How many hours in the infirmary?
I was always available. I didn't have a staff like they have now. Dr. Tom Gootee, just out of internship, was the physician. He was with us for close to 25 years. So I had that job for ten years plus teaching sociology and Latin. I also taught moral theology for a couple of years. This was all during my first ten years.

Then I was asked to be associate to the spiritual director in high school, which I did for three years or so with Fr. Lucien [Duesing, OSB]. After that, I was asked by Abbot Bonaventure to be instructor and novice master for the brothers. I had that job for three years. They were happy years for me.

But I fought my way out of a job. At the beginning of Vatican II, renewals were coming up for the lay brothers. I encouraged the union of what used to be the lay brothers and the fraters, who were studying for the priesthood, and lost my job as the novice master. Around 1967, the novitiates were combined. They're still combined, but that's another whole story in itself. I was still teaching sociology and in '63 led a seminar on race and then a seminar on civil rights in '65. I was also involved with the March on Selma, which I have written about.[3]

Tell me a bit about that experience.
Abbot Bonaventure had received a call from Cardinal Ritter in St. Louis asking that some representatives from the Archabbey be sent to Selma. We were to act as buffers between police and marchers. The abbot asked if I would go, and I said, "Yes." Frs. Cyprian Davis and Lawrence

Ward, along with Fr. Terence Girkin from St. Benedict's and the Rev. Charles King, pastor of Liberty Baptist Church in Evansville, and I drove to Selma. We checked in at St. Elizabeth's Mission, conducted by the Edmundite fathers and brothers, and went to Brown's Chapel, which served as headquarters for all civil rights demonstrators.

On Friday, we made our first vigil at the Selma wall. The wall was a single strand of plain white clothesline. It was a strong psychological obstacle to integration, voting rights, morality, human rights and dignity. On either side, the two ideologies clashed, two social groups formed and reformed for a confrontation. On our side was the singing of freedom songs, such as "We Shall Overcome" and "We Shall Not be Moved," and praying. On the other side, nightsticks, guns, glaring lights, horses and troopers stood preventing us from marching.

On Saturday morning, a large group of clergy and representatives of various religious groups met in the basement of the First Baptist Church to plan the day's march. We marched twice that day and were stopped by the troopers. A pattern of marching, a repulse and regrouping continued to build. There was no march on Sunday, just a vigil at the wall. After this vigil, we were hungry, thirsty and unwashed. The black community responded to our needs and gave us food and shelter. The charity and love they showed us came from the heart.

On Monday, March 15, after the federal injunction against the march to Montgomery had been lifted, a final triumphant march in silence to the courthouse came about. Until this triumph, the atmosphere of the demonstrations was marked by uncertainty and danger. We used the nonviolent techniques of love and peace. This whole experiences was a grace and gave me insight for teaching my sociology classes.

What happened after your early teaching years?

I was asked to be spiritual director in the School of Theology. Because things were so uncertain in the mid-'60s, I refused to accept the position of spiritual director because it made me look like the authority. I did agree with Fr. Adrian Fuerst, who was the rector, to be spiritual coordinator. So, along with the theology faculty, we had two years of preparation with a psychologist and psychiatrist every month in Louisville on how to do small group guidance.

This was a way of meeting the transition in the '60s. Each faculty member had a group of eight to ten students. Faculty met weekly, and also met with the students weekly. This enabled the students to say what was on their minds. Our role as faculty advisors was to listen to them and see what would come out. It's different from sensitivity training. I did it for the entire time that I was spiritual coordinator, from around '66 to '68. It was effective and I found myself using it more and more with lay people in my later assignments.

The '60s were very, very difficult years. We went from regimentation to self-responsibility. We eliminated bells. People had to be responsible, like other graduate students, for their own lives. They had to get up to be in class, to be in chapel and so on. They were allowed to drive their own car, go off the Hill and take a weekend off. There were also theological and devotional changes. It was a very difficult time.

During the '60s, students were restless. Things were changing and they wanted some actual experience of priesthood; they wanted field education. We started the Deacon Internship Program, which I led for seven years, from about 1968 to 1975. It was at the request of students. It was also a new experience in Catholic theological education. One or two very understanding and mature priests had students as deacons on weekends to help them preach, sort of unofficially. Students also went to their own home dioceses for the summer to help out.

Beginning in '73 and '74, students were placed in Indianapolis parishes selected by the Indianapolis authorities. I was there with them. During the last three years I was working in this program, students went to their home parishes. I would visit all of them and this was really an experience. I visited them in their home states. We had students as far north as Providence, as far south as Florida, and also in the west and here in the tri-state area.

I learned a lot, but I got in over my head. I knew it and I accepted it. I didn't really know what I was getting into. I went into a bad depression because bishops have expectations of their pastors, students have expectations of their instructors, and faculty members have expectations. I was in the middle and I was going in circles. I didn't know what I was doing. But I weathered it; it reached a climax and I finished up strong. The program still continues.

What was so difficult about this program was that we had no precedent for it. I hope this sounds modest enough, but in my early priesthood up until I left to go to the parish in '75, I was in innovative programs. I was invited to help work and to create them. I don't know why.

Why did you leave teaching and go into parish work?

A new rector was appointed. He's now Archbishop Daniel Buechlein in Indianapolis. His style was different. It's more consistent with the direction the Church is going now. He was more academic, more cerebral, more controlled than Fr. Adrian. Adrian had vision and imagination and was open to change, innovative programs and development. I think it's a terrible mistake how we are now undoing changes made after the Vatican Council. I do not belong to the contemporary school of retrenchment.

The new rector and I did not see eye-to-eye on things. I had trouble getting an appointment with him. We finally had an appointment to see each other and I said, "I'm happy, the program is going well, but if you need someone for parish work, I'm available." He said, "Fine." It took a year and a half to get assigned to do this. Abbot Gabriel finally asked me if I would be a pastor and I said OK. So in August 1975, the 25th year of my priesthood, I went to be associate pastor at St. Benedict's Parish in Evansville.

Fr. Alban Berling [died December 2005], who was there, said he would like to stay on as a school pastor. I was canonical pastor for the year, but we acted as co-pastors. When he left the following year, I became pastor by myself. I was pastor of St. Ben's for 15 years until 1991. Then it got to be too much for me, too many problems. I left, in the sense that I requested permission from the abbot to move to another parish. It was granted. I went to St. Henry, Indiana, just 11 miles from here in

Dubois County. That ten years at St. Henry was my Camelot! I loved it. I loved the people. I loved the smallness of the parish.

The reason it ended in 2001 is that canon law says that you have to offer your resignation at age 75. The bishop asked for it. I submitted it and he accepted it. It broke my heart. The people cried over it, too. But that's life. That's a monk's life—obedience. In August, Bishop [Joseph] Hart from the Diocese of Cheyenne, whom I taught in '56, saw in a newsletter that I was resigning and offered me work out there.

I was in the West for over four years. I was to have been in residence in Cheyenne at St. Mary's Cathedral parish taking care of the sick. However, while volunteering my vacation time at Holy Spirit community in Rock Springs, I was invited by the bishop to remain as associate pastor in residence there. After being there two years, I then helped as resident priest at St. Anthony's in Casper. Because of surgery last spring and losing some of my sight from small strokes a couple of years ago, I came back home this past summer.

So for the last 25 years, I was in parishes. In some ways, I went to St. Ben's as kind of a protest against just doing work at the Archabbey as the only way we could fulfill our vows. This changed with Abbot Lambert. His tenure can be characterized as having an emphasis on service to the Church and priesthood. Many of our monks now serve in parishes.

Prayer

From your experience as a monk, what would you wish to convey to your younger confreres or even the laity?

I would say the whole monastic formation, including poverty, obedience, chastity and stability, are the most important things in life. They go beyond us as individuals. As part of a group effort, we give witness to the world today that there are things more important than money, more important than material goods. The search for God, supported by the community here, is probably our greatest contribution. We are needed; I think we all know that. We also take pride in being a witness to society. We pay a price for it in isolation. We pay a price for it in the intrusions into monastic life and silence.

Have you learned anything else that you would pass on?

Yes, unless you've developed a sense of intimacy as a human being, as a counselor, as a priest, I don't think you can be a complete priest or even successful. I have discovered in the past decade, as a priest in Wyoming, women. This resulted in some beautiful, beautiful experiences. I'm not talking about physical, but psychological and spiritual intimacy and sensitivity. Most of them were church women. Four or five of them are coming here in May to make a retreat and spend some time with me. However, when I came home, I found that the women here were just the same. So who could have changed? I have, not the women.

I think it's the rigidity of the past and fear that kept me from being intimate. My sister said to me, four weeks ago when she came to visit, "Well, you show more affection now than you used to. I think you were afraid, weren't you?" And I said, "Yup!" So it's important to be open to discovery over your whole life. I have more sense of freedom now.

What is your favorite part of the Rule of St. Benedict?

In general, I see the holy *Rule* as a paraphrase of the Gospel way of living. It includes the sayings of Christ, his actions and his example. It is modeling his life here in the community, the life that is found in eternity. This is an evangelical life. Let me tell you a little story. When I was out in Casper, we said morning prayers. We said evening prayers and then had supper. There were generally seven people who came and they were totally committed to being a community. I would talk to them, but because of my sight, I couldn't read toward the end of my time there. However, I listened to them recite the Psalms and say the prayers. I told them that they were my little monastic community. When I came back here, I find they are always in my mind. They're not sophisticated, they're not refined, they're not educated, but we led the Gospel principles in our life together.

What is your key to living Benedictine spirituality?

This may sound strange after 50 years of being a monk—it's life in the community pursuant to the Gospel principles, evangelical principles. Life in the community, for me personally, is the key.

What has been your most difficult and what has been your happiest time over your lifetime?

The most difficult period is when I left St. Benedict. I had a conflict with a parishioner who put politics and money ahead of the welfare of the parish. This person put material wealth as more important than God and the spiritual. That was the most difficult time in my life. The happiest times were the jobs I have already talked about. I enjoyed them all. I enjoyed teaching. I enjoyed taking care of the sick. I enjoyed the innovative work in theology. I thoroughly enjoyed parish life.

Vatican II: Its Effect on the Church and Saint Meinrad Archabbey

Today some observers are of the opinion that society is once again indifferent to the meaning of a virtuous life and that it has a lack of spirituality such as was found in St. Benedict's time. How has this affected Benedictine spirituality in the Archabbey, in the Church?

I'll put it this way. Every social institution has changed, including family, church, recreation, professional sports, economic life and political life; they're all bad. They've all been radically changed. That's the given. I think the answer is positive, however, for Benedictine life and the Archabbey. Community life includes our vows, to properly act out and live. So I think our monastic ideology—values, way of life—is still very important.

I've heard, but I don't know if it's true, that Pope John XXIII thought that his call was to revitalize the human secular institutions in the same manner as the monks did in the Middle Ages. We're trying to hang on to the traditional values, I think. This isn't a negative thing. We know what we're doing, as we have worked at it, some consciously because of age and experience, and others, hopefully, are just beginning to grasp it. I think that's what we have to offer.

Some think Pope John XXIII was overly optimistic and that ever since Vatican Council II, the Church has been paying a heavy price for his initiatives. Still others applaud his gestures. What has this meant to you in terms of the Church and the monastery?

Where I'm coming from, personally, is that John XXIII was a hero. After the Council, we had priest support groups to work our way through the changes, you know, with the diocesan priests in Evansville. I don't know what I would do if we returned to the days of rigidity and formality. My personal life found fulfillment and a sense of comfort in everything the Vatican Council stands for. I loved John XXIII. I loved John Paul II, but not as well. I'm threatened by a return to pre-Vatican II and I see obvious evidence of it in the Church today.

With the new Pope?

Not so much with the new Pope as with the values of the bishops. John Paul probably had something to do with the appointment of the bishops. I see the Church in a retrenchment position. This includes the training of seminarians, issues of celibacy and homosexuality. I think this position is too inflexible and has a closed mentality. It's this mentality that created the problems we've had with sexual abuse among a few priests. I'm very much in favor of Vatican II. We struggled to internalize Vatican II. Desperately, we struggled, but we did get it internalized. Now there's a movement in the Church for moving backwards. I am not there at all.

How about the monastery?

We had group process before Abbot Justin [DuVall, OSB] was elected. We discussed things we considered important to the community. The number one priority was our obligation to maintain balance and continuity of monastic life. I lived through those periods of radical change from rigidity to a more eclectic, or open, look at theology and monastic life. I do not see a movement in the monastery back to rigidity; obedience to the Church, yes. Our theologians are pretty open. It would be a very serious error to go back to the past and return to the formation and values of pre-Vatican II.

Monks have a tradition of being isolated in the Church. But in the Church, there have always been monks who have precipitated changes. Monks have also been considered naïve by the Church, as they're removed from the real world. Well, I've been a monk in the real world for 30 years and I don't think it ever changed my effectiveness as a priest, or affected my monastic values.

I do not expect to live long enough, however, to see a balance between those who accepted Vatican II changes and those who want to go back to more inflexible ways. The Legionnaires of Christ, and other radical movements who want to return to the way it was before Vatican II, don't have my sympathy at all. I think they are mistaken and I think it is a serious error to try to return to rigidity. I do not find the monks in our community to be this way, however.

Compare the morale in the monastery today with that of 30, 40, 50 years ago.
It's just as good or better.

To what extent has the decline in vocations had an impact?
We're searching for new ways to address the decline here. It's a problem compared to the past, and it remains a challenge for the future. In general, our whole culture is against young people going into a religious vocation. Today's society and youth want pleasure first and it's difficult to escape the demands of our culture to serve Christ. The acclaim, the adulation and the privilege of being a religious are now gone. Now it's often loneliness. To go into the priesthood today calls for a lot of courage and sacrifice.

One of the most important changes in the seminary curriculum has been the de-emphasis of Latin. Even if the Mass is to be celebrated in the vernacular, was eliminating Latin from the academic curriculum a good idea?

I don't think so. I'm a little biased because I taught Latin. There might have been some people who left the seminary because they couldn't master Latin, but there were likely other factors along with this. I think academically, not only priests, but doctors, philosophers and teachers all need to know Latin. It's just too bad that it isn't taught anymore.

Striking changes have been made since the days of the Council. Comment on the positive or negative changes that have been undertaken in the recent history of the Church.

My first reaction was that I was against most of the changes. But then I grew to love them. I was first opposed to concelebration. I remember taking a survey while I was teaching in the old high school. I used red ink to answer the question, "No, to concelebration." I've changed. In terms of the liturgy, by being in the parish and seeing people participate, I really feel these changes are for the better. They have made it possible for people to give expression to their religious beliefs and practices. These include having the liturgy and lectures in English, and having an external ministry to the Eucharist.

This external ministry has led to lay people helping with worship. A priest is a priest and will always be a priest, because of the sacrament. However, I got special permission from the Bishop of Cheyenne to continue with what I have done for a long time. My hands have shaken all my life. If I tried to pour the wine, I'd spill it. I had permission, and folks accepted it beautifully, for the Eucharistic ministers to pour the wine. Other priests get the Blessed Sacrament for the ministers.

Just before I left Cheyenne, when I was recuperating from surgery, a very pious, very holy woman asked for the Eucharist. I didn't have the strength to administer it and had problems with my seeing, but I could say Mass. I had asked the ordained deacon to help me. I said to this woman, "Take it from him." She answered, "I only receive communion from the hands of the priest. Would you give it to me if the deacon gets it?"

And I said, "No, the deacon is an ordained minister of the Church. Lay people who give out the Eucharist are commissioned to the ministry. My hands giving out communion does not change the sacrament one bit. Most of our ministers here are holy. Their hands are just as sacred." I added, "You pray about it." And she said, "I will," but never came back again. Out in Casper, we had our share of families who had these old ideas about receiving the Eucharist only from the hands of a priest.

We have spent all these years internalizing the changes from Vatican II and seeing the results of their use. Now, we're asked to back off; we're asked to undo these changes and go back to the old manner of doing things. It is becoming more strict, you know. That's the direction in which we're heading. This is my personal opinion from personal experience, but I think that whatever can be done by lay people should be done. They're just as worthy as we are.

Assuming that you agree that there is no going back to pre-Conciliar days, what has been lost? What has been gained?
As someone said, "In some areas, they threw out the baby with the bath water." I think we have lost a deep reverence for the real presence of Christ. I have never learned to appreciate it, but I've met many people who spend hours in front of the sacrament for perpetual adoration. I try to do it now, since I'm home, at least a half hour a day. This custom has waned, but it doesn't need to be re-introduced rigidly. Some people have found their way to continue the reverence for the real presence.

There is very little that I would like to return to. Personally, I'm thankful we've shed the old Mass. Some of my classmates can still do it; I don't know whether I could do it anymore. I don't think we've lost anything there. There are some people who have an inordinate appreciation of the way things were. And I think they have a problem. It's their rigidity, it's their dependence on rituals as they grew up that have kept them from openness and exposing themselves. I could talk to midnight on this.

The number of religious vocations declines every year and the number of retirements and deaths increases in this population. What is the meaning of these changing patterns to the monastery and to the Church at large?

I really don't know the answer to that question. I would not want to return to the rigidity of the past and the formation methods of the past. The Church has survived in the past and it will now.

Comment on your hopes for the future of the Archabbey and the Catholic Church.

Hope for the Church, I don't know. I'm saying this more as a sociologist than as a priest. I don't know. It's up for grabs. I won't live to see it. It's one of the things I've accepted. I will not live to see stability. In the monastery, I feel confident, but where we're going in the Church, I don't know. I've seen the bad effects of rigidity and how it shows up in people's lives. However, a lot of good shepherds and a lot of heroes are parents. They are good Christian parents. I've known married men who have as much dedication and balance as any priest we have. I've met women who would make good priests, but it's not at all likely now.

You know, my personal opinion as a priest working full time in the parish and my opinion as a sociologist is that I would be in favor of married men becoming priests. Most women I've met, except a few radical sisters and nuns, would also make good priests. But until the day that the Church embraces everyone for service, and not just for menial, subservient positions or helpers, there will not be a fullness of the revelation of Christ's love and His message to the world. This is radical, I know, but I deeply believe this. I also know that I will not live to see that day, but I would like to.

Our present Holy Father Benedict represents the more traditional way. He represents an academic and cerebral approach to the Church. But I'm speaking as an American priest, a Benedictine, somewhat trained, with a lot of experience that includes personal and intimate contact with people and their lives. I think for the Body of Christ to be effective in today's world, we must be open and not threatening. I am threatened by retrenching rigidity. It's a sad, sad mistake. In the spirit of John Paul II, and especially John XXIII, the Church needs to function as a message of salvation to all people in today's society and world.

How about the Archabbey?

I am kind of hopeful for the monastery and vocations. Different kinds of people are seeking the priesthood today. In the Archabbey, we just can't return to rigidity. We have to be open, but this hasn't always happened for liturgical changes. For instance, up until a year ago, at the Eucharist, not only the priests, but the brothers, the abbot and all the lay people surrounded the altar. Now lay people kneel and brothers stand apart. I don't like this trend at all. I just don't like it. I was disappointed to come home to more rigidity again. As an older man approaching 80, I'm violently opposed to that type of inflexibility as being effective or healthy for people's spiritual development at the monastery. I haven't talked to monastic community members, but I think we're walking a pretty careful middle of the road.

However, I think the future of the Archabbey, in spite of changing times, is good. I think we've got good formation from both Br. Jacob [Grisley, OSB] and Fr. Harry [Hagan, OSB]. They see to it that the young men are cheerful and happy. These young men are better educated than we were. They're open and they like what they see here. They find support here. They are needed. They're needed very much. Now the rest is up to God. The monastic life is good.

Profile based upon: Fr. Camillus Ellspermann to Prof. Ruth C. Engs, September 23, 2005, Interview Transcription, Saint Meinrad Archives.

Also:

[1] *Ellspermann, O.S.B., Father Camillus "Len." Memories. Unpublished Essays, July 13, 2001. Saint Meinrad Archives.*

[2] *Ellspermann, O.S.B., Father Camillus. Reflections: A personal History, the Journal of my Years of Priesthood, 1950-2005. Unpublished essays, August 2005. Saint Meinrad Archives.*

[3] _____ *"Selma, March 12-16, 1965," Unpublished essay, n.d., Saint Meinrad Archives.*

Chapter Six

Fr. Simeon Daly, OSB

As a Benedictine monk of Saint Meinrad, Fr. Simeon's primary responsibility was as head librarian, a position he held for 49 years (1951-2000). He greatly expanded the library's collection, shepherded the building of a new library in 1981, and implemented the electronic cataloging system (OCLC-World Cat) in the mid-1970s, when this computerized system was still in its infancy.

Fr. Simeon was born May 9, 1922, in Detroit, MI. On August 10, 1944, he made his first profession and on August 10, 1947, his solemn profession as a monk. He graduated from the College (1945), the School of Theology (1948), and was ordained May 18, 1948. He received a Master of Library Science degree from Catholic University of America in Washington, D.C. Fr. Simeon was involved with establishing the "Experimental Office" of community prayer in the wake of Vatican II that was adopted by the community and is still used today. He served as Master of Ceremonies (1958-67) and as subprior (1975-78).

After his retirement from the library, Fr. Simeon has worked part time in the Development Office in communications, preparing news releases, contributing to the institution's newsletter and attending special functions for donors. He has written numerous essays on a variety of subjects and published *Finding Grace in the Moment* (2005), a collection of personal reflections and heartfelt stories, along with a CD of the same name.

Fr. Simeon was interviewed by Prof. Ruth C. Engs on June 9, 2005.

Childhood and Early Years as a Monk

Tell me about your childhood and family.

I had a beautiful family. A lot of my childhood memories and the relationship with my mother and father are found in my book.* Today, I weep for society that has lost the family values I treasure and the nurturing home that I had as a child. I was born Philip Daly on May 9, 1922, in Detroit, MI, to Philip and Marguerite Daly. My father was the bookkeeper in a business in which he was a partner, Gleason-Daly Sand and Gravel Co. I had two brothers and a sister. My sister Marguerite became a nun. My father was not particularly happy about our vocations, but in later life reconciled this. He was rather shy. My mother was warm and outgoing and usually took the initiative in social situations.

I grew up in a Catholic ghetto and was never more than two blocks from the church. All our friends were Catholic. All our neighbors were Catholic. At my grandparents' home in Wyandotte, MI, elderly Protestant people lived on one side of them. Although it wasn't a shunning, I was never in their house even though it was next door. I didn't know them, didn't know their names and never met them. It just didn't occur.

About 1932 with the Depression, when I was about ten years of age, we moved to Wyandotte, a suburb on the south side of Detroit. I went to Catholic grade school and to daily Mass. My friends were all Catholics and I couldn't name more than ten or 20 Protestants by name that I knew at all. In the sixth grade, I went to a private Catholic boarding school, the Hall of the Divine Child, which has since closed. I was a hothouse plant from the word go. Then I came here and was away from any other environment. So my total upbringing was a Catholic ethos. It just shaped everything I did. I felt I had a vocation—it was very vague. I was challenged when the opportunity came to go to Saint Meinrad.

How did that occur?

Fr. Columban Reed, a monk who was recruiting for Marmion Military Academy, stopped by our house in August of 1936. I had just graduated from the boarding school. When he learned that I wanted to go to a seminary, but as yet had made no plans, he talked about Saint Meinrad. I pleaded with my parents to allow me to go. Fr. Columban eventually made all the arrangements necessary for my enrollment that September. After I came here—which I did not reflect upon until recent years—I realized what a seismological shift there was in my world view. Before I came here, I was totally rooted in my family. And now that I was here, I was not likely to turn back. It wasn't rejection of my family, but Saint Meinrad became the center of my life and has remained so ever since.

On August 6, 1943, I became Novice Philip. For my college, seminary and even library science education, I had a benefactor. She was Miss Anna Casson, a retired schoolteacher from New York City. This little old lady, from her life savings, set aside some money to pay for my education. I will be eternally grateful to her and remember her faithfully in prayer.

How did you see the Church in your early years, what expectations did you have concerning the Church and have they been fulfilled?

The Church was an all-embracing prism through which I saw life and activity. Liturgical seasons were celebrated. Daily Mass and communion were central to the way I lived my life. My notion of Church was quite institutional and authoritarian. Priest friends of the family were like family members. Because of my mother, who attracted them and kept in touch, as she was a very gracious person, we had half a dozen priest friends. My personal perception of Church grew dramatically during the mid-'40s. With meditation on the *Mystici Corporis Christi* [The encyclical of Pope Pius XII on the Mystical Body of Christ of June 29, 1943]...I say my expectations have been fulfilled.

Reflect on your years in the novitiate. Has much changed in the Archabbey?

I think the basic values are the same today as what brought me to the monastery, but we carry things out in a different way. Basic monastic living of the principles of the Gospel is the life I feel that we have continued today. This includes seeking God, obedience, nothing being preferred to Christ, the work of God, fraternity, community and enclosure.

However, enclosure has changed probably more than anything else since my early years. Monks are much freer to be abroad than they were. And the world has entered into our cloister. These things are different, but they don't necessarily mean that they are bad. I think there is a danger of monks becoming too worldly. We were deprived of everything when I first came here in the 1930s. We didn't have radios; even the seminarians weren't allowed to have radios. In the school there was a public radio.

When did this change?

I don't know exactly. In the monastery, it changed slowly. There was not a day when we were told, "Now you may have radios." I think it filtered in and maybe at first it was tolerated by some and pretty soon it was kind of accepted. We weren't allowed to wear a wristwatch, either. Abbot Bonaventure introduced the wristwatch. I think some of those things were kind of extreme. They were a piece of, but they weren't the essence of poverty. You can still be a monk with values and the appreciation of poverty and still wear a wristwatch.

So the basic monastic values pre- and post-Vatican II are still here?

Yes, I really feel that they are still here. For example, reading the holy *Rule*, which itself is a document of formation. Prayer and work, with the guidance of a master, are tools to shape lives and create a community ethos of reverence for God and concern for one another. Enclosure, obedience and poverty are others. The *horarium* [the daily schedule of prayer and work] is still a framework for formation. The monastic ideals that we continue to try to profess are still represented in the life that we live today, but perhaps not in exactly the same way for some of them, like certainly silence and recreation have changed somewhat.

How is that?

In the house, we never speak in the corridor in a loud voice; in fact, we are not even supposed to speak or whisper in the corridor. We should go someplace else—move elsewhere so that the quiet in the house is maintained. This is still an important value. The purpose of this is to maintain an atmosphere

Fr. Simeon, as a young monk

of prayer and all the other things that go with a monastic life. After the manner of St. Benedict's fifth chapter in the *Rule*, the community has distinguished night silence and day silence. Night silence has always been strictly followed. Night silence begins after Compline, the evening Office that we now do on our own, and goes through breakfast. We can talk at lunch, but dinner is generally silent with table reading [someone reads aloud from a book or other material]. Up through the 1950s, table reading was also done at lunch although, in the past, silence was also supposed to have been observed in the workplace. I have my doubts that it was if work occurred outside the cloister.

Recreation is now different. Mortification and awareness of sin and the danger of uncharitable conversation was an emphasis in the past. No eating and drinking between meals were allowed. On non-fast days, one might have fruit during afternoon recreation period only. A bell for the end of recreation was the official signal closing down all eating outside meals.

After Vatican II, we spoke much more of community and of being brothers to one another and of sharing a life of faith and hope and love. Therefore, the idea of a coffee break was introduced as an opportunity for individuals in the monastery to get to know one another and to share more fully their personal lives. It was an opportunity to reinforce camaraderie, community and brotherly love. Sharing and support, and especially the concept of support, was now important. We were available to one another in a loving and caring way. This was seen as a greater good than mortification.

If your world view did not shift, then this new reality of communication and sharing was scandalous and we had men that were terribly upset. They said, "What is this place coming to? They are sitting around yakking, eating and drinking outside of the time of the monastery's formal dining hours!"

Was it primarily the older monks who were against the coffee break and the new spirit of communication and support?

Yes, some of them never reconciled, they never got it—and it hurt. They would stand aghast at seeing this lightheartedness. Some thought that these coffee breaks with conversation were not conducive to good formation as a monk and that providing pots of coffee and donuts was like going to hell, or whatever. Fr. Abbot Ignatius wrote a sign on the coffee urn, "If you are sick, go to bed and the infirmarian will take care of you. It's not proper for healthy monks to be eating and drinking outside of regular meals." It was a big change when the focus shifted from the individual to the community.

Can you describe this in more detail?

I came to the monastery with very little thought of community. I came as an individual responding to the Gospel. As closely as I can define it, it is Jesus saying, "Take up your cross and follow me." I wanted to do that. In my experience, taking up the cross and following was giving your life to God and the priesthood was the first criteria. When I came to Saint Meinrad and first learned of the community, monastic life was more strict, more enclosed. To me at that time, it seemed like a fuller response to the Gospel. So when I came here, it was a personal response and a personal journey. But by the late '50s and early '60s, I saw myself shifting from personal goals to being part of the community of faith, of being with brothers who support one another in faith and hope and love.

I'm still seeking as an individual, but brotherhood means much, much more to me than it did when I first came. And it continues to shape my life and my daily prayer. How grateful I am that I have brothers who share a faith. It is easy to live with my Christian values because there are other brothers who share these values, both in terms of prayer and practice, and in terms of respect for one another in living out these values. If I were alone in the world, I would not be as faithful, I know that. I know I couldn't pray in the same way that I do here. I am very dependent upon the community. That way of thinking was a major shift for me.

Have there been other changes in the Archabbey?

A major shift is that we have a unified community where all brothers and priests in solemn vows are part of the community. Prior to the late 1960s, the brothers, the fraters [monks studying for the priesthood] and the fathers were really part of three or four communities. There were two novitiates, one for the fraters and one for lay brothers. They each had their own liturgy. In the mid-1930s, two classifications of brothers had been created—the "junior" or American Brothers and the "senior" or the German Brothers. These older German Brothers were primarily farm workers and craftsmen that had come from Germany well into the 1920s. They prayed their daily Office in German.

Another great change is that the "work of God," or the Divine Office, is less onerous. It is less of a burden and more of a joy. Although I prayed the Office conscientiously and I loved the liturgy, there is no question that the old Office was burdensome. I can now pray more intelligently, not just because it is in English, but because the whole methodology of the pacing and the quiet has helped to make it more meaningful. Before Vatican II, the Office began like a train and just ran through as fast as it could. I think that Divine Office is now more of an expression of community. It is all of us being together, and I think the quality of Saint Meinrad's choir has also improved.

There were also a lot of little changes. I came across some of my *Bona Operas* [good deeds] for Lent from when I was a student in the early 1940s. In the seminary, we gave these to the abbot in an elaborate ceremony. On Ash Wednesday, we all came, one by one, to get ashes from the abbot. And on the way, we dropped our *Bona Opera* in a basket. It had to been folded in an exact way by the direction of Fr. Abbot Ignatius, so that when he unfolded it, he didn't have to fiddle to read it. He had to sign them and so he wanted them all folded alike. On this example [Fr. Simeon shows me one], it shows here by this crease that I didn't quite get it folded right the first time, so I had to fold it again.

This changed after Vatican II. They were simplified and went from Latin to English. We now get a form. We used to hand write them in Latin. The first year that I have one in English is from 1966 and it's on a form. All you had to do was to fill in. There were only three lines, as they said that three deeds were enough.

Can you describe the tone and nature of the discipline under which your vocation was formed?

I think, by and large, today we are less motivated by fear and more by personal responsibility. Also, authority is less authoritarian. I was a very fearful young monk and I was always afraid that I was going to be kicked out. Superiors were not the enemy and certainly from the start we were expected to be personally responsible. But now the ethos is that we have personal responsibility and someone is not constantly checking on you. However, it may be a personal perception or perhaps a sign of my own personal growth, but I moved from being a fearful subject to a cooperative monk. Today, I think there is more individuality and less conformity. People are encouraged to be themselves and, within parameters, to do their own thing.

Was there a difference in the lifestyle and routine compared to today?

Yes, it is entirely different. I think the seminary was run almost as if it were a pre-monastery. Although it was not unique to Saint Meinrad, or other monastic seminaries, there was little contact with the world. This was a time, anyway, before TV even came to southern Indiana. Occasionally, we had movies and they would always be pre-screened. During the film, someone would come up and put something in front of the projector to block off a kissing scene. We were protected. We didn't often have many visitors, and we went home only at Christmas.

How about recreation?

We did have a recreation place for ping pong and pool. But there was nothing like having drinks, such as the UnStable pub run by today's seminarians. You didn't leave the Hill, as there were no cars. You weren't even allowed to have a car. You were not allowed to go downtown to the local store or allowed to go into any of the buildings. You could go for walks in groups and we did that all over southern Indiana.

Were these restrictions for all seminarians or just for fraters?

It was for all seminarians. However, these restrictions began to change after my time as a seminarian. At some point, it might have been in the 1960s, a lady by the name of Julie sold ice cream downtown. I used to hear the students talk about going to Julie's and this was a big deal.

The UnStable probably opened in the '60s. By that time, the college students were having cars and were able to go off campus and some of them would drink. It just seemed logical to provide a place so that people did not have to go off the Hill to get some variety and a place where they could have a beer or pop. The UnStable provided an alternative recreational opportunity for college students, seminarians and lay theological students. But I am not sure if seminarians took part in the same way.

Work

What was your major job over your lifetime?

My major job—ultimately, I became the librarian. When I was in the novitiate, there were three things I didn't want to do—I can't remember the third one. I didn't want to be a librarian and I didn't want to be a barber. My first assignment was to be a barber.

I certainly didn't want to be a librarian. I had no ambition to be a librarian. I had no concept of what being a librarian involved. I was appointed and accepted it out of obedience; however, at the time I was not thrilled, to say the least. But one's perspective of major moments can shift over time. I have a story in my book, called "The Yoke of Obedience." I think this story was very telling. It was something I only looked back upon later and saw that it was really a transforming moment, as my motivations for not being a librarian were totally selfish. I was attached to recreation, especially handball, as a young cleric. The problem I saw in this library job was that we worked during recreation and I would miss all the fun!

I had started to help in the library during September 1949. Fr. Theodore Heck [the rector of the College] said that we would never be able to get accreditation for the college until we had the library cataloged in halfway decent order. He asked me if I would consider helping to do this. And I said I would.

In the meantime, we were in the midst of establishing Blue Cloud monastery in Marvin, SD, and they were in the process of assigning monks from here to move there. One of the monks, Fr. Justin Snyder, who had been at Blue Cloud, was the prior here. He was urging me to volunteer to go. I said, "No, I didn't think I wanted to do that." But he said, "They need you up there and you would love the work and I am going to recommend it."

So I kind of lived worried about going to Blue Cloud. Every monk, because of the vow of stability, has an affiliation with a particular place. In the event of a new community, every monk had the right to state his preference. However, the abbot made the final decision. There were three options: "I wish not to join the new community and I wish to stay at Saint Meinrad," "I am indifferent; I am willing to go but I am not asking to go," "I would like to go on to the new community." The state of my soul in those days was that I wanted to be indifferent in the good sense that I was open to what God wants. Therefore, I had said, "I was willing to go, but not asking to go." In my heart, I really didn't want to go.

Fr. Theodore had gone to the Abbot [Ignatius Esser] about me being assigned to the library. The Abbot called me in to his office. As was the custom in the pre-Vatican II days, when you went to the abbot's office, you knelt to kiss his ring and only sat down when he told you to do so. He told me to sit, told me that I was appointed to the library and that I should look upon it as my life work.

Although he was a rather formidable figure in my young life, I kind of relaxed after he made this appointment and sat back in my chair. I said, "Frankly, Fr. Abbot, I'm really kind of relieved as I was afraid that I might be sent to Blue Cloud." However, the Abbot replied, "Well, this is not settled yet. We're still working on that." I thought, "Oh my God, what have I done?" The Abbot had the philosophy of *Agere Contra*—it was good for your soul to do things that you didn't want to do. And it would have been characteristic of him to say, "Well, in that case, maybe you had better go to Blue Cloud," so I lived on pins and needles. All this by way of saying I was appointed to the library, November 13, 1949.

After being appointed, I realized that I couldn't continue teaching as I couldn't do justice to both jobs. I taught religion in the college and liturgy in the theology school. So I asked to be relieved of teaching. I only taught one year. I was in the library officially from November 1949 until July 31, 2000, although I started in September of 1949. I thus spent 51 years in the library. After I was appointed, I went away to school for two summers and a school year at Catholic University, 1950-51. I was appointed head librarian August 16, 1951.

Describe your early years as a librarian.

When I came back here after finishing my schooling, I established a budget. Our budget was a thousand dollars. I can hardly believe that this was all I got for books. I attempted to get more, but it was a struggle. Also the need to get the library cataloged was of high priority. I was part of a committee to search for a cataloger. We hired Miss Katharine Skinner from Yale, who arrived May 1, 1950, at the end of the school year. Miss Skinner was an Anglican, a high Anglican, and went to Compline every day and attended services on Sunday. About once a month, she went to Evansville [IN] to her own church. She lived here as a woman and a non-Catholic in a very Catholic and male institution. She stayed in the Gessner home down over the hill and walked up and down that hill every day.

Miss Skinner had been given the idea that she was to lead the cataloging project. When she got here, Fr. Placidus [Kempf, OSB], the librarian before me who only worked as a librarian on Tuesdays and Thursdays, pushed a cart in front of her that had a dictionary, cards, and a couple of pencils and said, "Go to it." She was dumbfounded, as she was thinking that she would be training young people, but there were no young people around as it was summer. So she did begin.

Was there no staff to help with the cataloging?

The library has always been short-staffed and the first years were terribly frustrating. Fr. Placidus was by himself. I was really the first one appointed explicitly to go on to library school to take his place and to look at the library as my life work. Although I became head librarian, as far as staffing went, I had little say about who should come and go. People were often put in and pulled out without me even knowing about it.

We did get fraters to help in the library, but they would be temporary. It takes so long to train somebody, as the work is very technical, and we were constantly training people. If they didn't have any place for people to work for a couple of weeks, they would assign them to the library. We were supposed to give them a job and keep them busy. After reflection, I realize these were obediences—my obedience and their obediences. However, it was frustrating.

Miss Skinner, perhaps because of her own frustration due to a lack of more permanent workers, wrote in her final report something to the effect that, "the library will never be what it should be at this institution until it is respected as essential as the kitchen and the powerhouse." She stayed with us for four years and was very professional and very demanding.

In order to focus on administration, were you able to obtain more permanent staff?

Br. Lambert [Zink, OSB] was assigned as my assistant in 1958. When he was appointed, I hardly knew his name. He was a plasterer at the time. Br. Lambert was not a professional in any way by training. But he was bright and he learned and he cared. He was a partner in everything and worked in the library until 2000. Fr. Placidus, whom I succeeded, worked in the library for about 15 years before he finally retired. Fr. Philip Mahin, who had library training, was an excellent cataloger and worked until his premature death in November 1971.

The first person I actually hired was Ruth Ann Denning in early 1972. She started as my secretary and then started cataloging. She helped me in all aspects of the library and is now the cataloger. Mary Ellen Seifrig came to work in the library in 1987 to help me in my position as executive secretary to ATLA [American Theological Library Association] at the time. She came to work fulltime in January of 1991. She is now assistant to the library director. So we have had a few long-time people.

What else did you do in your early years at the library?

Because of my training at Catholic University, I began to have a world view of librarianship. I realized that I needed to go to library conferences to keep abreast of trends. I am grateful to say that I would ask for permission to go to meetings and was allowed to do so. I immediately began to take part in the Indiana state library program. I went to the Catholic Library Association. I went to some ALA [American Library Association] meetings and then later the ATLA [American Theological Library Association]. I began to have a larger vision of librarianship than just cataloging books. The quality of my life was enriched by my professional life I had with the ATLA. For 18 or 20 years, I was involved with the nitty gritty of management of that association and established wonderful relationships with other people and institutions. This association awarded me lifetime membership, as has the American Library Association, the Catholic Library Association and the American Benedictine Academy. I feel blessed.

Over the past 30 years, library catalogs have gone from paper cards to electronic databases. How did that happen here?

In the mid-1970s, library procedures were becoming automated and we were on the ground floor on that. Saint Meinrad was the 16th library in the state to automate—do our cataloging on OCLC, a computerized database. There were lots of decisions on how this automation was to be done. At this time, OCLC was just getting established. The bigger libraries were scared because they had too much involved in their investment to make the move in this direction until it became obvious that it was a good move to make.

One reason for this automation was to bring better service around the state. Until the late 1950s, a county could only lend books to its own people. However, the Library Services Act, a federal law, allowed inter-cooperation between different types of libraries. The Indiana Cooperative Library Services Authority, called INCOLSA, was formed around 1974. It organized nine Area Library Services Authorities [ALSAs] in Indiana. We are in the Four Rivers ALSA. I became a key figure in this organization, mostly because there were very few people who would stand up and say they would do it. It wasn't that I had any special qualifications, but I learned in the process. Being willing to say "yes," frequently is the path to growth.

Institutions that were willing to enter the cooperative bibliographic program were asked to submit a grant proposal. If their proposal was accepted, they would receive a monitor and OCLC connection. We received the 16th terminal in the state and began doing all our cataloging on OCLC in September 1976.

I understand that you were instrumental in getting the new library building.

I began lobbying for a new library around 1966. I lobbied because the shelves were full and we sadly had thrown out whole collections of German books. I wrote the first request in 1966 for a new library. At that time, we began talking about redoing Benet Hall and they were looking for an architect. For all the architects interviewed, I was invited to speak to them about the library needs. Victor Christ-Janer got the job and I had a number of sessions with him. I drove him back and forth to the airport and we had sort of a personal relationship. He drew up a priority list for a long-range plan for buildings and the library was 15th! I was devastated, absolutely devastated.

So, at one point, I invited David Kaser, the head of the department of the Library Science School at Indiana University, to visit Saint Meinrad. He was a world-renowned expert in the architecture for new libraries. I had read an article about his world travels, so I called him up and, with tongue in cheek, said, "Have you ever seen Saint Meinrad and its very interesting Bavarian architecture? I think you would find it interesting to visit and then over lunch we can talk about the library." He visited, but I found I couldn't afford him. However, he said he would be willing to help and review any plans we had.

A Lilly grant became available to the college in the late 1970s. So I invited David and two other people to form a committee to survey the library and to see if it met our needs. They wrote up a report that is affectionately known as the "Kaser Report." David put the three parts together and edited it. In the document, he said that, "On a scale of 'A' to 'F,' the Saint Meinrad library scores an ignominious 'F'." Well, of course, this was according to my plan. It became a public document because it was a Lilly grant. After it was made public, the priority of building a library jumped from 15 to two.

In the meantime, we were beginning to discuss the need for a new monastery. The discussion of a new library came up in a chapter meeting in March or April 1978. The decision was made to use the same architect for the two buildings. The monastery would be built first and then the library. I think the meeting may have been Monday night. By Tuesday of this week, Fr. Gavin [Barnes, OSB] had been appointed to oversee the gathering of information that was needed for the library.

He came to me and said, "Do you think you could have a program document by Thursday?" I almost hit him. That I should be willing to make this all-important institutional document in two days just blew my mind. It generally takes from six months to two years to get all the input for this important document. In addition, it was Holy Week, but I did it. I had by Thursday night, the second or third draft. Over the years, I had been working on some aspects of it. I had already shown it to David Kaser, who had made suggestions, so the final program document was a very worthy piece.

I had also been collecting materials for prices of furniture and other kinds of things that would be needed in a library and so had a lot of data available. This program document was a key to the ultimate success of the building. The architects took over from there and now it's 22 years later and it's still functioning very, very well. We moved into the new monastery in July '82 and into the library in January '83. The building of the library was a period of great joy and fulfillment, and I am sure it has colored the quality of my life for the rest of my life—you can't take that away.

Prayer

Let's now look at Benedictine values and spirituality. What do you think is important to convey to some of your younger conferees or even the laity?

Well, I think the title of my book, *Finding Grace in the Moment*, embraces my whole theology—a belief in the presence of God. A monastic life is a call to respond to God's call and to become more and more aware, moment by moment, of God's presence in our lives. So being sensitive to the moment and being open to grace is the truth that underlies my life. I think this is the way to peace; all of the other things follow from it.

You can make universal principles and big things fit in them. For example, what is the greatest virtue? It is love because love includes poverty, chastity and obedience. Being more aware of God's presence and of God's action in our daily lives is a spiritual journey. It is opening up more and more to the reality that is there and letting the light shine through, so to speak.

What is your favorite part of the Rule of St. Benedict?

It's kind of simplistic, but Chapter 72 on fraternity is my favorite section. By the mutual support of brotherhood, we take up our cross together and follow the Lord Christ in obedience and do this as brothers in the community. That chapter has some beautiful things about obedience to one another. It throws the whole concept of authority on its ear, in a sense. It changes authority from domination to charity. It changes obedience from being someone giving commands and somebody obeying them, to someone anticipating what the wishes are of others and living accordingly. I think that the mutual obedience that Benedict describes here is most beautiful.

What is your key to living Benedictine spirituality?

It is hard to say anymore—seeking God. In many ways, the key to living Benedictine spirituality and my favorite part of the *Rule* are the same.

What has been your most difficult time or situation as a monk?

Fraternal conflicts—somewhat resolved but not always. That's the human condition. I have experienced this. In one of the psalms, we say, "From hidden faults acquit me," or something to this effect. But sometimes when you live close to one another, there is always a chance of offending somebody without even realizing it. If we are not open with one another, it can rankle and you might not even be aware of what you have done. Of course, that's not unique to monasticism. It was hard at the moment they occurred, but they have all been resolved.

What has been your most happiest time?

That would be difficult to recall. How can you describe happiness or our capacities for happiness? Certainly, making vows and ordination were very, very high moments in my life. My solemn vows were very emotional. However, I reject the idea, as mentioned by some of my superiors when I was a novice, that "This should be the happiest years of your life"—the heck with that! What I mean is that you build on what you have had. It would be pretty depressing if your young years were the happiest or the best. I think that what they may have meant was that you had time for prayer and a time for quiet; your life is less encumbered by major life burdens and serious human conflicts. So there is a certain amount of truth in their earlier comments. My happiness, I think, has blossomed. I enjoy each celebration, surely not to the same degree, but I don't like to make comparisons of what is best.

Are Benedictine values and spirituality still found today in the Archabbey, even though some have suggested that our culture is falling into indifference as to a virtuous life?

In terms of monastic values such as seeking God, obedience, silence and caring, all those values that are in the *Rule* are manifested today in the life we live together. Some purist might say that this isn't monasticism or this isn't Benedictine monasticism, but I don't know how you would judge that. I am very comfortable as a Benedictine and as a monk. I really feel that I have found my niche, so to speak. Conceivably, given my talents, like anybody else, I probably could have done other things. I could have been a professor, I could have been a researcher, I know that. I had ambitions to work with the poor—you can do only one thing with your life. I feel that I have used my talents constructively for good. I believe in the whole Divine Plan. I believe in Creation, I believe in God's providence. I believed each is created to know, love and serve God—the very basic things we learn in catechism—in this world so we can be happy in the next.

I have worked all my life to doing that and, in the process, I've touched other things and other hearts. I believe I have learned the meaning of love and I am very grateful for the countless people in my life that have helped me to blossom as a loving person, caring person. I have no ambitions outside this. Each day I try to fit myself into this plan of the whole creation. I really don't hear it, but I imagine myself hearing beautiful chords of music and that's the whole universe in harmony with God—each created thing doing its thing as it's been created to do. I try to keep in tune with that chord by living my life, by offering my praise and thanksgiving, by being a whole responsive creature of God making the sound that is harmonic with the rest of creation.

Vatican II: Its Effect on the Church and Saint Meinrad Archabbey

What have been some changes and challenges to the Archabbey and the Church since Vatican II?

First of all, I was probably considered somewhat progressive as a young monk and was very dedicated to the liturgy. I heard with excitement the liturgical developments beginning with the Holy Week transformation of Holy Saturday by Pius XII. It was a kind of beginning of making more sense out of what we do.

Pre-1955, we used to do a vigil of Holy Saturday at 6:30 in the morning. We had the Easter Fire in the morning and called it the "vigil of the Easter." But the liturgy was dictated by the Ecclesiastical Fast. We had to finish everything before First Vespers. We would be doing the whole Easter night liturgy at 7:00 in the morning. So a lot of changes that came about made more sense. I followed with excitement and with joy the whole Vatican II experience.

Perhaps one of the more difficult things, although it didn't affect me personally, was the contraception struggle and trying to find a happy solution to it. I found it very hard counseling people. My life was sheltered in many ways and I wasn't called upon for some of those hard family decisions. My brother and his wife had eight kids in ten years and they were very supportive of the Catholic decision.

I'm more comfortable now. My faith has been handed down to me and I am not to be the one to change it. If the tradition and my teachers say this is the truth of the Gospel, I bow. I may not understand it and I may have difficulty in accepting it, but I try to shape my mind and my heart to say yes.

As time has gone on, it has been easier to accept the Church's teachings because I see the things that they predicted in the 1960s would happen, have now happened. I think there is somewhat of a causal relationship between the breakdown of marriage and promiscuity. Our society, on principle, does not accept that contraception is wrong or relations outside of marriage is wrong. If you don't accept that as a basic principle, then your conscience can't be bothered.

Have there been changes in the community's organization or function over the past 50 years?

One of the major steps in the history of the community was the moving to lay boards, lay people becoming advisors to the community. Around 1965, we began with lay people on the Board of Trustees for the schools. There were moments when it was difficult. While we had a lot of expertise here, we didn't have a lot of expertise in every area. Most of us did not have the business acumen that an institution of this size needs. So the advice of lay people has been very helpful, even for the monastery. But the school and the monastery are so bound together that much of what we do is intertwined—it's hard to clap with only one hand.

In the late '60s, we were getting into dire financial straits. In the early '70s, one particular layman, who was rather outspoken, said, "There is no reason that just because you are a monastery that you can't go bankrupt." We began to experience the down side of being poor. Our credit wasn't being accepted. We began to cut back on things.

In the 1960s, farming got to a point where a small farmer couldn't sell produce for the cost it took to raise it. We sold the cattle and the dairy farm and auctioned off things that had been part of our history for over a hundred years. The money resulting from the sale was applied to the debt and reduced our annual interest. You are paying $200,000 per year for interest and the money is doing nobody any good except the bank. It was like flushing water down the toilet. That cycle repeated itself in the '90s.

In order to build the library and new monastery, were you better off financially by the late 1970s?

We were a little better off from about '78 to about '84 in connection with the capital campaign to build the new monastery and the library. The generosity of people helped to pay for these. This campaign also began a higher level of annual giving, which is a byproduct of a capital campaign. As you identify new development sources and people understand your mission and share it, more of them are willing to continue giving. In our current capital campaign, we hope the level of giving will be substantially better on an annual basis than it was before the campaign started.

What happened in the 1990s?

We closed the college and reorganized Abbey Press. There was a struggle with the college in the early 1990s. Around 1990, 250 students was our goal. But it kept dwindling. They tried different things to expand the outreach for the college. It was decided that, instead of the college just being for potential seminarians, it should be a regular college for lay Catholics. And that simply didn't work. Our grounds, the program and the whole ethos of the place are still aimed at men studying for the priesthood. A lot of the men who came for college were not particularly pious or enamored by the idea of going for the priesthood. We were not able to provide much for a social life.

In the meantime, we had a very high caliber of faculty of about 50 people. So the ratio per student was about three or four to a professor. It was top heavy and the hope was that eventually the situation would improve, but it didn't. Finally, a layman on the Board of Overseers just said—and I was very angry when I first heard him say it—"Shut it down this year. You can't afford this operation." To have someone from the outside come in and say you can't afford this operation was very hard to take. But it was the fact. So they closed the college and it was very traumatic.

The whole history of the institution, the life of all the people involved, not just monks, but also lay people whose livelihoods were stopped in midlife. What opportunities did they have and would they have to start all over someplace else? It was a very traumatic period.

Then Abbey Press had two or three negative years. It didn't take a rocket scientist to figure out you can't keep losing money and stay in business very long. Around 1994, they told the Abbey Press that if they didn't turn around financially, we would have to sell the Press. This would have been very traumatic since we have had a press from our very beginnings. Then we had "Black Monday" where we laid off 64 people at the Abbey Press. That was awfully traumatic. For some, it was early retirement; for others, they were just let go.

They leaned up the staff and dropped certain programs and restructured the Abbey Press. Within a year, it turned around almost a hundred percent. Not having to pay for all of the services and faculty for the college also freed up money. So within two years or so, the financial picture had changed dramatically. One of the professional men on our staff publicly said, "In my professional life, I have never seen an institution make such a dramatic change in such a short time." So it was a dramatic and, fortunately, a positive change for the community.

How is the morale of the community now compared to the past?

I used to say, when there was so much tension in the '60s, I wished that the Holy Father would declare a day of jubilee. Let's say, January 1, 1967, those who want to be monks and love the life say, "Yes," and stay. Those who are not happy and do not want to live the life, "Go with God's blessing." That day was never declared but, in the process of human events, many of the misfits, the disgruntled people and those who were not willing to go along with change left. So we have ended up with people who wanted to be Benedictine monks, wanted to live the life of the Church and wanted to live the liturgical life.

The younger men who have joined the community are not familiar with any other way and choose to be here because they want to be here. So today we're not stuck with unhappy people who feel they have been compromised. I think we have a community with a high morale. We have very dedicated people and unbelievable talent; the potential in this house is amazing. We're very blessed to have a high caliber of people gathered into one place. They all share the love for the Eucharist, love for the Divine Office and believe in the community values. Of course, you will have moments and failures, but I think if anything the morale is better than it ever was.

Was it a good idea to eliminate Latin from the curriculum even though the Mass was to be celebrated in English?

I think I would be partial to Latin and regret its elimination from our cultural heritage. The major documents are translated and are available in ways that there weren't before. However, there is a whole history of Catholic theology that is still tied up in Latin and not accessible to the average person, including most priests. But I don't think this has been a tragedy to the Church anymore than if we had held on to the Greek, because the Church was Greek before it was Latin. I think it has been a tragedy to the culture.

Striking changes have been made in the liturgy. Can you comment on the positive or negative aspects of this?

You could spend a week on this topic. The first real changes in the liturgy were for the Mass. Gradual changes were introduced about 1964. I love the liturgy, and Saint Meinrad celebrated the liturgy with great reverence and awe and perhaps a little more pomp than you might find in most places. But it was not pompous. The liturgy before was done very beautifully and was very meaningful. It was really a vital part of my religious upbringing.

I was fortunate, or unfortunate, I am not sure which, to have been a part of the structure that made the adjustment from Latin to English here. I had not had liturgical training, so I didn't pretend to be a professional liturgist. I was the Master of Ceremonies [MC] and that position was held in high regard. It was quite unusual for me to be appointed as I wasn't even ten years ordained. I was appointed MC September of 1958. In those days, I was primarily a rubrician. I was the person who directed the ceremonies and had to study what we were to do, train the acolytes, train deacons and so on what they should do so and then lead the ceremonies, so we would have a smooth operation.

How did changes in the liturgy affect the community?

Most of the time, the majority of the community was very much in sync and ready to move on and to cooperate. There were some who remained skeptical and that created little hardships. There were also some people who wanted to move faster than the community could move. There were tensions in this period. I was part of a committee of powerful and learned people who were really the decision makers and I was a broker of sorts. I called the meeting and kept the minutes and tried to keep people happy so that schedules were met. My opinion was consulted, but I would never pretend to have been a professional liturgical scholar. It was an exciting period and was hard work.

In terms of changes in the liturgy in the parish from pre- to post-Vatican II, what has been lost and what has been gained?

I think the change to the English liturgy was less beneficial to the average parish than it was here. The text that nourished and nurtured the theology of the liturgy was available to us in ways that are not available to the average parish, where they do not have a Divine Office. The English substitution of Latin hymns has some good points. But a lot has been lost in the average parish because you didn't have people who were trained in liturgy and in music. However, this might be changing. To guide the community in its worship, you need both. In some instances, music was taken over by grade school and high school kids with little knowledge of musicology and theology.

From what I read, I gather that many people are dissatisfied with their local liturgical celebration. That varies with the caliber of the staff and whether or not they have training in proper liturgy planning. Many, many convents had nobody to help them when the changes were required. When use of the guitar rather than the organ began to be used, few sisters in those early days knew how to play the guitar. Candidates and novices began to plan the liturgy without a clue of the liturgical seasons and celebrations and the propriety of various parts of the Mass. They just did ditties. There was a good deal of alienation.

Here at the Archabbey we had theologians and musicians who guided us though all those changes. We have been privileged because Fr. Columba [Kelly, OSB], from the very beginning, was able to provide musical settings from sound theological text. This has been a great boon. We did an "Experimental Office" around 1966 or '67. The Office was pared back to the bare essentials. There were about 20 of us and it included brothers for the first time. We would try something for a week or two and this ran for at least a year. I would post a sign and people would sign up.

For the Office, we had a booklet and it was the bare bones. Two of us, Fr. Philip and myself, were in charge of the Office and were there at all times but we didn't plan it. It was planned by Fr. Aidan [Kavanagh, OSB], Fr. Columba, Fr. Nathan [Mitchell] and others. Aidan and Columba were the key people. I would schedule a meeting and then we worked out the Office. In order to get it done, I typed the whole thing including the psalms. This little beginning was the core of what the Office is today. We paused between psalms, we slowed the pace down and, of course, it was in English.

What effect has the decline in vocations and an increasing older population had on the Church?

I don't even like to think about it.

What's the future for the Church?

That's a very good question and it remains to be seen. I certainly wouldn't be one to predict. There could be a shift, but it would still take 25 to 30 years even if we started to get lots of vocations to fill the gaps. I think that the lay leadership will come to the fore. I used in a homily a few months ago the following information. Since 1966, we have had something like 20 million more Catholics and 3,000 less priests in this country. Priests are not the deposit of the faith. The faith is found in the family, especially if we can maintain the family.

The Church is a combination of the people, priests and bishops. The faith will continue to be handed on, hopefully, by responsible people trained in theology. We now have more people in our lay theology program than we do in the priesthood program. Not all of those will function, but many of them will take up responsible roles in their own parish community. This is important because decisions that are made within the local parish will be made within the context of sound theology.

Now, as far as the Eucharist goes, the Church has lived through periods where people didn't have a priest available to them, even in this country a hundred years ago. They managed to pass on their faith. I read something the other day of some community in Russia that has not had a priest in 50 or 70 years. But they kept the faith. Now they are able to exercise the sacraments again. So it's God's Church; it's not ours. We have a responsible role and at least here, I think, we are doing what we can. So I wouldn't speculate what the future is going to bring—but I am hopeful.

*Essays and stories mentioned are from: Daly, Simeon, *Finding Grace in the Moment* (2005).

Interview profile from: Fr. Simeon Daly to Prof. Ruth C. Engs, June 9, 2005, Interview Transcriptions, Saint Meinrad Archives.

Chapter Seven

Fr. Rupert Ostdick, OSB

Fr. Rupert Ostdick spent most of his career as treasurer and his later years as manager of Abbey Press. He was born November 14, 1921, in Elgin, IL. Fr. Rupert professed his first vows August 10, 1944, made solemn profession August 10, 1947, and was ordained May 18, 1948. He received his theological training at Saint Meinrad School of Theology.

He worked as assistant treasurer (1947-48) and treasurer (1949-79). In 1972, Fr. Rupert also became business manager. In 1979, he became manager of Abbey Press until his retirement in 1991. In that year, he was transferred to the Human Resources Department, where he is claims administrator for the co-workers' health benefits program.

Over his long career, Fr. Rupert also served as assistant spiritual director (1958-61) in the Minor Seminary and in the College (1962-63). He became spiritual director of the College (1963-65), and served as subprior in the monastery (1986-96). From 1971 to 2000, Fr. Rupert was a member of the Archabbey Council.

The interviews for this profile were conducted by the late Professor Edward Shaughnessy (ES) on October 5, 2004, and by Professor Ruth C. Engs (RCE) on August 24, 2005. Initials before questions indicate the interviewers.

Childhood and Early Years as a Monk

ES: Tell me about your childhood and family life and how you came to your life in the priesthood and the monastery?

I was born in 1921, the first of eight siblings, and was given the name Howard. My first two years of schooling were at a one-room schoolhouse near the Ostdick homestead, just outside of Elgin, IL. At the beginning of third grade, I transferred to St. Mary's School in Elgin, and graduated from St. Mary's in 1935. There was no Catholic high school in Elgin at the time, so I enrolled in Elgin's public high school and graduated in 1939.

My father supported his family as a dairyman. My grandfather had raised a family of five sons and five daughters on a dairy farm. All of his sons became dairymen in one way or another. Some were dairy farmers; others worked in milk-processing plants. By the time I was 6 years old, my father had built and was operating a milk-processing plant in Elgin. He continued to operate that plant until about 1936 and peddled milk door-to-door in the town.

When I graduated from elementary school, two other classmates and I were invited to visit the seminary conducted by the Society of the Divine Word Missionaries at Techny, IL. My visit there was a very brief, one-day visit. I never discussed the vocation to the priesthood with my parents until our family moved from Elgin to Belvedere, IL, four years later, right after I had graduated from high school.

The first weekend in our new home in Belvedere, our family attended Mass at St. James Church. By the following Saturday, I had gotten a job as a clerk in the J.C. Penney Co. store; I went to church on Saturday evening during my supper hour to go to confession. At the end of my confession, the priest said to me, "What are you going to do?" And I said, "Well, I'm working at J.C. Penney Co." "That's not what I mean," he said. "What are you going to do with your life?" I was somewhat taken aback by the question, and I didn't say much in reply.

Next Monday morning, my mother was washing the kitchen ceiling; and from the view she had from the top of the stepladder, she could see through the window pane in our front door. A priest was coming up the walk. She came down the stepladder and welcomed him in. He introduced himself and, after a few brief pleasantries, said to my mother, "What does your son want to do with his life?" She said out of the blue, "I think he would like to be priest." I had not spoken to my parents for four years about this matter.

Thus began my guiding relationship with Fr. Sylvester Eye. He was a native of Aurora, IL, and each Friday he would visit his Dad. Often he would invite me to go with him so that we could stop at various religious houses in the vicinity, among them Marmion Military Academy. We visited Marmion a number of times and spoke with Fr. Norbert Spitzmesser, a member of our Saint Meinrad monastic community. He was serving as headmaster of the Academy at the time and arranged for me to visit Saint Meinrad for three days in October of 1939. After that visit, I returned home and continued working at the J.C. Penney Co. store for the remainder of that fall semester. I was 17 years old then.

After some weeks of reflection and prayer, I decided that I would like to come to Saint Meinrad and eventually enter the community. However, I knew that, since I had not taken any Latin in high school, I would have to catch up on Latin. I announced my decision to my parents, and my father said, "No, you're not going there." We were a very poor family with many mouths to feed; and his plan for my future was that I was to be the business manager of his dairy that he hoped to buy.

In the tradition of the Old World, since I was the eldest in the family, he thought it was my duty to help with the family business. He and I would discuss this each evening at the supper table when he had returned home from work. My poor mother had to listen to the altercation back and forth, day by day.

After that initial response from my father, I was guided by Fr. Eye who, while he counseled me never ever to ride roughshod over my parents' desires and directions, instructed me that parents are not endowed by God with the responsibility of making a life decision for their children. Their children, as they approached maturity, are free agents, so to say, and should make that decision freely for themselves.

Eventually, I made arrangements to come to Saint Meinrad at the beginning of the second semester. So, just after Christmas, one day my father, on his way to work, dropped me off at the parish church where I attended Mass each day, and as he said "Goodbye," he added, "Well, if you don't like it there, you can always come home."

In the next several years after I entered the community here, two of my sisters entered the congregation of the School Sisters of Notre Dame. By the time that happened, our Dad was used to saying "Yes!" to his children's vocations.

I came to Saint Meinrad January 5, 1940. I was a belated vocation in the sense that my studies were kind of disjointed. Since I went to a public high school, I had no Latin or Greek, so I enrolled in the "second-special" Latin course. I took two years of Latin that semester between January and June of 1940. The next two years, I doubled up on the Latin courses—taking two years in one each year. I came into the monastic community as a novice in July 1943.

RCE: How did you see the Church and the monastic community at this time? What were your expectations?

Well, the Church was the guiding star of our family life, and we were faithful in attending church. After I graduated from high school and was working for a semester and considering a vocation to the priesthood, I had a rather economic view. I wanted to do what would be the surest way to heaven and to get there the most efficient way. I saw the monastic community as a proven way of life that would model the family that I had come from. That was very attractive to me. That's how I saw it at that time. By and large, I still hold that view.

Fr. Rupert, as a young monk

I know that motivations are modified with experience and I have seen that happen in my own thinking because of interaction with my brethren. Some of them, especially in the earlier years after we made vows together, were tussling with the idea of the Benedictine way of life as a family. They thought this was an outmoded interpretation of Benedict, as we were adult people. This thinking was especially so when they came back to the monastery after being sent away for their education.

The interaction with their compatriots in the academic world was, I think to a large extent, reflected in their changing views. Most of them have now gone to God. I still hold rather tenaciously, now more than ever, to my view that the Benedictine life is a life of family. The abbot is the father and the brethren are the adult sons—as distinguished from babies, you know. I think this is a legitimate view from my own reading of the *Rule*.... I think that those expectations have been fulfilled.

RCE: How about family visits or vacations in the early years?

When I first came here, my family didn't visit me that often because they were poor people. When they did come, Dad would load the family in a blue pickup truck—it was a panel truck with the panels taken out and homemade windows put in it. Abbot Ignatius used to call it the Blue Goose. In those years just after the war, we still had gas rationing. I shudder to think of it now, but Dad would put an extra five gallons of gas in the back of the truck so he would have enough to make the trip. Before our monastery had a guest house, they stayed in the homes of local people in the town.

When my father came here, he would often go down to the powerhouse to talk with the men who worked there. He had qualified as a station engineer when he was younger. He visited them, not for that, but to talk German with them. This experience was a good feeling. In latter years, my family came less frequently. My two siblings who are School Sisters of Notre Dame now come here once in a while. They have come for occasions such as jubilees of priesthood and monastic vows. It's always a marvelous time to get together. The conversation is non-stop until they go to bed or go home. The last time my family came was to celebrate 60 years of monastic vows in 2004. In another three years, it will be for monastic priesthood.

ES: What was the tone and the nature of training in the novitiate? Is it different today?

We were more focused on the formation process taking place in us. The evidence for that, in my view, was that there were certain requirements in the School that we were excused from. For example, I don't think we had to concern ourselves with some of the thesis-like papers that were required of other seminarians in the School. But we had other formative responsibilities that took the place of those tasks. Academics, while praiseworthy and required for ordination to priesthood, were secondary to being trained as a monk.

ES: I get the impression that the tone is less serious and more light-hearted now?

I ponder on your comment about how it's more light-hearted now. I wonder if that doesn't follow upon a greater self-discipline and responsibility that was unavailable to us in those earlier years. In other words, our day-to-day activities were probably more regimented compared to today's pattern. Then, far less was left to our own initiative. The pattern back then was, frankly, a burden; but it was good training. For some of us, the year of novitiate and the three years of the clericate were an endurance course. We didn't appreciate it as we should have, and as we do now in retrospect—this was a kind of an unspoken feeling.

Once you were ordained and moved into the ranks of a full-fledged monk, you could finally admit this. After this transition, you had more personal self-responsibility. This was a new burden, but it was a relief, too. The things we found a burden, during the years of the formative process, now sustained us when we meet the challenges of living without the supervision that had been there for us. So the system worked!

ES: It appears that young men today come in already having a college degree or even advanced degrees.

Yes. You can just look at the backgrounds of the young men who are currently in monastic formation in our community. One has a PhD in psychology. Another has a master's degree in chemical engineering. Others have worked in professional arenas such as foodservice management, for example. Another is a certified Emergency Medical Technician.

I used to talk about myself as being a belated vocation because I didn't come to the seminary until I had graduated from high school and had been working for a semester. I was ordained at the late age of 26. The usual age was 24. I had at least one classmate who had to get a dispensation to be ordained to the priesthood at the age of 23. Now the youngest in the novitiate is 25, and ordination to priesthood is at least six years off for him.

ES: Is there any particular incident that helped you in your formation?

Our class, the novitiate class of 1943, was the last class that was under the tutelage of Fr. Henry Brenner. He had been novicemaster at that point for 35 years. In April of 1940, he was replaced by Fr. Meinrad Hoffman, who prior to that assignment, had served as the spiritual director of the Minor Seminary [high school plus two years of college]. So he knew all of the men who were in the novitiate. Fr. Henry was a very talented man. He was low key in his instructions and they were, frankly, boring to some extent. He gave a conference to the fraters every Sunday morning after the community High Mass.

One Sunday evening, I went for a walk with Fr. Julius Armbruster, who was one of the senior members in the fratery group. He told me in the course of our conversation how much he really enjoyed the down-to-earth valuable instruction he got from Fr. Henry. His comment made a deep impression on me. I began to listen to Fr. Henry with a more sympathetic and comprehending ear. Fr. Henry's conferences about the holy *Rule* and about the customs of our community were very practical and filled with common sense. Many times in more recent decades, I have harked back to his instructions.

Work

ES: What were your major jobs over the years?

Before I was ordained—I was still in simple vows in May of 1947—I received a letter, dated May 31, from Abbot Ignatius Esser. In that letter, he said something like, "Fr. Rupert, today (it was Decoration Day) you are being decorated with an appointment. Fr. Matthias Zinkan has to go to Marmion Abbey in two weeks' time. And you are to take his place in the Abbey Treasury. So take this letter and show it to your cleric master and then show it to the treasurer and begin to learn as much as you can from Fr. Matthias before he leaves for Marmion." Fr. Maurus Ohligschlager was the treasurer at the time. I was really not happy about that decision, but it was the first obedience that I had been given.

I had taken a business course in high school, at my father's behest, so as to be able to do the work he had planned for me. When I entered the monastery, I thought that would be the end of having to tend to the business end of things—monks are not too prone to want to be treasurers or business managers!

However, God had other plans. I was the assistant treasurer until that September. After I was ordained a priest in 1948, I was appointed Abbey treasurer. I served in that capacity from 1948 until 1979—a period of 31 years! The last seven of those years, I was also business manager when the two offices combined.

ES: When Abbot Ignatius sent this directive to you, what work had you been hoping for?

I yearned for the chance to study for a degree. The summer after I was appointed to the Business Office, I was sent to the summer school at Loras College, where I studied cost accounting and corporation finance—two six-week courses. That was the extent of my higher education experience. I learned years later that my academic records reflect the fact that I have an "imputed" BA degree based on the work I did in the "College Department" of Saint Meinrad Seminary.

RCE: Tell me about your first years as treasurer.

Several movements in the community were coming together and they drew one another along in my first years. Fr. Theodore [Heck, OSB] was director of studies and registrar for the schools. He laid the foundation for future accreditation by reorganizing the curriculum and improving the faculty by having men sent away for degrees. When I became treasurer, I knew that I had inherited a kind of a makeshift accounting system. It had double-entry bookkeeping as its core, but it was so adapted that it was hard for people to see what was going on.

My predecessor as treasurer, Fr. Maurus Ohligschlager, frankly did not understand double-entry bookkeeping. He followed the pattern of his predecessor in recording transactions. So when I was handed the reins, I began to investigate what other communities were doing. I went to St. John's Abbey and spent about three or four days with Fr. Ignatius

Candrian in their business office. I got a copy of their chart of accounts and all of its subdivisions.

In addition, there were textbooks written to teach auditing and book-keeping. Since I didn't study at the university, I read those texts and used them as patterns because they were so good. They were replete with examples. They had practice sets. In other words, they had the forms and the description of the transactions that you were going to record in the forms. You then posted that information to the ledgers and then summarized it all into a business statement. I used the book, *Twentieth Century Bookkeeping*.

RCE: What else did you do?

My recollection is that, in order to gain accreditation, we needed to develop a budget as part of the institution's operation. That is, the preparation of budgets and the discipline of staying within the budget became part of the institutional pattern. Basically, for most academicians, it meant anticipating the needs for the next year and having it approved. This approval would be a kind of permission to carry out those transactions. Because we were not able to receive public funding for our budgetary needs, it had to come from our own sources. As long as I was in the business office, the budget was a planning instrument. What it was not, was a legal right to go ahead and spend that money without checking first.

I remember my predecessor as treasurer, Fr. Maurus, going to the monastic chapter to give the financial report. It consisted of two 8 1/2 by 11 sheets of paper. We had the first audit in 1951 from a Chicago firm. During the second or third audit, one of our senior fathers who had been stationed at the Indian missions came back to the monastery. He came to my office one day and saw these men working. And he said, "Father, are these men from the outside?" And I said, "Yes, they're auditors. They are auditing our books." He said, "You mean they see everything?" "Yes, Father," I answered. It was hard for some of the seniors to shift gears into "let this be open." It was now open and the audit reports were made available to the community. Even though they didn't understand it, it was there.

RCE: Financially, what was happening with the community at this time?

We had substantial debt by the time we completed Bede Hall [1958]. Abbot Ignatius had a pre-development office kind of program. He called it "the pay as you go solicitation for funds." You see, the Development Office in its present form dates to about 1967. We had a Development Office before that, but it was run by a monk who was struggling to understand his responsibilities, as I had to struggle to understand my altered responsibilities through the course of time. Under Abbot Ignatius, we had been borrowing money for our current operations as 60- and 90-day notes from the local banks. That meant that the financial destiny of the community was on short-term notes.

One of the first things that Abbot Bonaventure [Knaebel, OSB] did after he was elected in 1955 was to contact an annuity bonding company in Wisconsin, B.C. Ziegler Company. Through them, we issued annuity bonds that were sold on the bond market. This meant that the payment back was staggered over the course of 10 or 15 years. That gives us a little breathing room to utilize our borrowing capacities with the local banks appropriately and not live from hand-to-mouth. Administratively, it was a prudent financial step and the right and effective thing to do.

RCE: Did you or the abbot decide on this? How about other business and expenditure decisions?

I couldn't have done it on my own. I think at least we would go to the Abbot's Council. You see, administrative-wise, canon law requires permission from the chapter for expenditures of fixed assets such as buildings. In other words, to go into debt to build a building, you had to have—over a certain level of expenditure—the permission of the chapter and, in some cases, the Holy See, through the office of the abbot president. That bond decision would have fallen into the area of current administration rather than concerns like fixed assets.

RCE: When you went to a business model, how did most of the community react to it?

I think that as much as they understood it, it was a comfort to know they could anticipate receiving tentative approval of the financial aspects of their work that helped the community. They didn't concern themselves too much with the details of providing the funds. I remember going to a chapter meeting and was recommending something when one of the confreres got up and said, "We don't understand this, but I guess the only thing we can do is trust Fr. Rupert." They were willing to leave so much to my administration. This was a terrifying responsibility when you look at it, because these were gifted men, to trust me that much!

RCE: I'm told that you started one of first profit-sharing retirement plans of any monastery.

I believe that was in 1967. When we developed our profit-sharing plan for the retirement of our lay co-workers, I know that we didn't have very many models to go by. I don't recall our being the first in the nation to develop such a plan among Catholic institutions. We were largely guided by people who had experience, like insurance agents, who could go to their parent company and provide us with typical models. In other words, other institutions didn't have this, but when I say that, the number of institutions that we did try to get information from was comparatively small.

I remember my predecessor as general manager of the Abbey Press, a lay person [Peter Kaufman], was the impetus whereby I went ahead with a profit-sharing retirement plan. He had first been an auditor for one of our auditing firms out of Louisville, KY, and was employed as comptroller of the Abbey Press. After he had been in that position for several years, he became general manager. One day he came to me and said that he thought we should start a retirement plan of some kind. He said, "A man, Benno Greulich, had retired from Abbey Press after 50 years of service and got nothing." That really touched me, so we took steps after that to develop a retirement program.

We set aside a percent of a co-worker's annual wages to put into a fund. When they decided to retire, they essentially got—this may have changed over the years since we've had that plan—a lump sum of whatever is accumulated in their account, either by way of contribution of the Abbey or interest earnings on the funds. When they retire, they have some decisions to make. Are they going to roll it over into another annuity in their own name outside the retirement fund? Are they going to invest it themselves in the stock market, real estate or whatever? They have so many options. That's great!

RCE: Tell me about the financial crisis of the '60s and early '70s.

I'm sure you've heard about the fact that we closed our high school and liquidated our agricultural enterprises.

RCE: Yes, and I understand when the high school was actually closed it was at peak enrollment. Was it closed for financial reasons or did somehow somebody read a crystal ball and see that enrollment would decrease?

All of the above. At the time, the high school was not the problem, or the cause, of our financial problems by itself. It was partly. This was at a time when seminary administrators were examining the advisability of taking a young boy from his parental home and isolating him in a high school seminary during his formative years. From where I sat, that was equally, if not more, influential in the decision to close the high school. Also, from my point of view, closing the school was a way of placing our financial resources in those educational enterprises that were not being questioned in terms of psychological needs of children.

In reflecting on our schools, in the context of other schools, there was the recognition that we did not have the ability to tax the general population for support. The only thing about an academic enterprise that could be treated on a for-profit basis would be such things as lodging, the book store, student stores. The rest of it, the instructional part of an educational institution, was not expected to be self-supporting.

RCE: How about the closing of the stone and agribusinesses?

You see, we were looking for any way of stopping the bleeding, so to say. The stone quarry was breaking even when we closed it, but for 18 months or so it had a diminishing net income. So rather than invest, not just capital investment but also labor we had to pay for, as there were no monks working there except the manager, we saw the handwriting on the wall. However, it had been a part of the monastic tradition in this house since the 1870s when the first stone was quarried at Monte Cassino. That was a tender point with the community. It was with a good deal of regret that we were unable to continue it.

The closing of the farm particularly helped in our survival. At the time it was closed, there were one and a half monks working there. We saw that this was an asset that could be liquidated, not at an advantageous price, but it would bring some cash in to pay a part of our debts. We paid off as much as we could.

ES: Tell me about your years at the Abbey Press.

In 1979, there was a change of administration at the Abbey Press. The general manager of the Abbey Press reports to the treasurer-business manager of the Archabbey. For an interim period of six months, I served as general manager of Abbey Press as well as treasurer-business manager of the Archabbey. During that six months, we made a search for a new general manager, but no satisfactory match was found. One very strong candidate, a layman, decided against accepting the position because of the isolation of Saint Meinrad.

No one in the monastic community was available to be assigned the position, though I had suggested a number of names of monastic confreres whom I thought could do the job. They were in other positions and were not able to be moved into that slot. At that time, seven departmental managers reported to the general manager of Abbey Press. Those seven managers petitioned Abbot Timothy [Sweeney, OSB] to have me continue as their general manager. So, I was relieved of the duties of treasurer-business manager of the Archabbey and spent the next 12 years working as the general manager of Abbey Press, from 1979 to 1991.

RCE: How long has the Abbey Press been associated with Saint Meinrad?

The first press was brought here in 1867, about 12 years after we started the institution. It will be here, hopefully, for several more centuries, at least. Abbey Press is very important to us and over the years has gained more importance. One of the reasons I, as a monk, was sent to Abbey Press was that we needed to improve our relationship with our co-workers. The morale needed boosting. During the late '60s or early '70s, we had begun a personnel office. We had never had one before. This office has been a help to the institution and a help to the local people, too.

RCE: How many people were employed when you first went there?

When I first went down to the Press, there were a phenomenal number of people who were employed at Abbey Press. The number 500 sticks in my head. There were so many people that it was hard to find a place for them to work. They would sit at small tables in the corridors. My predecessor believed in having the help you needed to get the job done. When I went there, one of my goals was to reduce this high number of employees to a more realistic number. I did this mainly by attrition. There were no major layoffs or firing of people.

RCE: When you got there, what were your products?

The products that we offered were basically of a religious nature. I fostered this because, at that time, our catalog was being mailed under a "not-for-profit" postal rate. The rationale behind qualifying for this postal rate was that the catalog fostered our religious apostolate for the family. In the succeeding years, I had to appear before various taxing entities to explain and justify our position, as we were in competition with other companies who were "for profit" but offered the same or similar products.

This mail order catalog was begun in 1963. This section of Abbey Press was well on its way to having a customer base when I got there. The dealings were in the hundreds of thousands. Products offered in the catalog included holy cards, religious greeting cards, prints and plaques. Later, we started to produce and offer plaster figurines. We finally accepted products from other producers. The focus, as we developed the catalog, was the Christian family, and home decor that would foster religious life in the family.

RCE: How about magazines?

The Grail magazine emerged out of some earlier magazines in the 1930s. Articles included those that fostered Catholic teaching, human interest stories about living the faith, catechismal explanation of Catholic doctrine, and the prayer life for people. It was promoted across the nation. In some ways, it was a partner effort with oblates. We had an oblate chapter in New York City and I believe we had an office to promote *The Grail* a short time in New York. In the early '50s, its title was changed to *Marriage Magazine* and then finally *Marriage and Family Magazine*. We discontinued publication in the late 1980s during the last years that I was at the Press.

By the early 1990s, I was getting up in years and too old for the heavy responsibility. So I was relieved. In the meantime, a younger monk was getting his master's degree in business administration from Indiana University. Upon the completion of his studies, he came back and was appointed the general manager of Abbey Press. After that, I had a period of about four months during which I was able to catch my breath a little bit, and then in 1991, I was appointed to the Human Resources Department, where I have been ever since.

Prayer

RCE: What is your favorite part of the Rule of St. Benedict?

I cherish the whole *Rule*, of course. But the part I go to often is Chapter 72. It's the summary of how our lives should be lived. It has a good ending—we look forward to life everlasting. That's my favorite part of the *Rule*. I think it clearly describes, in accord with the old views of Benedict, the relationships between the monk and his abbot and the monk and his brothers. And that, in terms of our final goal, is really very compelling for me. How our day-to-day conduct fits in with the description of those relationships.

RCE: What is your key to living the Benedictine spirituality?

If I were to pass the key to Benedictine spirituality to someone else, I would have to say two things in this order: humility and obedience. These basic life attitudes are the core of the way Benedict leads his followers to God. Humility is founded in reverence toward God. It's manifested by living in a community of monks and by accepting the requirements of obedience. That's how we spell it out. We didn't choose this conglomeration of different personalities because popular personality traits attracted us, but rather for fundamental ways of going to God. So I think that's the key to the living of Benedictine spirituality.

I must say that, over the years, especially since Vatican II, the approach to obedience is much enriched by the work of the Council on the Decree on Religious Life. It's called *Perfectae Caritas*. It means "the perfection of charity." The section on obedience discusses the search for God's Will by the individual as well as by the superior. This means, for example, that superiors, in general, now have to dialogue with the individual regarding assignments. And that's an enrichment of obedience. Without this consideration, it's a precarious kind of obedience in many ways. God, in His goodness and His infinite wisdom, can make up for the mistakes of any fallible superior. God and His Church, through that document, have ordained that this process of dialogue between the superior and the subject should be a part of the picture, where it wasn't before.

RCE: What have been your most difficult times?

We just talked about humility and obedience. When I was appointed to the business office, I would never, ever have chosen that work for myself; it was very difficult. It was doubly difficult because, as events turned out, my higher education stopped at about my kneecaps, because this job was a full-time responsibility. I was in the last year of theological studies and took the final year over a span of two years, because I was full-time treasurer and full-time student. I guess I got through it. I always had great respect for, and still have great respect for, the development of the human person that comes through education. This was, as I looked at it at the time, truncated because I didn't go away for advanced studies. Now, strangely enough, that circumstance that kept me here because of the work also gave me the privilege of going to choir every day with the community and that has been a blessing, a great blessing and a source of much peace.

RCE: What have been some of your most joyful or happy times?

I think some of the most joyful times have been in the last couple of years. I was very happy when we elected Abbot Justin. This was a joyful time of my life. It still is. With that thought, in the last years, you see, once you do administrative tasks for a good long time, it's time for other people to take that over in your advancing years. It's just a result of the passage of time, in a way, but the pressures that were there are now gone.

Since 1991, I've worked in the Human Resources Department and I have had the advantage of a supervisor who is very understanding when I have other commitments. These other commitments are mostly with reference to what I would call priestly work. For example, I serve on a team of about a dozen monks that are commuting chaplains to Monastery Immaculate Conception. I have done, in the last couple of years, a couple of retreats. I don't have classes to look back on and bring knowledge from the fruit of my studies. But somehow, an old guy's common sense has a value that is appreciated.

It's been one of the great privileges of my life in recent years to be invited to serve as extraordinary confessor for the school here. That's something I don't deserve, obviously, but nonetheless it's been a source of great joy because it puts me into contact with these young people and is so marvelously enriching for me. That's another plus about having to be here all the time. I have been involved, off and on, in spiritual direction and guidance in the schools since about 1955.

There came a point when, during one year, I was novice master, and then cleric master in 1964-65. At the end of that year, the Business Office was in full swing for a number of big projects, too. I went to Abbot Gabriel and I said, "I don't feel I can do both anymore." I was running the Business Office on about an hour and a half a day. He said, "Well, you know what? We'll make you stay in the Business Office." That wasn't what I had hoped for, as it limited my activity with the students at that time, but in the course of time, my load was lightened.

Vatican II: Its Effect on the Church and Saint Meinrad Archabbey

ES: In general, what is your attitude toward Vatican II?

Having lived through it, in my view, by and large, the Second Vatican Council has had a positive effect on the life of the people of God.

There are many challenges living in the aftermath of the Council. One such challenge is that life after the Council obliges people to focus on what is really essential. If people's practice of religion is grounded in doctrinal substance and expressed in ritual, which is more clearly expressed in their vernacular language, and they feel they are present for a mysteriously holy action, then their practice has radically changed for the better.

As I reflect now on what has happened, I think people understand better the Scripture readings of the Mass read in their own tongue, even though those readings have always been accessible to people in their Bible. And when the Scriptures are thus presented in the context of the Mass, there is a sacramental power at work.

We formerly depended so much on the sacramental life of the Church —and its grace-filling effect on people (and still do)—and on the theological dictum that the effects of the sacrament are produced by the fact of the sacrament's action being performed by an ordained priest. However, that dictum should not be applied to the situation where the holy Scriptures were read to God's people in a language the faithful could not understand. People can more successfully grasp the meaning of the holy Scriptures when those sacred words are read to them in a language they can understand.

ES: What are other effects of the Council?

I think that one of the very great enrichments in the Church from the Second Vatican Council was the greater responsibility assigned to, and received by, lay people. Some clerics looked at this and grudgingly gave ground for that transition to take place. The generous response so many lay people are giving to the call of responsible service in the Church makes the disillusionment they have had to experience in the past ten years, because of the clerical sexual abuse scandal, all the more understandable.

ES: After the Council, was there a different experience in the monastery as compared to the lay church?

There was a parallel experience in the monastery, I am sure. A monk, by being a monk, had as a vocational endowment a deeper understanding of the liturgy and what it meant. Because the monk had to comprehend Latin—and that was a blessing—he was equipped to withstand or tolerate the changes with less trauma and with the advantage of an earlier appreciation of the opportunities that came from Vatican II. This, of course, is only one monk's view of the question.

ES: For the layperson, a parish priest or a monk, was there a sense of psychological dislocation for a while?

The new experience was embraced by our monastic superiors. The monk who asked, "What does the abbot, the place-taker of Christ in my regard, expect of me?" realized that, "We should try to see the best in the Church." I think that is the way we have lived our lives since then. I should also say that the changes were more easily accepted by us monks, because we were living more abidingly in a religious context.

Also, the clearest manifestation of the Vatican Council was its greater emphasis on self-determination and responsibility that came with changing one custom at a time. For example, personal, para-liturgical devotions had been scheduled for the monastic community prior to Vatican II. Some of these were dropped from the community schedule. There was a time when, every evening in May, we had May devotions with Benediction of the Blessed Sacrament. But after Vatican II, that was dropped from our schedule.

However, certain things, we felt, as a community, we should hold on to. An example of this is the May and October pilgrimages at Monte Cassino. This was the tradition of our mother house in Switzerland. The pilgrimage shrine was part of the Swiss monastic lifestyle that our pioneer monks brought with them. And the German-heritage people in this locality expected this custom of us.

ES: Even if the Mass were to be celebrated in English, was eliminating Latin from the academic curriculum a good idea?

Latin in the academic curriculum has a place and I would hope that it would be retained. I sympathize, at the same time, with the depth of technological training that is required by living in the computerized era. The human mind is able to absorb a lot, and we don't challenge ourselves enough, but I think back nostalgically about the many benefits that came to me as a result of studying Latin, even though I am by no means a Latin scholar. We nevertheless had to study enough Latin to understand our textbooks. They were in Latin.

I think, for example, there are benefits from the study of Latin for those seminarians enrolled in the clinical pastoral experience program. You see, in that program they are working in the context of a group of doctors and nurses who are using medical terminology that's based largely on Latin and Greek. Without some knowledge of Latin, medical jargon goes over these students' heads.

Still, I think that if we were to try to reinstate Latin, with all of its academic benefits, in addition to all of the other disciplines into the current course load, the schedule would be taxed. Perhaps another way of saying this is that great benefits would come from a return of the central position of Latin in a classical education. At the same time, we have to be responsible enough to assess what is possible in the context of the burden of these other scientific and technological adjuncts to the theological curricula.

ES: What has been lost, if anything, and what has been gained since the Council?

There are always things that are going to be lost when one sees such a vast transition as took place after Vatican Council II. The way in which some of the faithful have, since Vatican II, reached back to their earlier experiences and have insisted, and worked toward, making available the Tridentine Mass tells me there is a kind of nostalgia that is legitimate, because it has been approved by the Holy See. Perhaps it expresses a sense of loss that is very acute for some people.

From this one monk's point of view, I see that the liturgy has been much simplified, and in having it so simplified, there is somewhat of a loss of solemnity. That, too, has been a value that we've seen go. Yet, this change has been in the service of the People of God because they came into their heritage in their native tongue to celebrate the liturgy. The complexity of a Solemn High Mass or of a Pontifical Mass would still leave them wondering about many things. When they can follow a more simple liturgical rite, that is much to their benefit.

As we experience the liturgy here in the monastery, we pretty much follow the customs that are now in vogue, and follow the directions of the bishops—particularly our own bishop. For example, when we made the transition from filling the wine flagon and putting it on the altar, as distinguished from putting all the chalices filled on the altar, as one of the more recent changes, we do that very properly and in accord with direction. So to summarize, one of the losses that I see—and it's balanced by some compensations—is the loss of solemnity in liturgical practice.

ES: With the loss in vocations, the death of priests and diminishment in the ranks, has this had a deleterious effect on the morale in the community?

Generally speaking, our community would rejoice in an abundance of members. But on the other hand, we have never placed our salvation as a monastic community on the number of the monks, but rather on the quality of their lives. Indeed, the number of vocations does affect the morale of the community, but that is so because the question of numbers makes us go back to the basic idea that vocations are a gift of God; the call comes from Him and not from a human vocation recruiter.

ES: Do you think, in that sense, we are a different Church, a different organization, from what we were a half century or century ago in America?

Yes. I think we are a different kind of Church. The decrease in vocations, the depletion of the ranks by death and by people leaving the religious life and the priesthood, those kinds of exercises of personal preference have made us a different kind of Church. In the past, people departing from religious life, of their own free will, was much more unusual. And yet, God is the judge.

God is the one who knows the tally, so to speak, of those religious in the past who, maybe on the surface conformed to the pattern of life of their particular congregation, but really whose hearts were getting farther and farther away from God because they were frustrated in their own personal lives. That kind of painful situation was given a sensitive, sympathetic relief by the dispensation of the Church to people who were in such circumstances.

ES: Would it take some of the pressure off the Church, especially in America, if the requirement for celibacy was lifted?

When we are reading St. Matthew's Gospel, Chapter 8 [verse 14], about how Jesus went to Peter's house and cured Peter's mother-in-law, all of a sudden it dawns on us that the first Pope had a wife. I don't mean to be facetious about that, but the discipline of the Church regarding clerical celibacy has varied over the millennia of the Church's existence. I really don't know that, if celibacy were made optional for priests, it would solve a lot of problems and have beneficial effects. I don't know that.

And I find it difficult to speculate about it, because I think our affection for those who have done this tends to prejudice our opinion. Many of those men, who had once been ordained, resigned their priesthood and were married, have still served the Church in ways that are really most admirable. They have made the transition from the celibate priesthood to the married state; and by their good work as laymen have enhanced the position of lay people who serve the Church. And that is a good sign.

ES: Some historians have suggested that the American Catholic Church is simply undergoing a late stage of Protestantization—a kind of last stage of American assimilation. Does this idea strike you as at all plausible?

Ecumenism in the life of the Church has always been fraught with ups and downs. I would like to mention a couple of very encouraging points from the comparatively recent past.

The first bishop of Gary, IN, was serving on the Ecumenism Committee of the United States Conference of Catholic Bishops. There was a Saint Meinrad alumni meeting held one evening in Gary where he spoke. He had just returned from attending a meeting of this committee and told us that, in his opinion, those closest to entering the Roman Catholic fold *en masse* were the Lutherans.

He didn't want to be quoted on that point. But then he proceeded to talk about how close Lutherans are to Roman Catholics in their liturgy.

About four years ago, in Augsburg, Germany, Bishop Victor Dammertz, the former abbot primate of us Benedictines, concluded a kind of concordat with the Lutheran Church on the subject of the significance of faith and Christian practice.

And so, if you judge on the superficial level about the Protestantization of the Roman Catholic Church, you're going to be able to cite this or that facet that seems to indicate this might be the case. And this doesn't surprise me, but I think that the term "Protestantization" is probably not accurate, because the process of ecumenism is ongoing— and has been ongoing since Luther nailed his theses to the chapel door at Wittenberg Castle. So, as we come closer together and discuss the things we have in common, I truly hope that we can grow in appreciative respect and love on both sides of the relationship.

Profile based upon: Fr. Rupert Ostdick to Prof. Ruth C. Engs, August 24, 2005, Interview Transcription, Saint Meinrad Archives; Fr. Rupert, OSB, to Prof. Ed Shaughnessy, October 5, 2004, Interview Transcription, Saint Meinrad Archives.

Chapter Eight

Br. Benedict Barthel, OSB

The primary work responsibility of Br. Benedict for most of his monastic life was in the Abbey Press, where he served in various capacities. In his earlier years (1939-70), this included different aspects of typesetting, composition and printing. In his latter years (1970-95), he was a mold maker in the Sculpture Division. Previous to being assigned to the Press, Br. Benedict served for three months at St. Paul's Indian Mission, Marty, SD.

Born November 3, 1919, in Evansville, IN, Br. Benedict was one of ten children and given the name Carl. He graduated from St. Boniface Elementary School, Evansville (1934), and attended Reitz Memorial High School in Evansville (1934-36), after which he spent a year at St. Placid Hall, Saint Meinrad (1936-37), in the new program that encouraged high school age men to become brothers of the monastery. He was in one of the first classes of "junior brothers." Br. Benedict made his first profession February 10, 1939. After Vatican II Council allowed brothers to profess final vows, he made his solemn profession March 21, 1973, his feast day.

With the closing of the sculpture operation in 1995, Br. Benedict worked in The Scholar Shop, Saint Meinrad's bookstore, until 2002, along with being assistant guest master. In this role, he still greets guests as they come into the Archabbey Church for daily prayers with the monks.

The interview with Br. Benedict was conducted on November 16, 2005, by Prof. Ruth C. Engs.

Childhood and Early Years as a Monk

Tell me about your childhood.

I was the eighth of ten children, three of whom died in infancy. Three of my sisters married; the fourth left her job to take care of the home after the death of my mother in 1948. This included my aging grandmother, an invalid uncle and my father as well. One of my brothers became a diocesan priest; the other—my youngest brother—a Holy Cross brother. My father, after several years as a schoolteacher, worked all his life in the office of a wholesale hardware company, Boetticher & Kellogg, ending up, after very trying years, as secretary/treasurer. In recent years, the building was demolished to make way for Casino Aztar.

All of our schooling was in Catholic schools. After graduating from the eighth grade at St. Boniface School in Evansville in 1934, I attended Memorial High school for two years. Then in 1936, I came to Saint Meinrad and entered St. Placid Hall. This was a school for young boys of high school age that Abbot Ignatius had begun several years earlier in the hope of attracting young men to a vocation to the brotherhood. It was designed as a three-year program and the first class, having completed the program, had just moved up to the monastery to begin their six-month candidacy when I arrived in September 1936.

Describe the St. Placid Hall program.

It was an abbreviated high school course. At that time, it consisted of two years of academic study, with the third year devoted to learning a trade. Classes were taught by monks, who also taught in the minor seminary high school. Since I already had two years of high school, the only formal schooling I had at St. Placid Hall was a course in typing and shorthand. In the year I was there, about 40 were in the program. We slept in dormitories and ate in the monastery. Classes and chapel were on the second floor and a recreation room was in the basement. We were called "oblates." At that time, oblates received no academic credits for their class work. Later, around 1950, the oblates began attending the minor seminary and received an accredited high school diploma.

A major portion of our time as oblates was taken up in caring for the dining rooms of the monastery and schools. At that time, this consisted of a major and minor seminary, totaling around 800 students and 150 monks. The oblates had their own refectory, adjacent to the monastery refectory. The work consisted of setting the tables for each meal, cleaning the refectories and washing all the dishes after each meal. A few also helped in the kitchen.

What were early influences on your vocation?

It's hard to say. After all, a vocation is, by definition, a calling from God, and who can fathom His designs? But as for human influences, our grade school was taught by Ursuline sisters and our local high school by Holy Cross brothers. Some of the religious atmosphere no doubt rubbed off on us, even though unconsciously. My dad was a daily Communicant and always made sure I was up when I was supposed to serve early Mass. While I can't say that any odor of sanctity pervaded our home, religious values were taken for granted. All this provided fertile soil for the Lord to work in, and what followed has to be credited to Him.

At the time I decided to leave high school to pursue a religious vocation, my brother was entering his diaconate year here, so it is hardly surprising that when he informed me of the Oblate Program, I decided to give it a try. To make joining easier, two other boys from our neighborhood, much to my surprise, also decided to come. Since I was the only one to persevere, it may have all been part of God's plan to make my path easier. God knows, I needed it, as I was a very timid lad!

Tell me about the early years of your formation.

In the Oblate Program at Saint Meinrad, after three years at St. Placid Hall, the oblates were to enter the monastery and become candidates for six months. After six months of candidacy, we were received into the novitiate on February 9 and made our first profession a year later, February 10, 1939, the feast of St. Scholastica. Back then, we were called the "Junior Brothers." This name stuck until the Junior Brothers were officially joined together with the Senior Brothers around 1945. This transition went very smoothly, because we already knew most of them quite well from working with them in various ways.

Even after this time, however, we were still often referred to as the Junior Brothers because we followed different schedules and recited a different Divine Office. The older German Brothers recited the Little Office of the Blessed Virgin in German, in what is now St. Gertrude Chapel. We recited an English adaptation of the Divine Office in our own oratory on the fourth floor of what is now Newman Hall. Eventually, the German Brothers recited their Office in the crypt of the Archabbey Church, while we took over their former oratory, which was then beautifully redecorated and dedicated to St. Michael and the Angels. However, it was commonly referred to simply as "the Brothers Oratory."

What kind of work did you do during your formation?

During our candidacy and novitiate, a major part of our time was spent in the peeling room, at present the offices for the kitchen staff. We prepared and cleaned vegetables and picked eyes out of potatoes after they had been run through the peeler, which abraded off most of the skin. At this time, most of these were raised in Fr. Fintan's [Baltz, OSB] vegetable farm. The farm extended over most of the area from the road past Lake Fintan to the highway. The lake was built primarily for irrigation purposes and supported quite an elaborate sprinkling system.

Br. Benedict, as a young monk

To help with the work, Fr. Fintan solicited help from anywhere he could find it. Many a boy from town got his start at the Archabbey working for Fr. Fintan. Students in the school were also invited to volunteer. To give them a spiritual incentive, they were told their pay would be donated to the missions. Fr. Fintan was a tireless worker and his garden effort didn't end until almost the day of his death. The lake, however, continued to provide many hours of pleasure and a relief from the summer heat before the days of air conditioning.

Because our work in the peeling room had to be given priority if folks were to eat, our novice instruction had to be fitted in whenever it could be arranged. Our novice master and brother instructor was Fr. Gualbert Brunsman, a very talented and ingenious person, who was given many tasks, so our instruction was rather haphazard. It was quite a loss when around 1948 he was sent to South Dakota to be superior of the Marty Indian mission.

Where did you live during the early years?
From 1935 to about 1940, we were all housed on the top floor of Newman Hall, above the students' chapel. It was just a long hall, the

entire third floor. This was a former student dormitory that, for us, was partitioned off with plywood dividers, open on the top. There were about 20 of us there. As the number of Junior Brothers grew, some of us were moved into the top floor of what was called "Brenner Pass"—now Benet Hall. Later, we were given rooms wherever they were available or more conveniently located to our work. At one time, Br. Lawrence [Shidler, OSB] and I lived above the bakery, although neither of us were bakers.

After the completion of the Brothers Wing, now called the Sherwood Annex [removed in 2007], many of us were assigned rooms there. Our former quarters in "Plywood Flats" were demolished to make way for other uses.

What did you have in your cell back then?

Just the basics; a bed, chair and desk, washstand, a closet or cabinet of one sort or another for our clothing. We had no bathroom facilities. We carried our water for washing from the bathroom down the hall. Space was at a premium at times. Some rooms—including mine—were divided by a partition to accommodate two people in a room. Now, in the new monastery, we have our own cells, with bath.

How did you see the Church in those early years? What expectations did you have? Have they, by and large, been fulfilled?

Not knowing what to expect, I had few expectations and, consequently, few disappointments. I just lived one day at a time and took things as they came. Basically, it was a happy experience.

Describe something of the tone and nature of the discipline under which your vocation was formed.

I guess I was a very disorganized sort of person, because I was never aware that we were being formed. We just lived in a situation that was very scheduled, and one just assumed that that was the way monks lived and we might as well get used to it. In that sense, I guess we were formed. As changes came over the years, somehow we just adapted and adjusted our perspective. This, by hindsight, because I was never aware that this was part of formation.

All told, I considered my novitiate year and early religious life some of the happiest years of my life. One fault I must confess to though—and one I have never overcome, and which must have been very discouraging to the novice master—is a tendency to fall asleep during conferences. I'm sure I missed out on a lot of the wisdom Fr. Gualbert had to offer.

What was the horarium—*your daily schedule—in your early years?*

My recollections are very foggy. But as best I can recall, we all rose at 4:00 a.m. for our Morning Office—recited in English—followed by Mass and meditation. For a time, we Junior Brothers were permitted to "stick in" once a week until 5:00 or 5:30, which was a welcome break. For the priests and fraters [monks training for the priesthood], Matins always began at 4:00 a.m. Apart from the things that we attended with the rest of the community—meals, rosary and a few other things—we pretty well had our own schedule.

Along with the fraters, we served the private Masses of the priests, which were said in shifts. These began at the conclusion of Lauds. The time varied considerably because of the length of the Office, and occasionally some of us had to leave our own Office to serve the private Masses. The ringing of the Angelus bell was the signal to leave.

Until later years, the brothers did not ordinarily attend the conventual Mass except on Sundays and major feasts, so for those who were not serving the private Masses of the priests, there would be an opportunity for a short nap. At 6:00, Prime and Terse were recited, followed by breakfast for everyone. This was a rather informal meal, come as you could. By 7:00, most of us were off to our various jobs, but our work schedule varied according to the needs of the day of our particular jobs.

At 11:45, Sext and None were recited, followed by dinner at 12:00. This was the main meal and was always accompanied by reading at the table. Following dinner, the community processed to the church to make a short visit to the Blessed Sacrament. At 1:00, we returned to our jobs until 5:00, followed by supper, which also was accompanied by table reading. Following supper, there was a period of common recreation until 7:00.

The priests, fraters and brothers each had their own recreation room, and separation was quite strict. Permission had to be obtained if one needed, or wished, to see someone from a different department. When the junior and senior brothers were joined together around 1945, we began recreating with them. Mostly card games with the seniors, pool or ping pong with the juniors. I think it can be said that these periods were thoroughly enjoyed. During the spring and summer, volleyball was a favorite.

With the elimination of a period of common recreation in recent years, I believe we have lost something important, and that is a sense of community sharing. If we are going to call ourselves a community and truly be one, I think it's essential that there be a scheduled occasion for sharing part of ourselves with all our confreres. Currently, an effort is being made to meet this need by serving the dessert in the calefactory— our recreation room—on Wednesday evenings.

How about the rest of your day?

At seven in the evening, there was about a 15-minute period of public spiritual reading in the Chapter Room for everybody. This was followed by the evening prayer of Compline. The priests and fraters recited it in Latin in the church, while the brothers went to their oratory, where it was said in English. After Compline, one was free to retire and night silence began. We all had to be in bed by 9:00.

How about vacations or visits from your family?

I don't recall that visits from family members were ever restricted in any way; all that was needed was permission. As for vacations, I don't think that any of us had vacations as such, apart from one week after our profession and again after our 25th jubilee. By the time I reached my 50th, I really don't know what the policy was, but I don't recall that I had a vacation. Permission to go home for family needs or for very special family events was usually readily granted—but not for weddings, unless the monk was to be the celebrant of the Mass.

As a substitute for vacations, each summer we spent a week at Camp Benedict, our camp on the Blue River near Leavenworth. For the first few years, the Junior Brothers all went together. With 40 of us, things were quite hectic at times and sleeping accommodations were primitive. Cots were set up on the screened-in porch and in every other available spot. These had to be taken down each morning. A rising time was not laid down, but after the first person got up, there wasn't much sleeping done. For several years, tents were also put up. A few brave ones chose the open air under the starry skies, listening to the howls of the coyotes. At least we were told that's what they were. Some of the local folks claimed to have seen them.

The major outdoor sport was swimming in the Blue River, but even that was problematic. With every good rain upstream, the river could rise precipitously, sending downstream debris of every sort, and no one could dare go in. In the flood of '37, it rose to a height several feet above the floor of the house—some 40 feet above its normal level. When it was fit to swim in, it was great fun. There was a rope swing that went out over the river, and at the high point of its arc one would drop 25 feet or so into the water. The less brave among us dropped off the swing before it reached that point.

There were numerous limestone caves in the area. Some of these were quite long, deep and winding, with passages going off in all directions. It was easy enough to get lost in them. Among our group, there were several avid spelunkers, for whom the high point of the week was the opportunity to explore, revisit or discover new caves. I had gone with them on several occasions. While it could be a fantastic, almost mystical, experience, caves always gave me the creeps and I never felt comfortable in them.

Mass was offered in a small chapel near the house. It was more like a doll house and at one time must have been a playroom for children. With crowding, it could hold about a dozen people at most. The rest gathered outside or, when the weather was bad, up on the porch. In spite of all the inconveniences, the week at camp was a thoroughly enjoyable experience, and Saturday came all too quickly. This was clean-up day, when everything had to be put back in shape for the next group that would arrive in the early afternoon.

Work

What was your major work over the years?

After I was professed in 1939, for most of the rest of that year, I continued working in the peeling room. I did have a three-month interlude when Br. Charles Guy and I were sent to our mission at Marty, SD, to learn a trade. He was to learn printing and I was to learn something about the machinist trade. Marty was founded as a school for Indian boys and girls that eventually became accredited from grade school through high school. It was taught by Sisters of the Blessed Sacrament and a few lay teachers. Looking toward the future, Fr. Sylvester Eisenman was instrumental in founding the Oblate Sisters of the Blessed Sacrament for Native American girls. He intended for them to be the future teachers.

Over the years, especially through the efforts of Fr. Sylvester, the mission complex became a totally self-sufficient plant. It had fully equipped shops and a farm, mostly under the supervision of Fr. Sylvester's brother, Leonard. However, for whatever reason, our stay lasted for just three months before we were called back to the monastery. Br. Charles took up working in the Abbey Press book bindery, while I went back to the peeling room until November of that year. Then I, along with Fr. David

Duesing, Fr. Maurus Ohligslager and Fr. Herbert Palmer—now at Prince of Peace Abbey—were sent to the Abbey Press. It was the intent of Abbot Ignatius that monks would again take over its management and operation, a noble idea, but one which time has proved unrealistic.

What did you do at the Press?

I started in the office as clerical help. At times, though, every available hand was called upon to help with stapling of the magazines. Eventually, I moved onto typesetting—both hand composition and operating the Linotype [Linotype—though a brand name for the make of the machine—had become by extension a sort of generic name for any typesetting machine of this nature. Ours were Intertypes.]

The Linotype was truly a marvel of human ingenuity and, for 60 years and more, the staple of the printing industry. Without it, modern book publishing would have been impossible. But with the arrival of the computer age, the Linotype has become a relic of the past and has gone to join the dinosaur in the history book. Nevertheless, in spite of its antiquity, the newer of our Linotypes was taken to Plant II of Abbey Press and, until quite recently, was used in the imprinting of personalized cards and other items. Elsewhere I have attempted to describe in detail this marvelous machine in my writings.*

Around 1950, when the Abbey Press started getting into offset printing, Fr. Robert Woerdeman, then-manager of the printing division, asked me to set up the platemaking department. This involved learning the basics of photography as well as layout and the platemaking process, plus a bit of construction. Along with this, we attempted to make our own zinc etchings for the letterpresses. But that didn't prove too successful, so that was given up and they were again sent to a commercial engraver.

How long did you work there?

I continued working in the platemaking department until about 1970, when Br. Maurus [Zoeller, OSB] asked me if I was interested in taking on the mold making for the sculpture operation he was starting. After

30-some years at Abbey Press, I was ready for a change, so I accepted the offer. At that time, it was to be an operation totally separate from the Press. But after a year or so, it, too, came under the management of the Press. We started with the religious statuary of Trina Paulus, who provided the original molds, but we soon expanded to producing almost anything imaginable. I would estimate that, over the years, we had produced a thousand different products, not all of which were selected for the catalog.

The sculpture operation began in the east chicken house, where, in earlier years, many of us younger brothers spent many a night vaccinating chickens under the tutelage of Br. Dennis Hickey. This was sometimes quite an ordeal, as we would often have to pluck them out of the trees in which they were roosting, but when we had finished—around midnight or so—Br. Dennis always provided a little lunch.

The department was under the management of Mrs. Rose Mary Sitzman, and the statues were originally cast in plaster. But later, because of shipping problems, due to breakage and other reasons, we switched from plaster to a polyester product, and later to a more stable urethane, which was used until the operation closed in 1995. In the late '70s, when an addition was made to the old dairy building, our entire operation was moved down there. Later, because of the objectionable fumes produced in melting the mold material, this part of the operation was moved back to the chicken house, where we remained until 1995, when all production was sent to China; the entire department was closed down and people were laid off.

After this, I was sent to work in The Scholar Shop, the school bookstore, and along with that, was made assistant guest master. The Scholar Shop was under the management of Mrs. Donna Hagedorn. I enjoyed the work there, and the opportunity to get to know most of the students. It was also during this period that I began the project of making up booklets for guests attending our church services. I knew nothing about computers, so I had to get the music parts from the choir books, and the psalms from the Psalter. It was a long-drawn-out project, but I think it has proved quite helpful to the guests. Experience had shown that, for most guests, trying to follow the Office from the choir books simply was not helpful.

My work in The Scholar Shop ended in 2002, while my role as assistant guest master presently continues. It's been an interesting—though sometimes trying—life. One thing I must say, though, is that in all my years of working with our lay co-workers, both men and women, I could never hope to find a nicer or more cooperative group of people to work with. It's been a very rewarding experience!

Prayer

What is your favorite part of the Rule of St. Benedict?

That would be difficult to say, but I can say what has been the greatest influence on my life in the past ten years, and that is Chapter 53, "On the Reception of Guests." I am not one who mixes easily with people, as everyone knows. Why Abbot Lambert [Reilly, OSB] picked me as an assistant guest master, I'll never know, other than that, at the moment, I was out of a job and available.

There have been trying moments, but also rewarding moments. And that is where the *Rule* comes in. St. Benedict says, in Chapter 53, "All guests who present themselves are to be welcomed as Christ," and later on, "Great care and concern are to be shown in receiving poor people and pilgrims, because in them more particularly Christ is received." It took a while for this to soak in, but eventually it did, and it is this thought that has enabled me to put up with the inconveniences and make the sacrifices that the job has come to entail.

When I undertook the rather daunting task of making up booklets for all the services in church, as time went on and by the grace of God, I eventually came to appreciate that it was a special way of receiving Christ, and at the same time fulfilling another prescription in that same chapter: "First of all, they are to pray together, and thus be united in peace." In a world so much in need of peace, perhaps I can thus contribute my mite toward achieving that goal.

Perhaps this same chapter can explain why I have come to have a greater tolerance for crying babies in church than some monks can appreciate. But the innocent little ones were Christ's special love when He walked the earth, and so I have come to believe that in them He is even more specially received. And where do their parents more appropriately bring them than to the house in which Christ is especially believed to dwell?

In fact, St. Benedict himself prescribes in Chapter 59 that, when a child is offered to God by a member of the nobility, and the boy himself is too young, the document of their oblation is, along with the boy's hand, wrapped in the altar cloth. What was the minimum age? St. Benedict doesn't say. And besides all this, tolerating the crying of babies is a great way to learn patience! God speaks in many ways, and if He so chooses, He can speak more eloquently through the voice of a crying baby than can the most gifted orator. And that message may be, for us, the more important message.

What is your key to living Benedictine spirituality?

I'm afraid I can't be of much help here. My life isn't that complicated and just trying to be Christian is about all I can handle. And here we have, as St. Benedict says, "the Gospel as our guide." I suppose one might call that the "key" to all spirituality, by whatever name you choose to call it.

What has been your most difficult and what has been your happiest and joyful time or experience over your lifetime?

This type of question I find exceedingly difficult to respond to. Sure, there were depressing days, frustrating days and disappointments. Lots of them. There were also the joyful and happy days. But none of these follows a pattern and my mind retains few specific memories of them.

One takes life as it comes, one day at a time: the good, the bad and the indifferent—and deals with each as best one can with the graces God provides us. Our responses aren't always what they should be, but that's why God gave us the sacraments.

But to single out any one of them as the best or the worst simply wouldn't be useful. God doesn't seem to work that way—at least not with me. While, to us, the trials as well as the joys may seem to be random and unconnected things that just happen, God undoubtedly has a plan. We can only hope that, when He closes life's curtain on our act, He will find us at least remotely resembling what, from eternity, He had in mind for us.

Vatican II: Its Effect on the Church and Saint Meinrad Archabbey

As you know, St. Benedict became discouraged by a general disregard for the spiritual ideal in his own time. For that reason, he developed a practice for living. Today, some observers are of the opinion that society is once again falling into indifference to the meaning of a virtuous life. How has this influenced the Church or monastic life?

There can hardly be any reasonable doubt that our society is once again falling into indifference to the meaning of a virtuous life—or even any life at all. Without question, there are many, many people in the world who remain faithful to a life of virtue, and even a deep life of prayer. They are the "counter-culture," not, unfortunately, the mainstream. That all this moral turmoil should be reflected in monasteries is, to a degree, inevitable. Each one has to deal with this in his own life as God inspires. It can be a serious problem for each one personally, and for the spiritual well-being of an entire community.

What were, and are, the influences that have led us down this road? I'm sure there are many. I will mention but one—yet one that has the potential of being, in different ways and at different times, good, bad and indifferent. That one would be television, and most of the modern technological means of communication. What is so sad is that all of these have such limitless potential for good, and yet I fear that, when all the chips are counted, the net result has not been in favor of virtue or spirituality, in the monastery or out of it.

When television was first introduced at Saint Meinrad and made available to the community at large, it was almost by coincidence. Br. John [Miller, OSB], in a downtown store, filled out a free ticket for a drawing of a TV set. As fate would have it, his name was drawn and the TV was set up in the third-floor recreation room of the old monastery. The reception was not the best and the viewing time was limited between supper and Compline. The vast majority of programs in those days were harmless, like "Little House on the Prairie," a detective mystery or comedians who were actually funny. Occasionally, we were allowed to watch at other hours a program of special interest.

The picture today is totally different. I don't know that anyone today would seriously claim that the technological marvels that have so changed our lives have been of benefit to their spiritual life or have enlarged their spiritual vision. There are, of course, a few very worthwhile and uplifting programs available, but by and large, these are not the ones being watched. On the whole, has the spirituality of the monastery been deepened? I would very much doubt it.

Would we be better off without TV and other communication technology? That depends, but I honestly believe that from a strictly spiritual point of view, things were better in the old days. Were we a collection of saints? Far from it! I know it only too well. Nevertheless, I sincerely believe that the underlying spirit, beneath the surface, was more deeply spiritual then, compared to today. Would I want to go back to those days? Not really, but that, too, depends. To summarize it all, I'm afraid that the amazing advances in technology that have taken place over the past half-century have not been the benefit to humankind that God had a right to expect that they would be.

The changes that have affected the contemporary Church may seem now to have been inevitable. Some think Pope John XXIII was overly optimistic and that, ever since Vatican Council II, the Church has been paying a heavy price for his initiatives. Still others applaud his gestures. What has this meant, in your view, to the Church and the monastery?

Not everything that has happened in the Church—both the good and the bad—can be laid at the door of Vatican II. Some things would very likely have come about, even had there been no Council. Society itself was changing, and even some of the things that flowed directly from a directive of the Council are far removed from the intentions and even the words of the bishops who wrote the decrees. Overzealous commissions and committees have sometimes gone far beyond the written word in pursuit of their own agendas. So I don't think we can blame the Holy Spirit for everything that is wrong in the Church, or in the monastery, today.

Things like diminishing Sunday Mass attendance, rare reception of the sacrament of Reconciliation, ignoring the Sabbath rest, the acceptance, even by some Catholics, of such moral evils as abortion, divorce, homosexual conduct and more, are in great part the consequence of a general deterioration in our society of a moral awareness in regard to man's responsibility for his actions.

The beginning of all this, I'm sure, the Council Fathers were aware of, and it was the hope of the pope and the bishops that a second Vatican Council could turn the tide around. But it was like putting one's finger into the hole of a collapsing dike. Nothing but direct divine intervention could have stopped it, and that is not God's usual way of acting. Man must face the consequences of his free choices and learn to deal with them.

What has this to do with life in the monastery?

Perhaps nothing, directly, but we are all products of our time and, consciously or unconsciously, we are influenced by the forces that formed us. So again, each one of us has, with the help of God in prayer, to deal in his own life with the influences of a society that has, in great part, turned away from God. In some things, we have done better than others.

Compare the morale in the monastery today with that of 30 or even 50 years ago.

The human personality hasn't changed much in 50 years, and there will always be optimists and pessimists. Both leave their imprint on us. I don't think this has changed in my short lifetime, so you can expect that my morale will fit somewhere in there, too.

Even if the Mass were to be celebrated in English, was eliminating Latin from the academic curriculum a good idea?

I had two years of Latin in high school, and while that makes me anything but a Latin scholar, it was enough to be very helpful in following the church services. Of course, it wasn't enough to translate the texts with any great degree of understanding, but I was glad I had at least that much.

Even as a typesetter, I had found it useful. Knowing the Latin roots of words was very helpful in knowing how words were to be syllabicated.

While I know that students for the priesthood already have all they can handle in the way of studies, I don't think Latin should be at the bottom of the list of required courses. Even apart from nostalgic or historical reasons, its usefulness as part of general education is being more and more recognized in the more progressive school curricula.

Striking changes have been made since the days of the Council. How have these changes affected the monastery and the Church?

I believe the changes, for the most part, have been positive. That some things of value have been lost, I don't think can be denied. Among the most important of these, in my humble opinion, concerns the ritual of the Mass. I believe we have lost much of the sense of "connectedness" with the Church Universal that the more ancient liturgy used to provide, not so much through its use of the Latin language as through the universality of the rite itself.

The number of religious vocations declines every year. What is the meaning of these changing patterns to the monastery and to the Church at large?

Many factors figure in the decline of vocations. Certainly, one major factor is the size of families themselves. With only one, two or three children in the average family today, there is an obvious reluctance on the part of a young man or woman to pursue a religious vocation when he or she faces the moral obligation to provide support for aging parents in their declining years. And for the same reason, there may well be a reluctance of the part of parents to encourage one.

Another obvious factor would be the temptation to embrace the more materialistic lifestyle in which most youth grow up today. The prevailing spiritual atmosphere today does not inspire the spirit of sacrifice and dedication that the religious life entails. This is not to say that there are not many young men and women today who do not respond generously to God's call. Only that they face an uphill climb and need all the support we can give them—in prayer and every other way.

Is the Catholic Church different today from what it was 50 years ago?

The Church, as we know, is the Body—militant, suffering and triumphant—with which Christ has chosen to identify Himself, and so, in its essence, can never change. Nevertheless, in its earthly trappings, the Church today is a far cry from the Church of the early centuries. This is true for every age of the Church's history.

What, then, is it that identifies us as the Body of Christ? In the Nicene Profession of Faith, the Church is defined as, "One, Holy, Catholic, and Apostolic." Hence, to be the Church of Christ, it must possess, at all times and in all places, all these attributes and characteristics, and it must proclaim them consistently. A thing cannot be true one day and not true the next. The Church today is sometimes on a perilous course, because many who claim to be Christians in good standing take different courses in regard to Truth than those laid out by the apostolic authority conferred upon Peter and to his successors, against which the gates of hell shall never prevail. How can we reconcile these contraries as we see them played out in history? How has Saint Meinrad fared in all this?

Thankfully, by the grace of God, we have survived thus far—with a few scars, of course, through more than one period of turmoil without any serious deviation in course. We can but hope and pray that Saint Meinrad will always remain true to the "Faith of our Fathers" and persevere in the Truth until God says, "The End."

What are your hopes for the future of the Archabbey and Church?

I don't have the gift of prophecy and I won't hazard a guess. But considering the continuing trends in our society toward materialism and the rejection of all authority other than one's own, I can't help but be a little pessimistic. If we live long enough, I fear we had better be prepared for some difficult times—which is not something new in the long history of the Church. In the end, the Cross has always triumphed!

Interview profile based upon: Br. Benedict Barthel to Prof. Ruth C. Engs, November 16, 2005, Interview Transcription, Saint Meinrad Archives.

*Barthel, Benedict. "Answers to Dr. Engs' Questions," which includes answers to items on the questionnaire, essays of personal memories and details about the operation of the Linotype machine, 21 pp, October 2005, Saint Meinrad Archives.

Chapter Nine

Fr. Eric Lies, OSB

Fr. Eric taught in the Minor Seminary, held management positions at Abbey Press and spent over 25 years in the Development Office in various leadership positions.

Born October 13, 1919, in Aurora, IL, Fr. Eric professed his vows on August 6, 1940, and was ordained on February 2, 1945. He received his theological training at Saint Meinrad School of Theology. He also holds a master's degree in English (1953) from the Catholic University of America, Dubuque, IA. For 13 years following ordination, Fr. Eric taught English, geometry, religion, speech and homiletics at Saint Meinrad Seminary. Also during that time, 1950-58, he served as associate editor/art director for *The Grail* magazine at Abbey Press.

From 1958-64, Fr. Eric was manager of publishing at Abbey Press. He then became general manager, 1965-68, of the Press, after which he moved to the Development Office, where he served for more than 25 years. He was associate director of development, director of public relations and graphic designer. Fr. Eric retired in 1994. Since then, he spends his time creating calligraphy pieces and giving retreats.

The interview with Fr. Eric was conducted August 22-23, 2005, by Professor Ruth C. Engs.

Childhood and Early Years as a Monk

Tell me about your childhood, your family and how you came to Saint Meinrad.

I was born in Aurora, IL, in 1919. I have one brother and one sister, both younger than I. My dad was an automobile mechanic at the time and we had a good Catholic life. A wonderful Catholic mother. We went to Catholic schools. I really began my vocation in sixth grade. Sister Emaline, my teacher at Our Lady of Good Counsel, kept me after school one day and said, "Have you ever thought about becoming a priest?" Well, I really hadn't, but I was honored that she thought so.

So I put it off. I went to high school at Marmion. It was run by our Benedictine fathers from Saint Meinrad and I was so impressed with them. They were very kind, but very strict. They offered Mass every day and it was marvelous. We had a "vocation week," where they brought in a farmer, lawyer, doctor and other occupations. On the last day, they had a priest, Fr. Ildefonse, and he was very interesting. I said to him, "You know, maybe I am interested."

He recommended that I come to Saint Meinrad when he went for a retreat that summer. Six others and myself did that. We had a wonderful time. But the thing that really impressed me was the spirit of the monks; the monks that I did meet were just so wonderful. I wrote in my journal that "I wanted to stay here the rest of my life." But when I got home, my dad was unhappy about it. He said, "You have to go to one more year of high school." So I did.

I didn't tell anybody during that year in my high school, but I knew all the time that I was planning to leave and come down here to Saint Meinrad after my sophomore year. And I did. I was a junior in high school…in 1935. And I was very happy and have been happy ever since. I've had a few times that weren't too wonderful, but generally speaking I felt marvelous. And I have had nothing but good luck since I have been here.

How did your family and friends feel about you choosing this vocation?

I think they were in favor of it once it happened. My folks certainly were, and my brother and sister seem to be. I came from a very good Catholic family, a big family…I mean uncles and aunts, a lot of children, we had a lot and we mixed frequently. They seemed to be very pleased that I had this vocation.

How did you see the Church in those early days? What were your expectations?

I don't remember specifically. But I do have a feeling that I was very pleased to be a Catholic and hadn't thought of being anything else. Being a priest and a religious, I hadn't thought of that either. But I certainly felt part of it, you know. I never thought about leaving the Church or being critical of it. I was very pleased.

Have your expectations been met?

Yes, they have. They've been met very much higher than I ever expected.

Describe your early years in the monastery.

Well, when I first came to the monastery, I expected it to be very difficult, severe and prohibiting. I never thought it would be any fun. But I am telling you, it has been absolutely fantastic. The work I've done, I have enjoyed it all. I have a little prayer in the morning where I ask, "Why did you bring me to this paradise of angels?" There are so many wonderful people I have known…most of them in the cemetery now. It's really been a great thing and wonderful work. It's been much more positive and enjoyable than I ever expected.

What was the nature of formation and how might that be different today?

It was very strict compared to today. For example, our parents were only allowed to visit once or twice a year. They had to come here and we couldn't go out anywhere with them. You never went home unless there was a death in the immediate family. Nowadays, a couple of times a year at least, the novice master takes the novices to Louisville [KY] or Evansville [IN]. They see a movie, go to some museum, have a nice dinner and then come home. People travel now in cars frequently. They can drive to the doctor. They can do things they are interested in. One of the novices took me to an art exhibit. We had a wonderful time. So, in general, the discipline is much more relaxed now than when I was a novice.

What was a typical day back then?

Well, we started out with Morning Prayer at four o'clock and it went until about five on ordinary days and longer on feast days. Then we would go down to the crypt chapel below the church, where we would have low Mass. In those days, low Masses and high Masses were quite different. After low Mass, then we would come up to the church. I remember the first time we came up from low Mass. I thought we were going to breakfast because we had been up quite awhile. However, we had another office called Prime, the Morning Prayer, which we don't say at all anymore. After this we went to breakfast. We had two Masses every day. One was a private Mass and the other was a conventual Mass as a community in the main Church. It was probably at 7:30 or something like that. Then we would go to study hall and study until class time…this was third year of college. We were not allowed to talk at all between classes.

Was silence different then?

Silence was much more strict than today…there was more of it. Nowadays, they are allowed to talk quietly in the calefactory and even in their quarters if they have something they need to say. Conversations were only allowed in the calefactory in those days. The reading room and the study hall were quiet, so you didn't do much talking except during the recreation periods after lunch and after supper. And then you just talked. Oh my gosh, how we would talk! Whoever you walked out of church with, that was your partner for most of the evening or most of the recreation. You also got to know the person in rank who would come out with you most of the time. We would walk around the block, around the monastery or play volleyball or sit on the benches and talk.

Fr. Eric, as a young monk

What kind of recreation did you have back then?

That's another big difference. Everything is free flowing now… individualistic because of television, air conditioning. In those days, we had recreation right after lunch for about half an hour or so. We would walk outside and talk. On Tuesday and Thursday, we would spend the whole afternoon playing tennis or volleyball or other sports and then go swimming and come back in time for Vespers. We sometimes would take hikes together, as monks, in small groups in all kinds of wonderful hills and woods around here. We wore regular clothes, lay clothes. But, by golly, we used to play tennis in our habits. And I know we ice-skated in our habits.

After the afternoon recreation—I know we didn't take naps in those days—we went back to study hall or class. In those days, everything was done together. We also had rosary and night prayers and Compline. I don't recall what time this was. We got seven to eight hours of sleep, I know that. We all got up at the same time. We all probably went to bed about the same time, too. Everything was done uniformly.

Every day when you were a novice, we would have about an hour with the novice master. We would sit around in a circle and do a lesson on the *Rule* and what we were here for. The novice master was Fr. Henry Brenner. He was a very wise man and a very good teacher. He had a whole stack of cards, three by five cards, that he turned when he used quotations. I think he was quite an author and had written several books. He was very strict, but a very kind man. He wasn't harsh when he corrected you. But he did correct you if you needed it.

Describe a typical meal, and who did you sit with?

You sat in the order of seniority of profession. The tables were long and I would guess at least 12 sat there. You didn't do any talking anyway; it was all silent…all three meals. We had reading at lunch and supper. The reading was very serious and always strictly religious. We took turns reading out loud. The meals were basically good and substantial. The brothers did all the cooking. Even when we had a total population of 700, the brothers did the cooking, family style. I don't know how they cleaned all the dishes and did all the work, but they did.

The food was a little simpler compared to today. We didn't have as much choice for a main course. Now we have a buffet and the main course may be fish or meat, and vegetables and potato. We have a whole array of things. I bet there are at least 20 items on the salad bar that you can pick nowadays and there are three or four kinds of dressings. In those days, it was all together on the table and you had no choices at all. When apples were in season, at some meals we would get three kinds of apples: fresh apples, stewed apples or apple pancakes.

What did you drink?

We all had what we called "bellywash," which was coffee mixed with milk and sugar. It came out in pots. Black coffee was available at times and I would call it "tiger milk." That's what we drank at all three meals. We had wine at the main meal. I believe it was the noon meal. You were allowed an eight-ounce glass, a regular water glass of wine. We novices never knew what effect it was going to have. Some would drink the whole glass after our meals were through. It was funny because they weren't used to wine and they had no idea that this amount was too much—they learned real fast.

How about vacations?

In those days, we didn't get any vacations at all. As soon as we made profession in the summer, we went to a resort cabin on the Blue River. It was a beautiful spot, full of life. We put up all the tents. Slept in the tents right under the sky. Later on, they built a little screened-in porch for the beds. But in the beginning, we slept right out in the yard. We just had a wonderful time the whole week. I was a cook for a while. Cooks were allowed to go both weeks. There were a lot of caves in the area. We used to go hiking. Hike into the caves and do a lot of swimming and boating down the river. It was really wonderful.

Work

What was your job after you made solemn vows?

I had no idea of what I would be doing. Monks had a lot of different jobs in those days. One of them was teaching in the seminary. Another was parish duty as a priest, and some were in the Indian missions. In those days, we weren't sent away to universities very much. At that time, I wouldn't have any idea what work I would be assigned to. I thought I might be sent to a parish because I had become interested in parish work. I thought Fr. Alban [Berling, OSB], my classmate, would stay here and teach. But instead, it turned out that I was always here except for short times away, and he was in the parishes for 50 years.

[Fr.] Don Walpole and I were interested in art. When we were juniors, they gave us a little studio room and a drawing board. We could spend an hour a day there. It became obvious after a month or two that Fr. Donald was the artist. He could do things in perspective with people's bodies and faces. I wasn't able to do that. So he was sent to the Art Institute in Chicago after our ordination and I was sent to teach geometry in the high school, because I could draw good triangles.

I taught for over ten years and I thoroughly enjoyed it. I started teaching English and then speech. I tried geometry for a year and it became obvious that I was not a mathematician. Then I tried chant for a while, but I didn't do very well at that. So English and speech were my real subjects. Eventually, Fr. Theodore [Heck, OSB,] took about four or five of us to Dubuque, IA, for graduate work. He was teaching there in the summer. We would go for six or eight weeks of summer school to get our master's degree. I got my master's in English. The fact is, that when I was sent to the Abbey Press, I was heartbroken for a while, but Abbey Press turned out to be a wonderful experience.

Tell me about your career at the Press.

I came into the reading room one day. They had just hired the first artist at the Abbey Press. He was using a template where you draw the lines along a square or a circle. On the cover of *The Grail* magazine was the face of Christ drawn with the template. It was so terrible. And I said out loud, "Oh, shit." Somebody was in the room and I didn't know it. I thought nobody was there. It was one of the magazine's editors. Sometime later, I was in bed with the flu. The editor came in and said, "Would you be willing to do the layout for the magazine?" I said, "Well, yeah, if you need me." He explained why they needed somebody. So I agreed to do it part time. I worked down there and also taught in seminary part time.

Then I got into it full time in the late '50s. It's hard to believe, but one day I was shaving and the abbot knocked on my door. He came in and said, "Father so-and-so who was in charge of the Press took an Abbey car and ran away. Who's gonna run the Press?" And I said, "I don't know." He said, "You're the only monk who knows anything about what goes on there. Hold it together for a few days." So I went down to see Jane, the secretary for the previous boss, and she helped me with all this stuff that needed help. I was amazed how well things worked out.

We did have a few problems, though. The previous manager had developed a line of wonderful Catholic fiction books for children. And they were very, very good. Mary Fabyan Windeatt, the author, lived up near Monte Cassino. She had done a number of books but had quit doing new ones. They had stacks of old books and people weren't buying them. We had sales and it helped a little. I had heard of an artist in Louisville, Ned Watts, who was doing marketing for an insurance company. I asked him if he would also be willing to do some art and also help with our sales. He said "yes," so I hired him.

Ned, Br. Maurus [Zoeller, OSB] and I then ran the show. Br. Maurus was in charge of printing at the time and invented note cards with holy cards on the front. We decided to start a catalogue. In it we put Christmas cards, note cards, the old books we had in stock and some other things from the outside. In the first issue of the catalogue we even listed scheduled retreats. Oh my, we blessed the mailing of the catalogue —80,000 of them. We blessed it in the delivery room and mail room. We were so excited. We had no idea what the results would be. The results were so good that even the abbot had to help us fill the orders.

During the last couple of years in the late '60s, I was getting a little depressed because the Abbey Press had grown to the point where it had gotten too big for me. I am not by nature an administrator. I enjoyed it until toward the end, when I was facing all these changes and did not have the courage to fire people. So I was relieved to get out of it and go to the development job, where I never had anybody under me. I was going from 150 to four people.

Tell me about your career in the Development Office.

There again, my appointments always came from somebody else not doing their job. Anyway, we had a new man, John MacCauley, who was going to develop our public relations and fundraising program. He had done this before at Notre Dame. He was leaving someplace in the southwest. Abbot Gabriel had talked him into joining us. I don't know, to this day, why John wanted me on the staff. He had someone who was not working out. So he asked Abbot Gabriel to put me on the staff. I can still see it. I went to the July 4th picnic and the abbot said, "I want to introduce you to John." I didn't even know what development meant. So John had a meeting with me and explained what development was about. As he saw it, it wasn't just fundraising; it was sharing the work of the monastery and seminary with people of faith who wanted to further the work of Saint Meinrad. He said, "Would you be willing to join us?" I said, "Oh yeah, if the abbot wants me to, I will." So I started out with John and one secretary, one of the first women that ever worked on the Hill.

Now before John's time, I think that Abbot Ignatius decided we needed to raise funds, so he hired a secretary for this purpose. She went through the telephone directory and picked out names that looked like they were Catholic. So they mailed a fundraiser letter to all the people who might be Catholic. They raised so little funds he had to fire her. Of course, this was before anything was known about development. It was too haphazard, going through a telephone book. But it was a first effort.

John set up development at Saint Meinrad and was the brains behind the whole thing. We became good friends right away and worked very hard. I did a lot of the work in the office and followed up on things. I wrote letters for different publication and for fundraising. I responded to alumni inquiries, filled in names on the certificates for donors and designed the mailings. I was in charge of fundraising for the first renovation of Benet Hall and was in Indianapolis for several months for that job phoning people.

Eventually, we started a program called Saint Meinrad Sundays. We would send one of our monks to a parish on a particular Sunday. He would talk about vocations and then ask for support for the seminary. I was in charge of that program for a while. That is, I had to go around and talk to pastors and persuade them to let us do that. Later on, I was director of alumni. But not in name, only in action, you know.

We would send out letters for annual giving. Besides the capital campaigns, some people would be invited to give larger amounts. One of the ladies, a good friend of mine, gave $13 million a couple of years ago. She was an oblate and very friendly. I knew her and her husband. We had no idea she was going to give that much money. I thought it was going to be about a million. And at that time, a million was fantastic.

John told us when we raised the first million dollars, back when I was first in the office, that he would take us to New York and have dinner on the top of the "Sixes." I don't know what Sixes is, but it must have been a fancy restaurant. And we said, "A million dollars, we'll never raise that much." But we did and he took us to New Albany [IN] to a Motel Six as our banquet.

John's successor was an ex-seminarian, Dan Conway, who was a promising member of the staff. He lived in Louisville and agreed to be an understudy for John. He did very well. Then Dan Schipp joined the staff when they knew that Dan Conway was going to move on. So we have had three managers and the staff kept getting bigger and bigger... and I retired.

How about your third career, calligraphy, how did you get into that?

I had done some signs for Fr. John [Thuis, OSB] here at the high school. One issue of *Jubilee* magazine, now defunct, had a centerspread of calligraphy type. I was so impressed with it. I thought, "Boy, that's something I could do." So I went to the abbot and said, "Would you mind if I studied calligraphy?" "Of course," he said, "you might use it someday." I found some information in a library book, but didn't take classes. When I was sent to Abbey Press and did some magazine layout, I got interested in it again because it was part of the layout.

When I got into development, I put the names in calligraphy on certificates of people who gave gifts. John MacCauley called me in one day and said, "Why don't you take some workshops in calligraphy?" But I said, "I spend a lot of time doing plaques for donors and designs for publications. They could be set in type, and I'd have more time to spend with donors." He leaned back in his chair, took a puff of his cigarette. "Ah," he said, "but we'd lose our trademark." On the strength of that remark, I started to attend workshops on calligraphy. That was the real beginning of my devotion to the art of the pen.* This gave me my hobby during my retirement. It was great. I love the work.

Let me tell you how I got started in color calligraphy. I had done a few black and white things for the Development Office and some for Abbey Press. When Fr. Simeon [Daly, OSB] opened the new library in 1982, he said to me, "We have a nice exhibit space in the library. Why don't you have an exhibit of calligraphy?" And I said, "Who would want to see my black and white stuff? I don't have enough to make an exhibit out of it." "Oh," he said, "why don't you try color?"

He gave me an assignment with two color renditions of Psalm 23, the Good Shepherd Psalm. And so I did that. Nobody in the monastery had ever asked me for a calligraphy before, but all of a sudden, every two or three weeks, somebody would come up and ask me to do a piece for them based upon a text. After three months, I had a nice exhibit, about 25 pieces in color. Fr. Noël [Mueller, OSB] said, "You just can't put it on the wall; you have to mat it and frame it," so he helped me in matting and framing. I had an exhibition for about ten years in the library every October and every single piece has sold. Isn't that wonderful?

Let me tell you about one of my pieces. I had a friend who had made a movie of Mother Teresa. He told me that she was very devoted to the Passion and did the Stations of the Cross every day. So I said, "I'll write her a letter and send her a piece of calligraphy." So I sent her a little piece. On it I had, "I asked Jesus how much do you love me? 'This much,' he said. And he stretched out his arms and died." I told her I thought she would appreciate it because of her devotion to the Passion. So I got a lovely handwritten letter…from Mother Teresa.

I have three letters from her. The first one was handwritten and at the end of it, it said, "Do small things with great love." Well, I have lived with that for all these years. I don't know how many years, but quite a few. About seven or eight years ago, friends of mine were going to Calcutta on a pilgrimage. So I did the ending of her letter in calligraphy. It was a nice big piece with a frame, and they took it with them. When they met Mother Teresa, the guide said, "Oh, she won't keep it, she'll hand it to the person next to her." But when she saw that the text was hers, she put it up in her arms and they took a photograph of it.

Prayer

Let's look at Benedictine values and spirituality. What do you think is important to convey to some of your younger confreres or even the laity?

Nobody ever thinks they are going to get old. I had no idea I was ever going to be old when I was young. You felt sorry for the old people, but you never thought you would be in their shoes. But now that I am in those shoes and have been for some time, I think of old age as a time of insight and, what's the word, a time where we prepare for eternity. Everything changes when you get old, you know. You don't think of future ambitions. You think of, "How can I make the best of what I have done, what I have learned?"

And that's a whole new way of thinking about things. I am not sure everybody comes to that perception. But it certainly is, to my way of thinking, a time of reflection and getting to the basics, such as prayer and reading, serious reading. One of the things I am noticing now, as I am approaching the end, is that I don't have any interest whatever in things that I used to that were very important. For example, fiction. I just can't read fiction anymore. I haven't watched a movie for almost 20 years. These are all peripheral kinds of things. I spend my time reading serious stuff. Even poetry. I was so devoted to poetry when I was teaching

English and now I don't read poetry. Perhaps that's a personal thing, but it's part of getting down to the basic things of life.

What is your favorite part of the Rule of St. Benedict?

Chapter 72. The prologue is wonderful, too. But I think Chapter 72 is the summary of the life, the practical life of which applies to everything else. It puts the emphasis on love, which is the most important thing in life. It shows that we have to love one another for the sake of Christ. And we have to show that love in action. First of all, in tolerating others because we are all different and we all have different gifts. Also to appreciate others.

So it seems to me that the chapter is a part of what I was saying about normal aging. You look at life as a personal relationship with other people, and with God, of course. That's the chapter I like the best. The Prologue I like because it's an invitation to loving God as the whole point of life. That's what it is. The Prologue makes that very clear.

What is your key to living Benedictine spirituality?

I think, to seek God, is the key. Because that is what St. Benedict put in all his chapters, seeking God above everything else. Seeing everything in life in relation to seeking God, whether it's relationships with other members of the community or people outside the community. Also whatever relationships we have, whatever work you do, whatever recreation that you take part in are all part of seeking God. St. Benedict said, "Prayer and work."

What has been your most difficult and your most happy time as a monk?

The most difficult time for me was the last year at Abbey Press because of the heavy responsibility. For example, Pope Paul VI had written an encyclical called *Humanae Vitae*. One editor was very liberal in his thinking. He started publishing articles criticizing *Humanae Vitae*. I couldn't imagine a magazine for families being critical of the Holy

Father. But I didn't have the guts to fire him or anything. It took Fr. Paschal [Boland, OSB] about two weeks to fire him when he took over managing the Press. But it's because I am not a manager type.

Because it was such a difficult time for me, I actually asked to see a counselor, which I never thought I would ever do. Instead, Abbot Gabriel surprised me. He came down to my office at Abbey Press and said, "I think you need a little vacation." I said, "Well, nobody gets vacations around here." In those days, we didn't take vacations. But he said, "You need one." I asked, "Where can I go and when?" He said, "Anyplace, anytime." So as soon as he left, I got on the phone and called my dad and said, "I can go to Canada fishing. When can we go?" He immediately got it lined up. He, his brother, my brother and I went up to Canada to go fishing. My first vacation! Soon after I came back, we had a Fourth of July celebration. Isn't it funny I can remember that particular thing? And he introduced me, as I mentioned before, to John MacCauley. I went to development and it was wonderful.

How about your most happy or joyful time?

In general, my time in development was a happy time. I enjoy travel and I enjoy being with people. I enjoyed the special sabbatical in calligraphy. I had a lot of experience in writing, because I was an English major and there was a lot of writing I could do. Those were very joyful years. I have a hard time saying what is the most joyful, because I really enjoyed teaching and I enjoyed the beginning years at Abbey Press. It's hard for me to identify just one good time.

Vatican II: Its Effect on the Church and Saint Meinrad Archabbey

What did you think about Vatican II?

Well, I think Vatican II was wonderful, a wonderful thing. It's strange, because if you read the documents from Vatican II, they are not the kind of thing John XXIII would have written. They are much more doctrinal, much more traditional. In fact, I am amazed that people criticize those documents, because they are very authentic, doctrinal explanations of the Catholic religion.

I think that Vatican II led to a marvelous improvement in the Catholic way of looking at things. For example, the use of the vernacular in the Mass and in Divine Office. I wonder how we used to understand and put up with Latin. Did you know we studied a lot of Latin but still had difficulty using it? Also, I was always thinking and plotting about how we could get the Catholic laity involved in the Church. And, lo and behold, Vatican II brought all that, both getting the vernacular and getting all kinds of things for lay people to do.

In those early days before the Council, organizations that were strong, such as the Christian Family Movement or Young Christian Workers, don't exist in the same form today. But the things they were setting out to do have now become very common. Today there are over a thousand oblates of this monastery. In those days, you had very few oblates. They were even afraid the program was going to fold. Retreats, you know, were just beginning in the Guest House. Now we have all kinds of retreats. Did you know I've been giving retreats, about seven or eight a year, for 55 years? Boy, that's been a big part of my life, also. I'll be giving "Gifts of the Holy Spirit" and "Roads to Inner Peace" next year.

How different is the Church today compared to the pre-Vatican II years?
In those days, there was a lot more faith, just a general kind of faith, belief in God's plan and little questioning. But there was also just a tremendous difference between the authority of the Church, priests and nuns, and the laity. They were very obedient, very docile and all, but they weren't involved. Nowadays, they are much more involved and, of course, that means they also are much more volatile in their expression of opinion. Neither is ideal, but the Church keeps going through all those periods.

When you think of it, there are some people now who are going for a kind of reformation of the Catholic Church. As soon as you do that, you start changing, little by little. I can't remember the figure, but the number of new denominations in our country alone every year is just fantastic. Because they disagree with the pastor, rather than accept the faith for the sake of the good, they want to be their own boss, so they start another religion. I've seen that happen so often with people that I knew very well. So, what I am saying is that the Church is in a period of change and it's hard to say where it's going to go. Hopefully, it will be better if it settles in a little bit.

What changes occurred in the monastery due to Vatican II?

Vatican II brought concelebration back. Apparently, this had been done in the early Church. I don't know when. But it was a brand new thing for us. Now we have one community Mass for the fathers, the brothers, the juniors, all together rather than separate ones that we had in the past. It's in English and it is simpler today than it was in those days. When I was a frater studying for the priesthood, there was a chapel, which is now the Health Service. It was called the Apostles Chapel. There were 12 altars in it. Some days there would be ten or 12 priests all having private Mass at the same time. We would all sign up to serve them. When I think of it now, I marvel that we didn't dislike it. The problem was that individual priests every day had to say a private Mass plus the conventual community Mass, and the students had to serve all those individual Masses. Now, this just looks like an impossibility. How we ever put up with it, I don't know.

Compare the morale in the monastery today with the past. To what extent has declining vocations had an impact?

You know, I really don't know the answer to that. My only experience has been with those who are satisfied and happy in their life here. A long, long time ago, years ago, there were some disgruntled characters,

211

people who weren't really interested in the dynamic values of the Benedictine life. They were a very definite minority. Some of them were people who joined as lay brothers. They didn't really like it when they became chapter members and had to come to our Office and Mass every day. Some seem a little unhappy in Church. As far as I know, everybody comes. But one or two don't sing and kind of sit there, even today.

What impact has the decline in vocations over the past 30 or 40 years had on the community, the Church?

I wonder about that often. We have been talking about that several times lately. People don't stop and count the numbers that have left and you don't think about it. You just forget it once they are gone. But every once in a while, somebody will bring up, like yesterday, when we were talking about several people who were very important in the community, theology teachers and director of studies. Then they were gone. We were thinking, well, that's quite a few people. I have never done this, but you could go through the *Ordo* and just be amazed at the number of people. Sometimes it's just one or two a year. I have been here since the 1940s. I can remember vaguely the first one who left. In my earlier days, nobody ever left.

I am not sure whether Vatican II had anything to do with people leaving. But around that era and especially when we closed the high school, many of those dedicated teachers were unhappy…not many, but some did leave. Then when we closed the college, the same thing happened. For a number of individuals, we don't know why they left. One or two fell in love and I don't even know how that happened. One of my classmates married and left because he was angry at the way the college was being run. I can't imagine leaving because of that. He did.

Even though the Mass today is celebrated in English, was eliminating Latin from the academic curriculum a good idea?

I think so myself. There are schools now that teach pre-medical Latin and some other schools that teach Latin. It's a great language. They first quit teaching in Latin in our time. We studied philosophy in Latin. When we first went to English, I thought it was a little funny. Now I can see that, with the vernacular in the present Church, there is no reason to have Latin. It's just an extra intellectual burden. It would be different if we were studying German or French or something where you could read and speak to people. Latin is a dead language. The Holy Father likes it. I think he speaks five languages. Latin is probably one of them. But I don't think it's significant anymore. It was there because the liturgy was in Latin and it was necessary to learn.

Since Vatican II, striking changes have been made in the liturgy and also in parish organizations. Comment on the positive and negative changes you have seen. What has been lost, what has been gained?

Positive changes include concelebration here in the monastery, as I've mentioned. I think there is much more participation by the community. You see, in my day, the priests did all the talking and people didn't answer anything. Nowadays, there's much more participation by the people at the Eucharist—monks and others. That's a good thing. That's a wonderful thing. In fact, I look back and think, "How did I ever put up with that as a stupid youngster?" I couldn't understand anything they were saying and it was all a mystery. They were going through kind of a monologue play. So I mean, it's a great blessing for the change in the liturgy.

I think the fact that everybody goes to communion, where they used to go once or twice a year, is positive. But nowadays they may be a little too free about that. Maybe people are going to communion, but not confessing serious sins. But it's better even imperfectly; it's better to be part of it. My impression is that there is much more involvement of the laity in parish affairs and in helping the priests meet the needs of the parish. He doesn't have to do everything by himself. And he gets the support of people on his parish council.

Is that good or bad?

Oh, that's good. It seems that way to me. When I was a youngster, as I mentioned, I started worrying about how we were going to get the lay people to be more involved in the Church. And it's so much better now than it was in those days. Oh, also another aspect is a rise in students studying theology. Many are now directors of religious education. Isn't that marvelous, the priest is now being helped by having a religious director? He doesn't have to do all of it himself. I am sure it is more effective that way, too, because the people who are involved in education are more in touch with what people are going through. A priest could be good by himself, or even a great catechist, but I think in general it's much better to have it shared.

Were there losses?

I am really not aware of any loss in the way the Church has been organized. There's a loss in terms of people's behavior. For instance, one thing that strikes me, now this is my own personal opinion, I think that the very fact that people have sued the Church for millions of dollars for a sexual impropriety of the priest is way out of focus. It shows that the people asking for a million dollars have lost their faith in what the Catholic Church means, because they could ask for therapy. They could ask for apologies. I have no idea how many millions and millions of dollars they have gotten. The lawyers get such a big chunk of that. So you know there is a loss of faith somewhere in there. I don't think you can blame the sexual misbehavior, for example, on Vatican II, however.

The number of religious vocations declines every year. What is the meaning of these changing patterns—to the monastery and to the Church at large?

I don't see priests encouraging young men or nuns encouraging anyone to go into a vocation. Sisters don't teach anymore. For me, my vocation started in the sixth grade because of the sister, as I've mentioned. I don't see that happening anymore. That is horrendous when you think of it. All of a sudden after Vatican II, sisters decided that teaching was not a religious vocation. And they all quit teaching, so schools had to get lay people. But those teaching sisters, you see, were getting nuns for their order. They were also getting priests for the monastery or for the Church. It's just a tragic loss. And that's one of the negative aspects of Vatican II.

In a sense, the same thing has been happening to priests. Back then, they were more aggressive in encouraging vocations. But I get the feeling now that few priests do this. You see at one time, I can't remember exactly when it was, at the 50th jubilee of a priest, all of the young men who had chosen the priesthood because of his influence would come back to the parish for the celebration.

I can't imagine that today. But it's wonderful to think of that. How wonderful it would be to have a whole group of priests there to celebrate with you. They were more aggressive in those days. It's true here also in the monastery. We used to go out to the parishes, give talks about vocations and things like that. I don't see much of that happening now. Fr. Anthony [Vinson, OSB] is doing everything he can. There is beginning to be an effort to be more aggressive and seek vocations. But it's still seems to me to be a lot of room for improvement.

What are your hopes for the future for the Catholic Church? In other words, where do you think the Church is going?

I really don't know. But I have faith in the rise and fall of civilization and the rise and fall of the Church. Fr. Adelbert [Buscher, OSB] used to talk about a cycle in history. The cycle would last two or three centuries. What always intrigued me was that leaders of the French Revolution killed all the nuns and priests they could find. So the Church was just decimated. Not only because of that, but because religion was held in very low repute. Well, after the revolution, the Cure d'Ars—St. John Vianney—finished his clerical studies. He became a patron of various priests and helped the Church to flourish again. Mother Teresa and also Pope John Paul might be beacons of hope. He always said, "Be not

215

afraid." My hope is that somehow some great saintly figures in the clergy or the laity will revive the faith.

How about here at the monastery?

I am not sure about that either. We don't have enough novices, but those who are here are a wonderful younger generation. For one thing, there are many good singers. Divine Office and public prayer are such important parts of our lives. It's so wonderful to have that music. I frankly can't understand why anybody would join if they didn't like public worship. Among the young people I see good sense, not only in music, but in other areas also. They are very promising.

I don't think they are worried about the future. It's just us older guys that are. But anyway, I have a feeling the monastery is also going to have a creative resurgence. The Einsiedeln Abbey [Saint Meinrad's mother abbey in Switzerland] has been around for over 1,400 years and at one point they were down to one monk. Whew! It's just incredible when you think of it. The membership grew back. So the monastery is like everything else; it goes up and down.

Interview profile taken from: Fr. Eric Lies to Prof. Ruth C. Engs, August 20, 2005, Interview Transcription, Saint Meinrad Archives.

* From Fr. Eric's farewell speech upon his retirement June 12, 1994, from the Development Office.

Chapter Ten

Fr. Abbot Bonaventure Knaebel, OSB

Abbot Bonaventure served as abbot from 1955-66 during a period of great change in the Church and monastery. Of the nine abbots at Saint Meinrad between 1871 and 2006, he was the "pivotal abbot," as four abbots have come before, and four after him.

Born September 6, 1918, in New Albany, IN, Abbot Bonaventure attended Holy Trinity School in New Albany. In 1931, he enrolled in Saint Meinrad's minor seminary and graduated from the high school in 1935. He received a BA (1940) and a theology degree (1944). In 1946, he graduated with a MS degree from Catholic University of America, and attended the University of Pittsburgh during the summers from 1949-51 to study mathematics.

Abbot Bonaventure made his first profession as a monk August 6, 1938, solemn profession August 15, 1941, and was ordained a priest

June 5, 1943. From 1946-55, he taught in the high school and college. He was assistant spiritual director for the School of Theology (1947-55) and assistant manager of Abbey Press (1952-55).

He was elected abbot of the community in 1955. Under his leadership, the old Guest House was built and he founded a community in Peru and one in California. After his resignation in 1966 and until 1979, Abbot Bonaventure was involved with the newly established Peruvian mission. He then served as pastor in two Indiana parishes until 1986, and then was administrator of Monasterio Benedictino in Morelia, Mexico. From 1989 through 2003, he served in several pastoral activities. During the past few years, he has worked in the Development Office.

Abbot Bonaventure was interviewed by Prof. Ed Shaughnessy (ES), August 3 and 4, 2004, and by Prof. Ruth C. Engs (RCE), June 15, 2005.

Childhood and Early Years as a Monk

ES: Reflect on your early years, such as family, early schooling and how you became interested in monastic life.

I was born in New Albany, IN, in 1918, the first of three boys, and given the name, Merton James. My brother Vincent was born four years later and Robert two years after that. We were all members of Holy Trinity Catholic Church in New Albany, except my mother. My mother had been raised in the Christian Church in Floyds Knobs. She did not join the Catholic Church until I was a deacon. My father faithfully took us to Mass every Sunday morning.

When I was in the sixth grade at Holy Trinity, a young man of the parish, Albert Walter, who had been ordained a priest, came to talk to us. After talking a while, he asked who thought they might like to be president of the United States. A couple of boys held their hands up. Then he said, "Who thinks they might like to be a priest?" I held my hand up, and I'm not sure whether or not that was the first time I thought of being a priest.

In the sixth grade, I had been one of the servers in the parish church. When I told my mother that I wanted to be one of the servers, she said, "Well, I'll get you an alarm clock and you can get yourself up." I would generally walk down to church, which was a good mile and a half away.

I was taught by the Sisters of Providence from Terre Haute [IN] and they probably talked about vocations. When I told the assistant pastor that I thought I'd like to be a priest, he said, "Well, you'll go to Saint Meinrad." After finishing eighth grade, he drove another boy from my class, Robert Sampson, and myself down here to register us on August 15, 1931. So I entered the minor seminary and had the benefit of Fr. Aemilian Elpers, the disciplinarian. He was in charge of close to 300 boys. He and the rector, Fr. Stephen Thuis, would sit at the head table. They were on an elevated platform and could tell what people were doing and what mischief was going on.

ES: What was the discipline like?

Fr. Aemilian was our Latin teacher for our first Latin class. He was quite a taskmaster, but he did teach us a great deal. I always had more trouble with languages than I did with mathematics. I did quite well with algebra, but my Latin was poor and I also discovered at that time that my English grammar was a little deficient. Anyway, as I picked up English, my Latin became better by the time I was in the third class.

In the minor seminary, we had a regular schedule. I was able to keep out of most of the mischief that might possibly have gone on. Now, Fr. Aemilian, as mentioned, was the disciplinarian during all my years in the minor seminary, from 1931 to 1937. He would tell people, "Remember, the heel is also a part of the shoe."

Let me tell you a story about discipline. There was a place called Hell's Bend, where "beaver boards" [compressed paper cardboard sheets] formed compartments for sleeping. The front was open but they were such that each individual had some privacy, you see. The only thing students were supposed to do is sleep there and make their beds after breakfast. We weren't supposed to be there at any other time. Most of us just slept in full dormitories with lockers along the wall. Nothing separated the beds. The fellows who were the seniors, in other words the second-year college men, were the ones in Hell's Bend.

It so happened that one of the fellows had gotten a nice cake for his birthday. He invited four or five other fellows up there and they were sitting around on the bed eating the cake. Fr. Aemilian looked in and said, "Am I intruding?" This fellow was never bawled out. Fr. Aemilian never said another word about it and must have thought the embarrassment was sufficient punishment. But the student never knew whether Fr. Aemilian was going to wait till the end of the year to throw him out.

ES and RCE: Describe your daily routine as a high school student in the minor seminary.

The first thing in the morning we went to a communion Mass. We didn't attend the whole Mass. We got there about halfway through. After communion, we had breakfast. Shortly after breakfast, we all lined up and went over to the Archabbey Church to attend high Mass there. After that, we began classes at 8:30. Six times a week, the first thing in the morning was always Latin. There were classes on Saturday, also, because Tuesday and Thursday afternoons we had recreation.

For recreation in the first year of high school, we were divided up into five-person teams. We played basketball a lot. We had a separate gym for the minor seminary [four years of high school and the first two years of college]. The major seminary [two years of philosophy and four years of theology] also had their own gym. I guess I was in the second or third class when I was trying to play back and forth with a baseball with another fellow. I broke a finger that had to be set. I was never much of an athlete.

RCE: What did you wear in terms of clothing then?

In those years, all students wore cassocks from the first year in high school to the fourth year of theology. We also wore a Roman collar. As far as I remember, for recreation, we had shorts for basketball and didn't have to wear the cassocks. We could wear pants and shirt and just regular clothing. I think most of us had tennis shoes.

RCE: Was there a difference in clothing when you became a novice?

When you started your novitiate, you got a best habit, which was a new habit. They were woolen and about three times as thick as the material we have now. You got one that had some wear and then another one that was more or less patches. That was called your work habit. You wore it to clean the corridors or to work in the monastery. When we went swimming, we wore that habit down to the lake, put on a bathing suit and then took the habit off. When we got out of the lake, we put the habit on and took off the bathing suit and came back up the hill wearing that habit. We played softball and volleyball in our habits.

Abbot Bonaventure, as a young monk

Of course, at night, when you hung those up, it would be wringing wet in the summer and still pretty wet when you put it on in the morning. At night, as a novice, we also wore the night scapular [a small piece of black cloth]. Most of us wore them until after Vatican Council II and then after that I don't remember whatever happened to them. I haven't seen one since.

ES and RCE: What was the tone and nature of discipline under which your vocation was formed?

It was in the second year of high school that I read the life of St. Benedict. And I thought that maybe I should become a monk. I talked to Fr. Stephen Thuis, the rector, about it. They put me on the list as a possible candidate for the Order in my third year at Saint Meinrad. I entered the novitiate August 1937, after my last year in the minor seminary, when I had finished high school and two years of college work.

Our lives were quite full. When you joined the monastery in those years, you had to be in the Archabbey Church at 4 o'clock in the morning for the beginning of the Office. Even though we had six years of Latin, it was quite difficult. The psalms are not easy in the first place. We had to sing or say the Office according to the *Rule of St. Benedict*. It was considerably longer then. It was shortened when changes were made after Vatican II. After the morning Office of Matins and Lauds, we often served at Mass or attended a full Communion Mass. Then came the Office of Prime at 6 o'clock. After that was over, we would have breakfast. So we were quite busy for two and a half hours in church in one way or another. After breakfast, we had the conventual Mass at 7:30 and then classes beginning at 8:30.

The novice master, Fr. Henry Brenner, was excellent. He spent most of his conferences with us talking about the holy *Rule*. He would tell us stories about people who had been in the monastery. He had been novice master for about 30 years when we had him as our novice master. We were under his supervision, not only during that one year of novitiate, but he was also the junior master. He was still our superior, even after we made solemn vows, until we were ordained priests. He was fair. He would occasionally mete out a punishment for something rather small. You were supposed to offer to say culpa and you got a little penance of some kind. Culpa was the discipline if something was broken or you were late for something.

ES: You have suggested that things were more rigorous than today. Do you think that the men who are coming to the novitiate now, in the 21st century, have it too easy?

No, they have their problems with the life, too. It's just that after going through the minor seminary and being in that frame of discipline, it was not too hard to adjust to being in the monastery and doing the various things required of us. At recreation in the evening, we were expected, as we left the Abbey Church, to go out and walk around in the "paradise"—a little area to the north of the monastery—with the person who was right next to you in seniority. In the early years, we were always seated in seniority in the choir and in the refectory. Sometimes that was a little difficult because being next to a certain person all the time could be hard to deal with. You might think that, "Oh, he recites too fast or he doesn't sing right." I can't always blame people about singing, because I don't have any ear. But it is true that just being next to the same person all the time can be a little difficult. We don't have to do that now in choir.

ES and RCE: What was the monastery physically like when you were a novice?

In the novitiate, we slept in a large dormitory and it was often cold in the winter. The room was partitioned off with hanging sheets to create a rather small space—from eight to 13 people slept there. Though each individual cubbyhole was surrounded by sheets, it could not keep you from hearing the snoring in the next beds. In this small space was a bed and, I think, a trunk at the foot of the bed to keep clothes in. The sheets that divided the cells were sort of on wooden slats that went around so you had a place to hang your habit up there. There was also a washstand.

There was no running water in the rooms of the monastery, except perhaps in the abbot's room. We walked down to what we called the "double O" to get water that we used for washing. That's where we also had the toilets. One sink was deeper and you could put your pitcher under the water and carry it back to your cell. We each had a little wooden washstand with a wash basin and a little soap dish. Your towel and wash rag hung on one side of the stand. You poured the water into the bowl and washed. Then you poured the dirty water into your wash bucket and had to carry and empty it in the same sink where you got your water.

The other clerics, those not yet priests, lived in rooms where there would be two beds in a room and a sheet down the center and a sheet across the front. You couldn't look in and see anybody in their bed, but there were two people in the room.

ES and RCE: When did you get your own cell? What was in it?

When I was ordained as a priest. There was a bed, a desk and predieu—something to kneel at. In those rooms as a young priest, you also had a washstand, a basin, a bucket, a pitcher and so on with running water down the hall. My cell was on the top floor right underneath a nice tin roof and, of course, there was no air conditioning or fan in those times.

Some nights in the summer, I hardly slept at all. You would put on your habit in the morning and it would still be wet from the day before from perspiration. Air conditioning was put in the new monastery when it was built in 1981. In the old monastery building, when Abbot Gabriel [Verkamp, OSB] was elected in '66, they put air conditioning in his office and bedroom, but it was just one outside unit. We're spoiled now with air conditioning.

Brothers got their own cell when they made perpetual vows. [When the new monastery was built, each professed monk received his own room with a private bath. Today all candidates and novices also have their own cells and bath. Besides the usual bed, desk, bookcase, bureau and easy chair, in some cases, a computer is found. A few elderly monks also have a TV. Some monks have religious or other objects or pictures hanging on the walls, which are painted white. On the windows of each cell are wooden shutters. Most cell floors are carpeted while hallways are usually concrete or tile].

RCE: What else was different then compared to now?

We had the full fast in Lent, for instance. We also observed more rigorously than we do now what are called monastic fast days that begin in September and go up to the time of Lent. But the Lenten fast was each day except Sunday, when there was no fasting. We had a piece of bread, coffee and some butter for breakfast. Then we had our full meal at noon and in the evening you were not supposed to eat more than eight ounces of food. So we would have the dish "nonsense."

Nonsense was something like cornbread, although it was sweeter and it was broken up. You would take some spoonfuls of it, put it on a plate and put some butter with it. All the tables had containers of corn syrup or molasses or, as we called it, "molaseeds." They brought this in by the tankful, in 50-gallon drums. Our breakfast for many, many years was something like the rosary: Monday would be pancakes, Tuesday cornbread, Wednesday nonsense, Thursday pancakes, Friday cornbread, Saturday nonsense. On Sunday, "grey dogs"—some kind of sausage—and occasionally some eggs.

RCE: When you weren't in a fast, what would you eat for breakfast?

We would have more things. There would be more fruit, apples for instance. We had an apple orchard so we had a lot of apples. Sometimes we were served a bowl with cornflakes that had milk already in it. That bowl was to be divided among four people. The brothers did all the cooking. Their menu was limited in the sense that they didn't buy much from outside. We raised it—tomatoes, potatoes. We had a potato cellar. In our slaughterhouse, we killed two beef one week and five or six hogs the other week. So we had meat and a dairy.

We had whole milk, although some of the cream was taken out to make butter. There was no pasteurization. The only safety to our milk was that the cows were given the tuberculin test. We had our own eggs. We must have had a thousand or more chickens. One of the brothers took care of them. We were self-sufficient in a lot of ways at that time.

We had a regular farm with one brother or priest in charge of it; laymen worked it. The lay people did most of the milking. They milked at four in the morning and four in the afternoon.

Work

RCE: Can you tell me something about your years as abbot?

I was only 36 years old when I was elected. I never had an administrative position. I had been appointed by Abbot Ignatius to the Abbot's Council a couple of years before my election. However, at that time, the council was a much smaller group. I was an assistant spiritual director and also was an assistant manager at Abbey Press. The present abbot, Justin DuVall, was prior for 11 years under Abbot Timothy [Sweeney, OSB]. This kind of experience gives you much more knowledge of what's going on in the community than what I had.

RCE: Was being elected abbot something you wanted or didn't want?

At that time, it was generally felt if you were elected, you should accept it. Now with the *scrutinium* [a process of discernment used by the monastic community prior to an election], a person can say, "I ask not to be considered," which indicates that you prefer not to have the job. But we didn't have that kind of option then. We just started voting. So I guess I had butterflies in my stomach a lot. I did develop an ulcer within two or three years after becoming abbot.

RCE: Did you find the job stressful?

I think it was, yes. It just seems like something always came up. I can't say much about those situations, of course. For example, you have a couple of men in a parish and they are fighting with each other. Not only are they doing that in the privacy of the rectory, but they are letting everybody else know about it. They might say something about the man in a sermon. It was a problem.

RCE: Describe what it was like to be abbot the first few years and also some of your achievements over your tenure.

It wasn't long until I found the community cooperating. In '61, I presented the idea of going to Peru and the community was generally receptive. In August of '61, the Vatican, under Pope John XXIII, had sent a high-ranking monsignor from the Secretary of State, Monsignor Casaroli, who later became a cardinal and secretary of state, to a conference of religious superiors at Notre Dame. He told us the Holy Father wanted each community of men and women to send ten percent of their personnel within the next ten years to work in Latin America.

Shortly after I got back from that conference, I got a letter from the papal nuncio in Peru inviting Saint Meinrad to take over a minor seminary in Huaraz, Peru. So Fr. Alcuin Leibold, a Spanish teacher, and I went down there shortly after Thanksgiving. Then I came back and told the community that I would like to send three men to investigate this situation—Fr. Kenneth Wimsatt, Fr. Benedict Meyer and Fr. Germain Swisshelm.

They were sent to the language school of the St. James Society in Lima in '62. It was a group that Cardinal Cushing had started with priests from his diocese. The society worked in Peru, Ecuador and Bolivia. They had established an intensive language school; it was five days a week for almost four months. There was a teacher for every two or three students plus a language lab. You really got bombarded with Spanish.

In the late '50s, I felt it was now possible to start a new foundation. So I said, "I would like to make a foundation in Oceanside, California." I presented this idea as starting out with a few people to see how it would work. So we started what is now Prince of Peace Abbey in 1958.

We built a Guest House in '61, but it's now gone. A new one is to be finished in a couple of months [it was completed in October 2006]. We had to build a new water filtration plant. A sewage disposal system was built because raw sewage was going into the Anderson River. We had 735 students here, among others, and a thousand meals a day.

RCE: Discuss the role of the abbot as administrator then and now.

Administratively, he is still in charge of everything. He's the one who officially appoints the rector of the seminary. Now they have a board that votes on it, but still the abbot is the one who has to make the final decision. He can be guided by procedures that they have set up. When I was abbot, we didn't have a Board of Overseers or Board of Trustees.

One thing, though, that was different during my 11 years as abbot was that we had a least a 114 novices. We would have an average of at least ten novices a year. It kept the abbot busy investing novices. Now we have two novices and some years we might not have any. So that's a big change. In 1954, the year before I was elected, the community was 237 men. Then some of them were assigned to Blue Cloud Abbey and they made their stability to Blue Cloud. So in 1955, when I was elected, we were 197 people. It kept growing until the high was 219 one year, around 1964, I think.

Another change is that the abbot is now a very necessary part of development. For instance, Abbot Justin has spent the last two days with the Development Office people seeing prospective benefactors. Since we didn't have a Development Office when I was abbot, I didn't have to do that.

RCE: How about changes in farming, printing and other operations when you were abbot?

Up until my time, it was considered that a person in charge of anything almost had to be a priest. For instance, all of the teaching was done by priests. There were no brothers who taught at all. I appointed Br. Gabriel Herbig to manage the Guest House. This was an innovation. But a priest said to me, "What about if somebody wants to go to confession?" In fact, it was the man I was replacing. I said, "Well, we have all these priests in the monastery and one of them can come over and hear the confession." At Abbey Press, there had always been a priest in charge, but I went ahead and appointed Br. Maurus Zoeller as manager of the printing division, as he seemed capable of taking care of it. He came with a printer's apron when he joined the monastery.

On the farm, we had about 300 hogs that we had raised. We were feeding them slop—the leftover food. The state came in and said, "No, you have to cook it." So they rigged up a tank with a large pipe inside and put 100 pounds of live steam through the leftover food. After a while, you had to feed them hog feed that you bought. So that was the end of it for us. All of these other farmers around us had ten or 20 hogs and there were no state regulations on them. We could buy hogs from the farmers cheaper.

Also, during my time, we had our own coal mine. It was down the road toward Fulda, not far from here. I didn't have anything directly to do with it. Somebody in the monastery was in charge of dealing with these individuals. We also had our own dynamo to make electricity. We only took electricity part time from the Southern Indiana Gas and Electric Co. in Evansville. By the time I was abbot, St. Bede Hall had been erected. I had a lot of debt from this to pay off during my time.

When St. Bede Hall was erected, our need for electricity was such that they said to us, "In order to get full service, you will have to give us all your business." In other words, we had to shut down our dynamo. The powerhouse is still there for heating and all the steam. We still run 100 pounds of steam through the kitchen, because we have those beautiful steam kettles in there. That was part of the construction in 1932. When I came here, the building with the kitchen that is now called Newman was being built.

RCE: What has changed since Vatican II in terms of abbatial ceremonies and customs?

The first official blessing that I saw was my own because Archbbot Ignatius had been blessed when I was in the seventh grade. Just preparing for the blessing was strenuous; however, it was quite an interesting ceremony. Fr. Bernardine Shine, the master of ceremonies, must have had me rehearse. It was all so new and unusual, but it's been modified since then. It was a much more complicated ceremony then.

For instance, you vested in priestly vestments. You did everything in the Mass. You read the Epistle and the Gospel and so on privately, but you didn't say the words of consecration. You ended up going to Holy Communion, but you did not concelebrate the Mass. The blessing of an abbot was different than an ordination or a consecration of a bishop, because those individuals also concelebrated the Mass. For centuries, a newly ordained priest said the words of consecration along with the main celebrant. So did someone consecrated as bishop. But the abbot did not have that privilege of concelebrating. Now we all concelebrate when we go to Mass. We have that privilege every day.

The ceremonies pre-Vatican II were much more elaborate. We had a little keg of wine and a special loaf of bread that we presented to the presiding archbishop. It looked as if it were the gifts for the Mass, but they were not used for the Mass. They were ceremonial gifts that also thanked the archbishop for the abbatial blessing. You gave your allegiance to the Pope. You read a special document that said you would defend the Holy Father. You almost said that you would raise an army for him! It was much different from today and has been modified and changed.

There was much more to the Pontifical Mass and some of the regalia have changed. For the Pontifical Mass, the prelate came in and vested from the altar. All of the vestments were laid out on the altar—the amice, the alb, the cincture and so on. There were 12 servers and each one brought a piece over to the throne. The master of ceremonies presented it to the Abbot and he put them all on. The abbot had to wear gloves. The bishops had to wear gloves. You put on a tunicle, dalmatic and chasuble over the alb. If you were going to wear green vestments, you had green sandals and green cloth stockings halfway up to the knee. Buskins they were called.

RCE: How about everyday customs and rituals associated with being an abbot in your time?

I had lived under Abbot Ignatius for 17 years, so I had the experience of seeing him act as abbot. He became abbot in the '30s and I joined the monastery in '37 as a novice. There was much more ritual connected with being abbot. The monks could be kneeling in the choir stall at four o'clock in the morning. When the abbot came in, everybody stood up. They could all be seated in the refectory, like at breakfast, and if the abbot came in, we all stood. Then when the abbot finished and got up, we stood while he left.

When you went to the abbot's office, you came in, knelt, kissed his ring and got a blessing. If he asked you, you sat down. If he didn't, you stood there and discussed your business. But that was just understood. That's what you did, as it was a custom that had come down from years before. As far as I know, we were still doing this when I retired as abbot. I am not sure how long Abbot Gabriel did it. I can't recall when they changed it because, after '66, I was away from the monastery in Peru.

Special reverence was also found at the Mass. The celebrant would come out of the sacristy with the servers. They would bow to the abbot, bow to one side, and then bow to the other side of the choir. There were other things of reverence to the abbot. When you came into choir and the abbot was there, you would bow to the altar and then bow to the abbot before you went down to your place. A lot of that has changed over my lifetime.

RCE: What was your work after you retired as abbot?

After my resignation in 1966, I went to our mission in Huaraz, Peru. In 1974, I became mission procurator until 1979. I became pastor of Sacred Heart Parish, Jeffersonville, IN, from '79 to '81. Then I was pastor of St. Michael Parish, Charlestown, IN, from '81 to '86. In 1986, for two years I acted as administrator of Monasterio Benedictino, Morelia, Mexico.

From 1989 to 1995, I was chaplain at St. Paul Hermitage, Beech Grove, IN, and then administrator of Corpus Christi Abbey, Sandia, TX, for almost two years. From 1997 to 2003, I was administrator of St. Michael Parish in Bradford, IN. Then I came back here and began working in the Development Office.

Prayer

RCE: What is your favorite part of the Rule of St. Benedict*?*

Chapter 72. It gives guidance on how the monk ought to feel and deal with his abbot. It has the line, "Let nothing be preferred to Christ"—to the love of Christ. As far as I'm concerned, it's such a great part of what makes the *Rule of St. Benedict* outstanding. Benedict uses much from the *Rule of the Master*. But the "love of Christ" that he expresses is not found in the *Master* in quite that way. So it's a very great improvement. Benedict wants us to live our lives according to Gospel teaching and that certainly is the way to carry that out. Mother Teresa's summary of the Gospel in five words is, "You did it to me" [Matthew 25:40]. It's the love of Christ. It's so overwhelming.

I can't remember all the things that are in Chapter 72, but it is strong on love, based on the office of abbot, that you should have toward the abbot. It's a love not depending upon how he treats you or whether he's doing a good job, or is good at finance, or a good manager of meetings or a good chairman, because Benedict says the abbot takes the place of Christ in the monastery.

As a younger monk, I was having trouble with obedience and fraternal charity—what's this guy doing and the like, and many other things that keep you from seeing the importance of that text. We study the *Rule*. If you look at all the things it says, you finally wake up and realize that's what it's all about—the individual's way of treating others. It's this one sentence in Chapter 72 that I would like to keep working toward.

RCE: What is your key to Benedictine spiritually?

Prefer nothing to Christ. The "love of Christ" is a good summary, I think, of everything that the *Rule* has; that sentence is outstanding in the way of spirituality.

RCE: What's been your most difficult and your happiest time or experience in your life?

It was hard being abbot. There were just enough little aggravations and decisions to make it difficult. For example, what do we do now about the liturgy, what about the business of the vernacular? Even though I rode with these changes pretty well, still there was discussion. People expressed their opinions one way or the other. You always had somebody stirring the pot, you might say, about the different things.

Some of the things were personnel problems. Some of the monks now tell me that if I found out that two men were fighting, I would go to one who was the most amenable and tell him to back off so there would be some peace. If there are two people fighting, if you can get one of them to back off a little, it seemed to help. You try to give guidance here and there, so you don't remember a lot of the things you have said.

RCE: What were your happiest times over your lifetime?

I think I've always had more of an optimist's view of things than a pessimistic one. Although, as I grow older, I sometimes wonder if I'm not becoming more like my mother who, if she didn't have something to worry about would start to worry about that. People coming in to the community, being ordained, being able to take on various projects and study. As abbot, it was a nice feeling to be able to send men to study Scripture and theology. We prepared a lot of people for many things.

I seemed to have a good bit of apathy. I'm a 9 on the enneagram, which means you try to keep things at peace. Number nine isn't the one who tells his wife every morning or evening how much he loves her. He thinks, "We did get married didn't we, so that's my proof." One of the things I feel is that, as abbot, I did not affirm people enough. That was perhaps, as I look back, that it keeps you from rejoicing too much in the different things that the community has been able to accomplish. Maybe that's more on the negative side than on the positive. However, there were times that captured joy. Having people come to the monastery and try it, and see them develop. So I had many joyous experiences in the abbatial office. My pastoral work in the parishes in general was a happy time.

Vatican II: Its Effect on the Church and Saint Meinrad Archabbey

ES: What is your opinion of the overall effect and changes since Vatican Council II? Have they been good for the Church, the Archabbey?

I approved of what happened. I have a little story about the Holy Spirit. Some time during the Council years, I'm not sure just when, we had changed from saying "Holy Ghost" to "Holy Spirit." It didn't come from the Council. Anyway, this elderly lady was complaining to a priest about some of the changes that had been made and he said, "Well, Mary, the Holy Spirit is behind that." And she said, "Well, how come the Holy Spirit said we should do something and the Holy Ghost never did say that?"

At the Archabbey we now, for instance, initiate newcomers into a better understanding of the *Rule*. The times allotted for spiritual reading are much more definite now than they were; in fact, there is more time allotted for spiritual reading. Of course, the Office is somewhat shorter, but that came about mostly because of the work that is now done, such as teaching and other types of activity. Vatican Council decided that it was possible to mitigate, in some ways, the Office.

So our arrangement fits well with what has come out of Vatican II. I sometimes think that for all of us, perhaps, our own personal prayer, apart from the Divine Office and the Mass and liturgy, is so very necessary and is what helps us more than anything else to gain benefits from all that we do in an official manner. Because our prayers, to me, are prayers for the Church as a whole and, also, as individuals.

RCE: Specifically, what was your view concerning going with the vernacular, concelebration and also having the fathers, fraters and brothers saying one Divine Office as part of the changes in Vatican II?

I had no objection to any of those things. I was in favor of them. That's why I had the experimental Office in English started here. As soon as the Vatican had approved it, I felt we should go ahead with these changes. They were part of the whole change of society, the economy and a lot of things. In other words, in the late '40s and '50s, some of the men who entered had come back from the war and were interested in religious life. Thomas Merton's books and his monastery, Gethsemani, for example, helped with this trend and resulting changes. As it turned out, I am glad that I didn't have to make some of the other decisions. Some communities put the habit aside completely. They could come to choir with a clerical collar and a shirt. These things came up for vote after my time as abbot.

RCE: The community was originally based upon the old European model of priests and brothers having different roles and privileges in monastic communities. Can you describe this and the changes after the Vatican Council?

There were differences then. In the refectory, the brothers were not given as many things as even the clerics—those going on for the priesthood—and the priests. The priests' places were set with a regular plate and a soup bowl on top of it. The brothers, and I think the clerics, or fraters as we called them, who were not yet in orders, got only the soup plates.

There was a ranking. First of all the priests, then the fraters and then the brothers. After Vatican II, there were certain innovations. Now we are listed in the ORDO [annual publication that catalogs information about the Swiss-American Congregation of Benedictine communities and their members] according to seniority. At that time, the priests and clerics in the house were all listed and then the brothers were listed. I think that continued all during my time as abbot.

Another story that relates to the differences in the past. One of the priests told the brothers, "Well, we, the priests, have to go out and work on weekends so the brothers can eat." In other words, what the brothers were doing here wasn't bringing in any money. It was because they were doing all the services and all the physical work of the Archabbey. There were 60 brothers. They ran the slaughterhouse, they ran the powerhouse, they ran all the kitchen work. We now laugh about these stories.

Today we are intertwined. In other words, the distinction between priests and brothers has been minimized a great deal. In fact, it was one of the good points, as far as I'm concerned, coming out of Vatican II. Some of the seniority rules still remained during my time as abbot, but it was possible for me to appoint someone to be in charge of the Guest House or in charge of Abbey Press who was not a priest. That was a great innovation.

ES: Was there a difference between the monk-priests and the brothers in their morale about the changes?

I think more priests were upset over the changes than the brothers. The brothers, as I mentioned, were no longer in a secondary status. At one time, they were not allowed to make solemn vows, but after the Council they were able to make solemn vows, which they make regularly now. The perpetual vow was not as complete as it did not include the strictest poverty. The brothers also had the opportunity to do more things, such as teaching. In all my 12 years of study at Saint Meinrad, all the classes were taught by priests.

ES: Were the monks optimistic about changes such as the liturgy?

Even though I was abbot at the time, I am not sure that I know what a lot of other people were thinking. It is one of those things where some might resent all these changes and not say much about it. Others might talk about it a bit, but only in jest, so you didn't know whether they meant it or not. But I do know we started having the concelebrated Mass as soon as the bishops, or whoever was responsible for accepting it for this country, approved it. We also kept the choir in Latin, but under Fr. Simeon Daly we started having monks recite the Office in English in the Chapter Room at the same time. This was on an experimental basis to see how it would work.

ES: How were changes in the liturgy, more openness and involvement of the laity in decisions accepted by the clergy in parishes?

My impression was that these were well received by everyone. When we were down in Peru, the laity were able, because of the decision of their bishops, to receive communion in the hand. This was earlier than here. Br. Xavier had noted this in a little notebook that I used when I was writing the history of our Peru mission. At Christmas time [1964], they had been able to receive communion in the hand and also both species. All those changes came about because of what the bishops in the Church, as a whole, had decided.

Some priests, before the Council was finished, thought that it wouldn't be long before they would allow priests to marry. The predictions about married clergy did not come through, of course. Some were disappointed about this and left. However, we know that a number of men who left and were married either divorced their wives or their wives divorced them. They had common marital problems.

In the Church today, we can't put all the blame on Vatican II. We know that, in the last five to ten years, the number of Catholic marriages has gone down. The number of priesthood students has declined. In my files, I have a brief outline of a talk that I gave at the beginning of the school year in 1960. There were 735 students for the priesthood here at Saint Meinrad. I just don't see how this large a change was because of the Council.

ES: Even if the Mass were to be celebrated in English, was eliminating Latin from the academic curriculum a good idea?

Latin was certainly cut down. When I was in the Minor Seminary, for six years we had it six days a week, the first class every morning, Monday through Saturday inclusive. But later, after the Council, at least here at Saint Meinrad, I have the impression that we reduced it to just two years and not for six days a week. There was still some benefit from Latin and those who were really interested in it could continue their studies.

All of the documents of the Church down through the centuries have been in Latin. If you want to look up what the congregations discussed in 1600, you will have to know Latin. It's still the official language of the Church, which still puts out documents in Latin all the time. So the Latin language still has great importance in the Church. It will be too bad if it's completely forgotten.

I think we may swing back to using more Latin again. I know we do that here in the monastery, but not as much as is found in some monasteries. Fr. Cassian [Folsom, OSB], of the monastery in Norcia, Italy, where St. Benedict was born, has established the Benedictine Office, as St. Benedict prescribed it; it's recited daily in Latin. This means their members have to learn Latin well enough to handle this. Academically, it is a wonderful thing to know. Much of our own English language comes from it and it's the basis of studying many other languages.

ES: What has been lost, if anything, and what has been gained since the Council?

There was a certain rigor about everything then. For instance, in the Mass, everything the priest did was described in rubrics—every move was designated. It was written in such a way that everybody, everywhere, offered Mass in practically the same way. They genuflected at the same places and held their hands a certain way. Everything was regulated. This was also found in religious life. All the nuns had to have the same type of shoes, the same type of stockings. Everything had to be the same and there were also certain rigors about rules and regulations. There was a swing against these tendencies.

However, I believe that it swung a little too far the other way. In many communities now, no one dresses the same so that it is hard to recognize them as religious. That's a certain loss, I believe. I think that some communities found that these changes contributed to the loss of vocations. However, I know there are convents in different parts of the world where the cloister is still kept. The religious are wearing their habits, but still vocations have decreased and they are in danger of having to close because those remaining are all so elderly. But I don't think we will go back to all that rigor again. To my mind, there is more of a middle way and some of the older things will come back again.

ES: What is the morale when you were first here compared with the morale in the monastery today?

I came in 1937. That's getting close to 70 years as a member of the community. It was a different time and we, as individuals, were different; the formation then had a certain rigor. We had certain things we had to do that were a part of the life. When you carried them out, you became accustomed to it. We were told, at one time or another in those early years, that it takes ten years to become a monk. But we were able to do what we were supposed to do even though it was not always something we might have chosen to do.

In those days before I came in, I didn't have a car, I didn't smoke that much, I didn't have much money. We just didn't have expectations. Nowadays, when people come in, they have their own car and maybe an apartment, and a TV and radio and everything else. It's quite a change, but I think that the young people today seem to be striving to become part of the group, striving to become part of the community. We are dealing with different people and different times.

ES: The number of religious vocations declines every year. What is the meaning of this changing pattern to the monastery and to the Church at large? Is it a different Catholic Church than it was 50 years ago?

I think the Church hasn't changed that much. In other words, the things that it teaches now it also taught 75 years ago. It's that the world itself has changed, along with the philosophy of life. For example, the sexual revolution, the attitude toward marriage and birth control. Anyway, it was difficult for people many, many years ago to keep those rules. They had their failures, but change wasn't as easily allowed. It wasn't as easy for people as it is today. Young people in their early 20s with a girlfriend or boyfriend aren't bothered if they aren't married. Things that the culture would not allow people to do then are now what people practice.

It is true that here at Saint Meinrad you generally saw more people coming to the monastery. You always knew that many more would come than would stay. Right now there are 111 of us. I have been doing a little research and looked up the numbers over the years. In 1917, Saint Meinrad had 111 monks. Then it kept growing and growing. In 1934, there were 143 members. Twenty years later, we were another 60 more than that, over 200. That was a lot of growth. I think this was a result of the wars and the Depression. However, today we have to more aggressively seek out vocations.

ES: Even with all the changes and a decline in vocations, is Benedictine spirituality still found within the Archabbey and Benedictine communities in the United States?

I think it is. Of course, all of us have the same problems with vocations slacking off and going down. Part of the solution is for us to live the Benedictine life here the way we really ought to; that's the best advertisement for vocations.

RCE: What do you see as the future of the Archabbey, the Church?

The fact that we received a couple of bequests, totaling $27 million, I see as a very, very positive sign. It's an affirmation of how two women found the hospitality of our community. Hospitality has always been quite good here. Abbot Ignatius would even take the ladies down to the dairy barn and point out, especially if a woman's name was Dolores, the cow that was called Dolores; each cow had its own name. Tours were part of the hospitality. Abbot Lambert [Reilly, OSB] has been exceptional in hospitality.

As for the Church, in the psalms all the time, we read that the Lord has His covenant with us and with His people. The people go astray, and are afflicted; they suffer, and are sent into exile. Still the idea is there and they continue to come back. So I think that the Lord sometimes deals with His Church this same way.

Profile based upon: Archabbot Bonaventure Knaebel to Prof. Ed Shaughnessy, August 3-4, 2004, and to Prof. Ruth C. Engs, June 15, 2005, Interview Transcriptions, Saint Meinrad Archives.

Chapter Eleven

Fr. Theodore Heck, OSB

Fr. Theodore was the leader in seminary education reform at Saint Meinrad. He served as president-rector of the School of Theology for 11 years from 1955-66 during a period of great change in the Church and monastery.

Born January 16, 1901, in Chariton, IA, Fr. Theodore attended Sugar Creek High School in Terre Haute, IN. In 1918, he enrolled in Saint Meinrad's Minor Seminary and graduated from the College (1925) and School of Theology (1929). He received a master's in education (1933) and a PhD (1935) in school administration from The Catholic University of America in Washington, D.C.

Fr. Theodore made his first profession as a monk September 8, 1923, his solemn profession December 8, 1926, and was ordained as a priest

May 21, 1929. From 1929-32, he taught Latin, mathematics and religion in the minor and major seminaries. He was director of studies (1936-56) and was in charge of modernizing the seminary curriculum.

Other positions held by Fr. Theodore over his long life have included subprior (1938-55), pastor of St. John Chrysostom Parish, New Boston, IN (1970-87), secretary to the Archabbey Chapter (1938-47), president of the American Benedictine Academy (1949-55), and prior (1966-69). He retired in 1987 and is the oldest living Benedictine monk in the world.

Fr. Theodore was interviewed by Prof. Ed Shaughnessy (ES), July 7 and 9, 2004, and by Prof. Ruth C. Engs (RCE), June 13, 2005.

Childhood and Early Years as a Monk

ES: Tell me about your childhood.

I was born in 1901 in Chariton, IA, and given the name Henry. My father was a house decorator, that is, he did work both inside and outside the house. When there was a heavy snowfall, he would clear a path from home to church with a snow shovel, a distance of about a mile. Automobiles were something of a rarity then. We kids used to run to watch a car, a Rush, as it came up the road. We could hear it coming. In 1904, the family moved to Kirksville, MO, where I first went to school, and then to St. Mary of the Woods, IN, in the summer of 1915.

My parents were good Christians and emphasized Christian service. They required that service of their children as well. We had a high regard for the Gospel. Most religious training took place at church or at home. Most mothers, like mine, taught catechism at home. My mother was very faithful in this. We had a wonderful home life. We had a little farm with cows, horses and chickens. We did all the chores and we were committed to them and to the family. In those days, you had a bicycle or a horse, so you couldn't go too far.

I found that coming from a large family—three brothers and three sisters—was good foundation for communal living. I grew up in a very religious family. Two of my younger sisters also joined a religious order. We grew up under a tradition where the German language was spoken. At home, light was provided by kerosene lamps; cooking was done on a coal stove. We had a telephone before we had electricity in the house. On the phone, my mother would take orders for father's work. Things were very simple.

ES and RCE: Why did you come to Saint Meinrad and decide to be a monk?

During my school years, I had expressed a desire to become a priest. I came to Saint Meinrad in the fall of 1918 with the intention of studying to be a priest. I didn't know at first what Benedictine life was. It was not until I came here that I learned what a monastery was. While I was studying at Saint Meinrad's seminary, I read a biography of St. Benedict and was very intrigued. I also witnessed the spiritual life and the work of the Benedictine monks here and I gradually became interested in a Benedictine vocation for myself, along with the priesthood. There were also other students studying at the seminary who were drawn to the Benedictine way of life who helped to encourage me.

The group praying of the Divine Office seemed to me a wonderful way to praise God. The Benedictine way of living was appealing to me. The impression of spiritual growth, the fuller service to God in talent and way of life led me to seek through prayer and example the Benedictine way of life. After completing the minor seminary course, I made my application to enter the abbey.

RCE: Were your parents and friends happy that you were going to the seminary?

Oh, yes, they were happy. I was ordained in 1929 by Bishop Joseph Chartrand. In 1932, I was given the opportunity to pursue graduate studies at Catholic University of America in Washington, D.C. In the three years I was there, I earned both a master's and a PhD. On my return to Saint Meinrad, I was given charge of modernizing and modifying our seminary curriculum with the title of director of studies.

RCE: When you were first here, were you allowed to have visitors?

They were not forbidden, but we're so isolated here very few people ever showed up. Once in a while, my folks came. They had difficulty getting here, but they would come. And that was true with others, too. It was because the roads were bad. When I first came here, you could hardly use an automobile because the roads were not paved; they were mud roads. I first came in a horse and buggy. You could also take the train part way.

From Ferdinand, it's about seven miles and Dale is about ten miles to here. It depended upon what train we came on. If we came on the Southern from Evansville, we usually got off at Dale. But if we came on the train from St. Louis through Huntingburg, we got off in Ferdinand. There was a small six-mile railroad called Ferdinand Flyer from Huntingburg to Ferdinand. In Ferdinand, or Dale, somebody from the monastery would meet us with a horse and buggy. My brother was in the Army [World War I] and he came one time for a visit. My father came a couple times. But that's about the only visitors I had. It was so hard to get here and people didn't travel that much.

RCE: What kind of transportation developed over the years?

We had bus service. It wasn't until the late '30s that the roads were improved, so the buses didn't show up until that time. We had good bus service from Evansville through here to Louisville. I think it was about 12 times a day a bus would come one way or the other through here or to Jasper. But the bus service just petered out, as we say. People used automobiles. They just didn't use the bus service anymore. That happened here, too, because if we had to go to Evansville or Louisville, we went by car as you could make the trip in one day, where taking the bus you couldn't get back that night.

RCE: What did you do on summer vacation when you were in the seminary?

I stayed at home with my parents and worked for the Sisters of Providence. They had different jobs in the summertime. My father was a decorator there and I helped him sometimes and sometimes I worked in the orchards. Whatever work they had for a young person, I did during the summer. I picked apples and cut weeds and so on.

ES and RCE: Describe your living conditions when you entered the minor seminary.

I entered the seminary when I was 17 years old. For sleeping, there were about 40 boys in a large room. It's now called Newman Hall. At that time in the high school dormitory, there were no divisions between the beds. One bed was here and another there with a chair between them. We had hooks to put our clothing on. The novices lived on the upper floor in a kind of dormitory. Each man was separated from his fellows by cur-

Fr. Theodore, as a young monk

tains that were intended to serve as partitions. Each one was closed and separate from the others. It included a bed, a chair, a table, a kneeling bench and a cupboard to put clothing in for storage. As novices, we kept our books at our desks in the study hall. Later, after we were professed, we were assigned to private cells.

ES and RCE: How about bathing and bathrooms when you first came here?

Our frequency of taking a bath depended on the water level of the Anderson River. When it wasn't high enough, we took sponge baths in our own quarters. Around 1923, we got indoor plumbing. Before that, we had no toilet inside so we had to go outdoors where there were toilets in an outbuilding. At night we hoped we didn't have to go. There was an emergency bathroom in the building next to the hallway, but generally we had to go outside.

The heating was not good in the winter. The Abbey Church was cold for Matins and Lauds. We had a dynamo that operated from about 4 a.m. until 9 at night. Thereafter, night silence prevailed. More electric current was brought into the monastery in the days of Franklin Roosevelt, under the Rural Electrification Act. As I recall, most of the monks voted in the elections.

ES: Reflect on your years in the novitiate. Describe something of the tone and nature of the discipline under which your vocation was formed.

Many years ago, discipline was stronger. Much of the time we were not permitted to talk socially, and night silence [no talking from Compline to after breakfast] was enforced. We did not have conversation at noon meal. Someone would do spiritual reading, such as the lives of saints, while we were at table. Very often, the reading was done in German. Sometimes the reading would introduce three languages: German, Latin and English. At that time, everyone would have to take his turn at reading. Today, the abbot appoints five or six readers, who divide the task among themselves. Of course, the holy *Rule of St. Benedict* influenced the style of our lives. It served to remind us of what we were—monks. Years ago, when I was a novice and young priest, we wore the habit nearly all the time. We always wore it when we prayed the Divine Office. The habit reminded you of your vocation.

ES: Does wearing the habit change the tone and rhythms of life in the religious community?

Yes, in many ways it does. We feel more secular, for instance, when we don't wear the habit. Nowadays, outside duties and commitments away from the Holy Hill affect the spirit and pace of community life. Concessions have been made in light of circumstances. We often come to noon prayer in our informal attire because other duties demand that we make accommodations in our schedules and routines. This is partly for convenience, but it is also necessary. Adaptation is considered, for the most part, both necessary and good. Today, the monks are freer than years ago. There were not many options left to the individual monk. At night, we had a little scapular. It was a little square piece of cloth with a hole in it. We'd put it over our shoulders and we wore that over pajamas.

The routines here become second nature. We have our lives together. We have our communal meals; we have an infirmary and all the medical care we need; we have our abbot to give us spiritual instruction. All these things give us a way of living. It may seem we are repeating the same thing over and over, but in truth, it is a constant program of growth.

RCE: What type of clothing did you wear when you went away from the monastery?

We always wore what we call a Roman collar and black clothes. I notice now many of the young people don't follow those traditions. When I go to a formal occasion, I still do. But if I am just going over to the hospital for a checkup or something, I just wear civilian clothes.

ES: Are there other differences between and now?

Friday evenings were for recollection and confession. Now we have the abbot's conference and a day of recollection on the first Monday of every month. Many monks are now committed to spending the weekends doing parish work. This also has an effect on our monastic practices. For example, a man's annual retreat has been cut down from eight days to six. More men seem to want to try out monastic life, but today we have more dropouts. Perhaps they are not as committed when they come in.

ES and RCE: How about health care when you were a young monk?

Another aspect of life in today's monastery has been the vastly improved health care available to the monks. We had one room set aside as an infirmary. It was on the second floor of what they call Newman Hall now. I think there were only two or three beds there. If we needed more room, they would put the beds in some of the other rooms. A brother was a nurse. He had been a nurse before he came to the monastery and was from New York, or someplace in that region. The materials were primitive. I don't believe we had the care that we have now. Remedies were more simple in those days.

The advances in science and medicine have been extraordinary, and we are the clear beneficiaries of new discoveries and medical techniques. Many monks have been given added years of life because of the improvements in health care. These have been changes for the good. I also believe people were stronger in those days. They were more resistant to sickness. We didn't have very much sickness. They were outside more and I think that helped them. Also, they were mostly younger people.

RCE: If somebody was very sick, was a doctor called?

Yes, a doctor would drop in. In the early years, he came by horse and buggy and later on by automobile. For a time, we had a doctor living downtown so he served us very well. Before that, we had the doctor from Tell City [IN]. They had a small hospital there at that time. That was before Jasper had a hospital. The doctor left Saint Meinrad sometime in the '40s.

We also had good service in the hospitals at Louisville and Evansville. We used the old St. Mary's Hospital before the newer one was built and different ones in Louisville. When people were very sick, they were always taken to the hospital. We didn't have the facilities to take care of them here.

RCE: Since you came here in 1918, during the Spanish flu epidemic, did anyone in the community get it or die from it?

I think we had the flu here, but nobody died of it here at Saint Meinrad. Two in theology went home during Christmastime and they both died. They were deacons. Those two were the only ones that I know of who died during this period. We are pretty well isolated, so I guess the flu germ didn't get around here as much as it did in the cities. The two men, the deacons, were to be ordained the following May. One was from Indianapolis and the other from Illinois. They probably got the flu when they got home. As far as I know, they were not sick when they left. They had two weeks' vacation. It was very sad.

RCE: Was anyone in the First World War?

We had one who was going to go, but he died of pneumonia. He died in the parish before he got to the Army. Other than him, I don't think there was anybody from the First World War.

RCE: How about the Second World War?

Oh, yes. The Army and Navy were always asking for help. Finally, the abbot gave permission. Those who wanted to go were able to go. We had eight or nine who were chaplains; they were volunteers. They served in all three services.

They were in Europe, Africa and Asia. It's hard to say just where, because they didn't report this information to us. The government didn't want them to tell where they were. This was especially true with the ones in the Air Force, as they were all over the world. Fr. Barnabas [Harrington, OSB] was a pilot in the service, but then he died later in an automobile accident. He was a pilot before he came to the monastery. He had a lot of friends who were pilots and they would take him along sometimes. Fr. Urban Knapp was in the Navy and Frs. Joachim Walsh, Cyril Vrablic and Basil Mattingly were in the Army. I have forgotten the names of the rest.

RCE: Did they all come back from the war?

No. A few of them, unfortunately, left the priesthood. We didn't have anybody who was killed in the war. But all of them who were in it have now died so there's nobody in the monastery who was actually a former chaplain. They've all passed away.

Work

ES and RCE: Tell me about your work.

In the fall of 1932, I was assigned to the Catholic University of America for a master's degree in education and for the degree of Doctor of Philosophy in school administration, sociology and psychology, which I received in 1935. The title of my dissertation was "The Curriculum of the Major Seminary in Relation to Contemporary Conditions." For this study, I visited 30 seminaries around the country and interviewed the officials of these institutions. This study was of special interest to the diocesan bishops and copies were sent at the request of the National Catholic Welfare Council to each diocese in the country.

When I returned to Saint Meinrad, I was appointed the director of studies from 1935 to 1955 and was assigned to revise the curriculum. We began the work for accreditation of the high school. It was accredited with the State Department of Education in 1931, and with the North Central Association of Secondary Schools and Colleges in 1937. Then we began to work for the accreditation of the college. This was begun with the State Department in 1938 and with the North Central Association in 1949.

Later on, the schools were affiliated with The Catholic University of America. The School of Theology was approved in 1943, giving the fourth-year students the choice of completing the fourth year in Washington, D.C., with the degree of licentiate in theology. The high school and college were affiliated with Catholic University in 1950. The college was accredited in 1961.

The traditional Catholic seminary was based on a six-year plan. It had six years in the Minor Seminary and six years in the Major Seminary; that's the old European tradition. Our college was the last two years in the Minor Seminary and two years of philosophy in the Major Seminary. These came before theology, which was a four-year course. Eventually around 1960, we changed the seminary's academic organization from these two six-year sequences to three four-year programs: high school, liberal arts college and graduate studies in theology.

RCE: Was financial separation also changed?

Not much financial separation, as the monastery had a department called the treasurer. They took care of the finances. We didn't have three treasuries. We had one treasurer and they took care of the high school, the college and theology finances. They are a very large department and so they could handle that. They still do that.

An external board, the Board of Overseers, was started about 1958-59. I was interested in this, so we started it when I was still the rector of the major seminary. It's been going ever since. It started out with a few men, but later on women also participated. We took people who were recommended. It now works very well and is over the whole school and the seminary.

RCE: How did you go about getting the college accredited?

To get the college accredited, I conversed with a number of men from different schools. I worked with the North Central Association and they helped me out. They suggested we separate the high school from the college. We had to have a special principal for the high school. We had to change to a rector, or president, for the college and a rector for the Major Seminary. So we had to separate into three different schools with three separate operations. The main difficulty of obtaining accreditation was getting the required subjects in our schools.

One of the major reasons for getting the college accredited was because many of our students wanted to transfer to other schools, but had difficulty getting in because we were not accredited. So we felt that we had to do something about this. Even the Army complained about the lack of accreditation. You see we had a number of men who went on to serve as chaplains. They were very effective as chaplains, but they didn't have a degree. So this was another reason we needed accreditation. A number of chaplains later on got their degree before they went into the military and having a degree was a big help to them. It's surprising how many of our students who transferred to other colleges went on for higher studies and became doctors, lawyers and professors.

RCE: What changes did you make in the curriculum to meet accreditation standards for the college?

We had what was called "classics training" here, where we focused on social studies and history. We had a pretty good history and English program. Mathematics was one of our weaknesses. We only had a couple of years of mathematics and science. We had to have more science to become accredited. Several of our fathers went to Purdue and got their science degrees and they started a science department.

Bede Hall was built [1952] for all the sciences. It had rooms and laboratories. After the college closed [1998], there was no need for science. They needed the room for dormitory space and so in the last few years they changed Bede Hall into guest rooms. During its time, it was a very fine building for the sciences. We had physics, we had chemistry and we had biology courses. We had advanced courses so students could get a degree later on if they went someplace else. They could get 16 or 18 hours of credit and then could take courses at another college and finish up. We didn't have a degree in science because it wasn't our focus, but we provided a good background for it. For priests, it's necessary to have a background for the kind of work they will be doing, but, at least, they had some science.

Traditionally, we had Latin, Greek and German as languages here. However, for accreditation we needed more modern languages, so we introduced Spanish. We had a sister teaching it for a while until one of our fathers had the necessary courses and then he took over the course. We've had French from about 1955 or '56, which continued until they closed the college.

RCE: Why did you close the college?

Lack of students. It became too expensive to keep it going. We were down to about 110 and you just can't run eight departments on 110 students. We were losing money so fast that we just decided we'd have to give it up. I'm sorry we had to do that, but we had to.

RCE: Is this the same reason that the high school was closed? Did Vatican II have anything to do with that?

I would say there are probably a couple reasons. Some of the bishops wanted the students to stay at home, so more Catholic high schools in local communities were built. Students then finished their high school at home. Of our three schools, the number of students in our high school was the largest. They would come for high school and then stay for college. When we had fewer people coming to our high school, fewer of them went into our college and then fewer of those went into theology. I would say that the high school broke the bridge. From then on, everything became smaller. By 1965, we had to give up the high school. We just didn't have enough students anymore. It had only been about five or six years before when we had the most students—around 1960.

RCE: What happened to the monks who were teaching in the high school?

Some of them got jobs right here in the monastery and some did parish work. Some of them were getting older and so they didn't have to work. We were able to let more people who seemed qualified to go out for graduate work. From this time on, we had more people going to universities than we used to. We had them go to Indiana University, University of Chicago, New York University, St. Louis University, Oxford and the Catholic universities in Rome.

From that time on, we felt we had to get these men more fully prepared, so more went to college. The younger ones went to college and some of the older ones went into visiting parish work. We had a number of parishes then and there was always need for a parish priest. Prior to that time, we usually sent people out on weekends to help out. Now they were able to take over some of the parish work itself.

RCE: For accreditation, were there requirements for the faculty to have doctoral degrees?

That was encouraged by Rome, so we tried to carry it out. We've had people get doctorates in Scripture, sacred theology and history.

RCE: When did Rome start to encourage the faculty in the theological school to have doctorates?

I think they always wished the seminaries would do this. About 1955, Rome encouraged it more and more. When summer schools developed, we were able to send more people for higher degrees and graduate work in the summer.

RCE: Was it only monks who taught in the schools?

Up to about 1960, practically everybody who taught was a monk. But from then on, we had some lay men and women and some sisters also teach. Our first teacher in Spanish was a sister from Ferdinand and then, after a couple of years, one of our fathers took over. Our French teacher was always a man who had studied in France. But in the fields of social studies and English, lay women and men and some sisters taught.

RCE: When did women students start to attend the theological school?

In the School of Theology, we didn't have any woman students prior to around 1980. They are not really students in theology. They can take courses with the theology students, but they are separate from the theology school. We had a summer school and most of the people who came were women, mostly sisters. This program was dropped in the last couple of years because people found it very hard to stay six weeks away from their work and their homes.

So now we have short courses of a week or two weeks or over Friday, Saturday and Sunday. It's often women who come down for these programs. They're not considered theologians in the School of Theology. It's kind of a separate school that they have for outside or lay people—lay degree students. They can do graduate studies in theology work and can get a Master of Arts [Catholic Thought and Life] or a Master of Theological Studies. They usually have to have a bachelor's degree before they come here, because we don't have a college anymore.

RCE: What did you teach over your lifetime?

I taught educational courses so we'd have the required courses for teaching licenses. Through the special interest of the Archdiocese of Indianapolis, a program for high school teacher training was worked out with the college and theology. We had this program for about 20 years, between 1940 and 1965. We had about a hundred students get their licenses to teach in English, Latin, social studies and history; and a few got it in Greek.

I remember when I asked Indianapolis if we could get a license for teaching Greek, they said, "We've never had a request for Greek from a high school," but they gave it to us anyway. We only had a few students who wanted to take on the Greek and I don't think they had many opportunities to teach it anyplace. But many of them still wanted to have a knowledge of Greek. This program provided many priests with licenses to teach in Catholic high schools throughout the area. When the shortage of priests for parish assignments became acute after 1965, we dropped our education curriculum for a lack of student applications.

RCE: What other work did you do?

During the years, I was subprior [1938-55], rector of the School of Theology [1956-66], prior of the Archabbey [1966-69] and parish priest [1969-87]. During several summers, in addition to parish work, I taught summer school at St. Benedict College, Ferdinand, IN [1936-43], and Loras College, Dubuque, IA [1944-57], in the fields of education and religion. Since my retirement in 1987, I have spent my time in the monastery living the daily life and schedule of the institution.

Prayer

RCE: What is your favorite part of the Rule of St. Benedict?

The Prologue and Chapter 73. The Prologue sets the stage for the entire *Rule* and Chapter 73 is the conclusion that brings it all together.

Faith is the steel that keeps us together. People won't believe if there are bad examples and might easily drift away from the Church. The very expectations of life in our society at large have changed. People, if they do not live by a moral code, will surely lose their sense of judgment. We need to acquire virtue from our natural and spiritual natures. We need more charity to reach out and help others. We profit from communion with God. Happy are they who have kept the faith with a gentle heart. The *Rule* teaches us that respect for life and social justice are very important values.

ES and RCE: What is your key to Benedictine spirituality?
    I feel that the Benedictine *Rule* provides guidelines for both religious and laity to lead them to the goal for which they were created: to know, love and serve God and one's fellows. The *Rule* defines our values very clearly, even though it was written 1,500 years ago. The monastery serves as a great safeguard for our spiritual lives and happiness.

ES and RCE: What has been the most difficult time of your life?
    I suppose when I was making the decision to become a religious. Thinking about giving up the world and so on. I finally decided to go to the seminary. I think that was the biggest decision I've ever made.
    When I think about it, I have not had a deep sorrow in my life. The passing by death of relatives and confreres brings grief, but there is always the hope of eternal life toward which we all are striving. It is a sorrow that religion does not seem to have a hold on many people. People who have abused their lives, morally or physically, cause me to feel sorrow, but prayer and the mercy of God bring hope.
    On the whole, even the difficult days had a silver lining. I appreciate all the more when I look back at the opportunities and problems that have been a part of my life. I see how they have been solved and I am thankful more and more for my monastic life.

RCE: How about your happiest times?

I would say when I made my profession and later on when I was ordained. Those were two great things for my life.

Vatican II: Its Effect on the Church and Saint Meinrad Archabbey

ES: Changes as the result of Vatican II seem to have been inevitable; what has this meant to the Church?

We can't remake yesterday. It once took three weeks to cross the Atlantic Ocean; now it takes only a few hours. The world changes. There is nothing wrong with all this, of course. When I was a boy, very few of my classmates went on to high school; even fewer attended college. The opposite is true today. I remember when most people lived in a rural world. Now two-thirds of the people live in cities and other urban areas. Yet we have approximately the same amount of territory as we had in 1776. Things change.

Science and technology have developed at an astonishing rate. Just this morning I saw a tractor pulling 16 plows. In the horse-and-buggy days, I recall, a horse or mule pulled two plows. All in all, the modern world is well served by the new technology. Even so, it presents one problem: we're still trying to catch up.

Bishops have a hard job nowadays to fit everything together, especially since they've lost the grade schools. Because of the many problems that have come up in recent years, they have a hard job of managing the Church. I think that's true in other fields, too. In other words, all the churches have the same problems, so it's universal. People are moving out so much now that they don't have the family life anymore that they had years ago. That was what held us together, spiritually and emotionally, the family, a close family life. Now the kids go out to preschool, from three years on. It used to be they didn't usually go out of the home until they were six or seven. Ideally, it would be nice if they could just be centered in the home during that whole period of pre-adolescence and adolescence, because that's where they learn to settle down.

I think Christian social life is suffering very much nowadays. We all feel it in a way, but it's hard to put your finger on something to do. Some of the bishops are trying to get the parochial schools started again, but the expenses are so high. People don't like to make the commitment anymore. For instance, years ago when the sisters taught, they got nothing, maybe $600 a year. Now they want $17,000 or $18,000 a year.

People, teachers and the parishes just don't have that much gift money to give. Many of the parishes are struggling just to keep the church and their families going. Many people now have lost their jobs. They don't have any source of income. They especially don't have the insurance. It's a real hardship, I think, all the way around. I don't know what they are going to do. Someplace along the line, people are going to have to work out something.

RCE: Is this unique to our time period? Think back to your experiences in World War I or the 1930s.

The First World War was worse. I had two brothers in the service during that time. Of course, we had financial difficulty, but it was not as bad as it is now. I think it's worse now. More families are hard-pressed for income to support their families. More people are going into debt and more people are moving around. They are restless.

Over a million people are moving from Mexico into the United States for jobs and we're not able to handle this very well. People are complaining that these immigrants take their jobs. But the types of jobs they take are very menial. I don't think many Americans care to do that kind of work. So they can't say much about it as the immigrants help keep some of the prices down by making things cheaper. Still, things are pretty expensive. Those companies that go outside our country to establish their businesses still charge as much as they did before. They went to these other countries because it had cheaper labor, but they didn't reduce the prices. That's a problem.

ES and RCE: How has change over the past few decades affected the Church, the Archabbey?

All in all, the health of the Church is good today. But the secular world does not pay much attention to the role of religion. People want freedom from the commandments. Of course, this has an effect on our Benedictine community, too. In any case, we are free only to do what is right. Tradition, custom and obedience fit better into our lives under obedience. Cardinal Hume said that an obedient religious has acquired an interior freedom. Hume believed that too much independence destroys freedom. "I do not believe," he said, "that the work of an individual, if it is not done well, is in accord with obedience."

We founded three abbeys during the [pre-Vatican II] era and we gave them a lot of our members. It made us much smaller. But we should consider ourselves lucky, as we still have the School of Theology. The main function of Saint Meinrad has always been training priests. The bishops dropped some of our parishes, so we didn't have as many outside parishes anymore so that gave us a few more priests. Each one of our foundations became an abbey once it became independent. There is an organization of all the abbeys, but the maintenance and governance of the abbey is independent.

ES: Even if the Mass were to be celebrated in English, was eliminating Latin from the academic curriculum a good idea?

I have not been disappointed by the change from Latin into English. In plain chant, the major work has been done by Fr. Columba [Kelly, OSB]; his adaptations have been outstanding. Liturgy is our external form for keeping faith alive. We use this form to carry on our Christian life, an asset that the secular world lacks. Many of those who complain today that the Mass is no longer celebrated in Latin or who don't like other aspects of the revised liturgy are simply homesick for the old days. Many Catholics have not yet caught up. This shows up in the parishes, where pastors are sometimes slow to inaugurate the changes. But gradually they will catch up!

261

RCE: Why do you think there was a decline in vocations post mid-1960s compared to the 1920s when you first came here?

Prior to the 1960s, many bishops or dioceses paid for part of the students' board and tuition. After the 1960s, they cut off funding, so many students didn't have the money to continue their education. I'd say finances had a whole lot to do with it. Some students were able to be supported by their parents, so they could continue. Others just gave up and went into secular life.

Also, for some people, the priesthood program was too severe, too tough for them, so they didn't want to go ahead. For others who got out, I think they had problems, personal problems, and so decided not to go on to the priesthood. Some wanted to get married and so the priesthood was out of the question.

RCE: What is being done now to increase vocations?

We give talks in various parishes nearly every Sunday where we encourage people, and families, to think about getting some of their children to give service to God. We have a summer school for young people to visit and think about it. If they're thinking about a vocation for the priesthood, they're advised to come for a week or two. We have several of them doing that every summer. Not many of them are deciding to become priests, but at least they're thinking about it. I believe there are a lot of young people who are worried. They know that there are problems in society and their generation has to do something and so some of them are thinking about a vocation. Some come and some don't.

It used to be if a young person had brothers or sisters or other relatives going through priesthood or religious life, they often followed suit. Now there are fewer people going into a religious vocation and so young people don't have those models to look to. Some say that since they don't have the sisters in the grade school, we don't have as many vocations in the sisterhood. I think that's true, as many sisters thought about their vocation from the time they were in grade school.

ES and RCE: What are your hopes for the future of the Church?

Now that I am in the latter days of life, my hopes are primarily spiritual, accepting God's will for the future. I do a good bit of reading in the field of sacred Scripture, history, biology, social science and current events. I have kept a record of the books and booklets that I have read. The total is now well over 2,000.

In the final analysis, the community must demand the truth and practice faith. The individual must be supported by a believing community. If it's everyone for himself/herself, the community will lack cohesiveness and a pervasive rationality and morality. When parishes were made up of basically individual ethnic groups, there did truly exist a sense of unity within the community; one had a feeling of belonging. People felt more settled and at home in their parishes and neighborhoods then.

ES and RCE: How about the Archabbey?

I think we've got to try to hold together more carefully and be more modest in our expenses. I am looking forward to the time when we have our garden again. In one way, Benedictine life is an endless adaptation because changes in the culture affect monastic life. Change must be seen in this context. This is similar to the Congress and the Supreme Court, who have to keep the Constitution up to date. The abbots meet every four years to make sure that the Order adheres to the true spirit of the holy *Rule*. Prudent adaptations should be made as needed. As Fr. Henry Brenner used to say, "We all have to keep poking at the fire to keep it alive." Good advice!

Profile based upon: Fr. Theodore Heck to Prof. Ed Shaughnessy, July 7 and 9, 2004, and to Prof. Ruth C. Engs, June 13, 2005, Interview Transcriptions, Saint Meinrad Archives.

Heck, Theodore, "Typewritten paper," n.d., Saint Meinrad Archives.

Chapter Twelve

John MacCauley laid the foundation for Saint Meinrad's Development Office.

Finance and Fund Raising: Support of the Abbey

Rupert Ostdick, OSB, Eric Lies, OSB, Daniel Schipp, John Wilson, with Ruth C. Engs

Writing about finances and "fund raising" (now called development) might appear to be an unusual companion chapter for an oral history of older monks. However, the financial cycles of Saint Meinrad during the lifetime of the monks profiled in this book present a model of wise investing, acceptance and survival strategies in a post-Vatican II world. Without solid financial management, there has always been the danger of demise of any institution.

The finances of monastic communities, like other institutions, have waxed and waned.[1] Although individual monks, friars and nuns took vows of poverty, the community as a whole, in many cases, did not have these restrictions. Old established orders such as the Benedictines and Cistercians became very wealthy in the Middle Ages. They were often founded and supported by aristocrats whose family lands became the monastery's holdings. The monastery generally owned the town and surrounding countryside and collected rent and tithes from tenants and gleaned income from crops, livestock and forests. With good fiscal management, the monastic community was able to obtain much from these enterprises and increase its assets.[2]

However, as evidenced by the ruins of abbeys that dot the European landscape, monastic communities also ceased to exist due to internal mismanagement or external social, political and economic forces. In times of trouble, monasteries with much property, wealth and power were often able to survive, and adapt, to changes. Others found their rich holdings confiscated by new political elites or hostile forces and were forced to disband. During the Reformation, monasteries almost disappeared from countries where Protestantism became the official religion and even dwindled in Catholic countries. A few like Monte Cassino, the traditional home of Benedictines, fell into ruins several times over the centuries, only to rise again.[3]

One secondary reason for the foundation of Saint Meinrad was to provide a place of refuge from the late 18th- through early 19th-century political suppression of the Church and its holdings in Western Europe. Like other communities established in the New World, the Swiss Benedictines who founded Saint Meinrad struggled to survive initially under the patronage of its European abbey.[4] Communities in the United States, such as Saint Meinrad, as part of their mission and as a mechanism for financial survival, established schools, presses, farms and seminaries to train priests.[5] By the turn of the 20th century, most American communities were independent of their European founders.[6]

Through the mid-20th century, communities survived financially through a mixture of activities. These included agriculture, parish donations, cottage industries, endowments and fees from students. Staffs for schools and other enterprises were inexpensive, as they were largely composed of nuns or monks with a few lay people hired to do certain activities. However, the financial and personnel situation in many monasteries began to change in the 1960s. With a decrease in religious vocations in the wake of Vatican II, lay people increasingly began to teach and work in Catholic schools and monastic communities. This increase in lay employees led to financial problems in many institutions, as salaries and benefits were needed to pay outside co-workers. Schools and colleges attached to monasteries found decreasing enrollments and new governmental regulations forced them to give up business not specific to their missions. By the last decade of the 20th century, many monasteries struggled to survive.[7]

In an effort to remedy these trying times, traditional "self-sufficient" monastic enterprises that were losing money were often sold off and development offices were established to work hand in hand with the business or finance office to help generate funds. Saint Meinrad is an example of a community that has survived, although it was forced to make painful decisions in the process. By 2005, it was seen as a model of success by other religious communities and theological schools. Of the monks interviewed in this book, Fr. Rupert Ostdick, OSB, was integral to the finances and business aspect of the community and the Abbey Press. Fr. Eric Lies, OSB, was a major player at Abbey Press and the Development Office. Fr. Simeon Daly, OSB, and Abbot Bonaventure Knaebel, OSB, worked in the Development Office during their retirement from other duties.

Finances and Support from the 1950s through the Early 1970s

Many schools, hospitals, and not-for profit institutions changed to a more business-like management in the post-World War II era.

Responsibility for financial matters "on the Hill"—the colloquial term for the Saint Meinrad community—until the 1950s had generally been confined to the abbot and a small group of advisors. Changes to a more transparent system resulted in monks having more knowledge of the state of the finances of their institution and personal involvement in hard financial decisions.

Budgetary and Accounting Reorganization of the 1950s

Not-for-profit enterprises through the first half of the 20th century generally did not require budgets for their departments within the institution. The Business Office just covered their expenses. In 1948, Fr. Rupert Ostdick became treasurer of the community after first serving as assistant treasurer for a little over a year. Around 1950, he asked department heads to prepare budgets to present the financial records of the community in a more business-like manner. This information was also needed as a requirement for accreditation of Saint Meinrad's schools.[8]

Over the 1960s, a decrease in the number of vocations, monks leaving to found Marmion and Blue Cloud communities, and an increase in students in the Archabbey schools led to a large number of lay co-workers being employed in the schools and other Saint Meinrad businesses. On January 1, 1951, these workers fell under the amended Social Security Act. They also had health and optional life insurance, which increased the community's expenses. The first certified public audit of the community's finances was held in 1951. The new recordkeeping system pointed out the financial drain of the schools upon the community in terms of teachers' salaries and continued education, maintaining present facilities and building new ones.[9]

These expenses resulted in a re-evaluation of the monastery's fiscal policies. By the early 1960s, it became evident that its financial operation would have to become more efficient if the schools were to maintain their high standing. In 1963, Fr. Martin Dusseau, OSB, the new business manager, was appointed to supervise the reorganization of the Archabbey's business procedures. As part of this process, an analysis defining the duties and function of each department and encouraging better coordination between them was carried out. The evaluation of the economic productivity of a unit and the phasing out of unproductive ones, based upon a business model, were discussed.[10]

In early spring of 1963, the community began discussions of the future of the Archabbey complex in terms of finances. These included the high school, new building construction and the various business enterprises of the Archabbey.[11] It was realized that "something must be done to supplement income from tuition if the seminary was to remain financially stable. But what?"[12]

Abbey Press

The Abbey Press has been a major source of income for Saint Meinrad for decades. A chapter titled "The Abbey Press: The Illumination of the Abbey" is found in this book. Therefore, only highlights of its history and activities as it relates to finances and development will be touched upon here. The Press began in 1867 with the purchase of a secondhand printing press for community and seminary needs such as leaflets, programs for the college, memorial cards and other small items. Many of the early printings were in Latin or German.[13]

Several magazines were started in the 1890s by the Press, but were soon discontinued as they created debt. In 1914, Fr. Edward Berheide, OSB, was assigned to manage the Press. He was the first manager to envision the potential of the operation as a method of financial support for the community. With the purchase of new printing machinery, the Press began to print hospital forms, stationery and the like, which made a profit. Fr. Edward also hired men and boys from the town to help the monastic brothers with the printing. Under his leadership, *The Grail*, a family magazine, was introduced in 1919; it was in English. By 1930, the Press was turning a profit.

However, by the mid-1930s, due to the Depression, the building of new facilities to house the operation, and limited sales of its products, excessive debt ensued and Fr. Edward was relieved of his duties in 1934. A variety of people and committees succeeded him. In 1941, Fr. Paschal Boland, OSB, took over management of Grail Publishing and expanded it to include the publishing of books; its financial state turned around. The operation was divided into two divisions: Abbey Press, a print shop; and Grail Publications, a publisher and book dealer.[14]

By the early 1950s, 27 full-time workers were employed at the facility in addition to a few monks. The Press printed a variety of material including doctoral dissertations, reference books, pamphlets, the ORDO and scholarly journals.[15] In 1950, Fr. Eric Lies was appointed associate editor and art director for *The Grail*. In 1958, he became manager of the Publishing Division of Abbey Press. Br. Maurus Zoeller, OSB, who had worked in printing for several years, became manager of the Printing Division in 1960.

In December 1959, *The Grail* changed its name to *Marriage*, with more focus on marriage and family life.[16] By 1962, the Press was printing 14 periodicals.[17]

A major reorganization of Abbey Press took place in 1966. Fr. Eric was made general manager of the whole Abbey Press and the Publishing Division. Br. Maurus remained as printing manager and Ned Watts, a lay artist from Louisville, KY, was named marketing manager.[18] In that year, Abbey Press acquired the publishing rights of Berlinger & McGinnis, a religious card company, and expanded further.[19]

As part of continued reorganization, in 1967 the printing and publishing units combined into a single entity.[20] Still more changes occurred in 1968. Br. Maurus became product development director and Fr. Eric began working at the newly formed Development Office; Fr. Paschal became general manager.[21] From 1962 to 1966, the income of the operation averaged around $800,000 per year and it was the primary financial support of the Archabbey.[22]

The Beginnings of a Modern Development Program

By 1966, the operational deficit of Saint Meinrad College was $218,000, and the School of Theology $122,000.[23] The community leadership realized that "St. Meinrad College and School of Theology will, like all schools, have to turn to outside sources to make up the differences between the cost of education and student fees."[24] This led to Saint Meinrad being one of the first religious communities to institute a comprehensive development program.

Before the foundation of a complete development program, small fundraising campaigns aimed at alumni for specific projects had been carried out.[25] The seeds of modern development at Saint Meinrad were planted in the winter of 1963 by Abbot Bonaventure Knaebel, when he appointed a Development Program Committee of monks to formulate a comprehensive program for Saint Meinrad. In 1965, a second committee was formed.[26] The current vice president for development, Dan Schipp, in 2005 suggested that the community "had the wisdom to establish a development program, even though there was some resistance to that at the outset, because Benedictines are not mendicants and some in the community…saw development as 'begging.'"[27]

The recommendations of the development committee resulted in three major actions. The consulting firm of Gonser, Gerber, Tinker, and Stuhr of Chicago was hired in 1965 to plan a development program. It helped Saint Meinrad formulate a comprehensive long-range plan with major objectives so that specific programs could be measured against attainment of these objectives. This type of planning had been common for many years in industry, but was relatively new to education.[28]

Secondly, the Board of Trustees (the governing board of the schools) was restructured to include both clergy and laity in 1966. A Board of Overseers, an advisory board to the presidents of the College and School of Theology, was also created. It was also made up of both laity and clergy. Thirdly, the architectural firm of Victor Christ-Janer & Associates, New Canaan, CT, in association with Design Environmental Group

271

Architects, Louisville, KY, was retained to develop a master plan for the future needs of the schools and monastic community, which it presented in 1966. The master plan divided Saint Meinrad into four main sections: Monastic Life, School of Theology Life, College Life, and Guest Accommodations.[29]

In 1967, shortly after the installation of Abbot Gabriel Verkamp, OSB, the consulting firm's recommendation of a full-fledged development program was put in place. John S. MacCauley, a layman who had worked in development, began as director of development and public relations on July 1, 1967. MacCauley had about 20 years' experience in these fields. Soon after he had graduated from the University of Notre Dame, he had formed a public relations firm in New York City. In May 1954, he returned to his alma mater as assistant director of the Notre Dame Foundation and helped establish their development program. He also served in public relations. From 1962 until 1966, he had been vice president for development and public relations at St. Norbert College, DePere, WI. He then worked for a year at the University of Albuquerque before joining Saint Meinrad.[30]

MacCauley's program and development philosophy, still in place today, is based on three simple concepts: 1) to facilitate institutional planning, 2) to communicate the values, mission and goals of Saint Meinrad, and 3) to invite participation and investment in Saint Meinrad and its work. Another goal, "building and nurturing relationships with alumni, benefactors and others who share in Saint Meinrad's mission," was later added.[31] As part of the overall philosophy, two important values of the Archabbey are "hospitality and service in the Benedictine tradition and gratitude toward all who participate in the prayer and work of Saint Meinrad."[32]

The first goal of MacCauley's development program—institutional planning—was to facilitate the community's and its various units' efforts in long-range planning. This planning was not to be done by the Development Office. The office was to serve as the catalyst for planning by the Archabbey and to insure that both long- and short-term planning was a continuous process. Out of strategic planning on the part of the institution, the agenda and priorities for the Development Office could be established.[33]

The full-time staff of the new department in the summer of 1967, besides MacCauley, included Arlene Schipp in a secretarial role. There were several part-time monks.[34] Janet Werne, in a secretarial role, joined the staff in the fall. Fr. Eric, a member of the two Development Program Committees (1964-67), became associate director of development in 1968. He was "MacCauley's right-hand man and a co-architect of the development program."[35] He had experience in layout and design. In addition to administrative duties, he entered names on certificates for donors in calligraphy. This artform became a trademark for Saint Meinrad.[36] By 1973, the office staff also included Paul Stabile and the former Fr. Louis Range.[37]

Communication is the second goal of development at Saint Meinrad. MacCauley in 1973 wrote that when he first came to the institution he found a "serious lack of communication" both within the tri-communities of Saint Meinrad [members of the monastic community, the College and the School of Theology] and also with Saint Meinrad and its major constituencies such as alumni, pastors, friends, etc.[38] MacCauley warned that the three Saint Meinrad groups needed to come to a consensus as to their values and mission before "any effective fund raising would result."

Therefore, a major task of the newly formed office was to facilitate effective communication within the community. After this had been achieved, a consensus among the administrators of Saint Meinrad, the Board of Overseers and the Board of Trustees deemed that the primary mission of the institution was a continuation of the education of men for the priesthood. Long-range planning was then undertaken by the College and School of Theology to meet this continuing goal.[39]

Better communication to "tell the story of Saint Meinrad" to friends and alumni through its publications was organized. To reduce potential confusion and misunderstanding from printed materials put out by different departments, key people at the Archabbey and the development staff reviewed all material before it was published.[40] The office reorganized the publications schedule of its various newsletters. In the spring of

1957, the *Saint Meinrad Newsletter* had been launched. It had news from the Archabbey, seminaries and alumni. Ten years later, this newsletter was redesigned for specific audiences. A monthly *Alumni News Bulletin* for clerical and lay alumni and the *St. Meinrad College Newsletter* for the College were introduced in the spring and early summer of 1967. Another edition of the *Saint Meinrad Newsletter* began to focus on events at the monastery and, in the fall of 1967, a Theology Edition of the newsletter began.[41]

The newsletters have changed names and formats several times; from 1980 to 2003, the *Alumni News Bulletin* became the *Saint Meinrad Alumni Newsletter*. In September 1980, news concerning the Archabbey, the College and the School of Theology were combined into one newsletter. In 1996, with volume 37, the newsletter became smaller in size. The *Saint Meinrad Newsletter* merged with the *Alumni Newsletter* to become *On the Hill* in the summer of 2003. It is sent to friends and alumni four times a year and gives general information concerning all aspects of the Archabbey. The *Saint Meinrad Annual Report*, with variations in subtitles, was launched in 1967 by the Development Office. It is sent out yearly to benefactors and friends of Saint Meinrad and focuses on the financial status of the institution.

The last leg of the tripod of development, outlined by MacCauley, was inviting others to participate and invest in Saint Meinrad and its work. MacCauley did not like the word "fund raising." He contended that the "ultimate goal of Development is to enable the institution to achieve its mission. Financial support is not an end in itself. It is a means to an end. Our primary task in development is to make sure that the end, the work of educating priests, deacons and lay ministers, remains clearly in view at all times."[42] Therefore, he believed that if the goals and values of the community were effectively communicated, people would respond to continue the prayer and work of Saint Meinrad.

Various programs evolved to tell the story of Saint Meinrad and to invite participation. Annual alumni dinners in cities where many lay and clerical alumni resided were held. Reunions on the Hill, regional gatherings of alumni and friends, overseas tours and personal contact with alumni were instituted. These programs made it possible to seek out alumni leaders, who then began to discuss Saint Meinrad and its work.

In 1968, a program called "Saint Meinrad Sunday" was started and led by Fr. Eric. On a particular Sunday, a monk would be sent to a parish in a local diocese (with the bishop's permission) to discuss the need for vocations and support for the seminary. Through this program, Catholic communities would learn that between 95 and 97 percent of their priests have received education at Saint Meinrad and the importance of continuing this mission.[43] This parish program became successful. All these new ventures, including a challenge grant in 1970, resulted in increased monetary investments in Saint Meinrad and its work. Total gift income rose from $253,000 in 1968-69 to $623,000 in 1973.[44]

Finances and Support from Late 1970s through the Early 1990s

A capital campaign, shrewd investing and the redirection of Abbey Press allowed Saint Meinrad to prosper through the 1980s.

Financial Decisions, Investments and the Abbey Press

In June of 1978, John Wilson, a native of Evansville, IN, with a degree in accounting from the University of Evansville, was hired by Abbey Press, but was transferred almost immediately to the Business Office. In May the following year, Fr. Rupert was appointed interim, and in November, general manager of the Abbey Press by the new Abbot Timothy Sweeney, OSB. Former Br. Luke Hodde, OSB, was appointed treasurer/business manager and Wilson became his assistant. About 11 years later when Br. Luke decided to leave the community, Wilson was appointed treasurer/business manager June 12, 1989, the first lay person to hold this job. As financial officer, he works closely with the Development Office and has been involved with the finances of the community through the present.[45]

The Abbey Press grew dramatically over the 1970s and 1980s. It had its largest growth in terms of personnel, productivity and profits and evolved into a direct-mail order business. In addition to printed materials, a religious sculpture operation began in 1971. Three divisions now made up the Press: printing, publishing and sundry products. They had "the common goal of making known the Word of God through the media of the graphic arts and other allied arts and to provide resource materials and products."[46] Abbey Press "Care Notes," first published in 1988 for hospitals, waiting rooms and religious organizations, quickly became popular.[47]

From the 1980s, Abbey Press made most of its money from July to December. For two or three months, money was needed to cover expenses. This was most often borrowed from funds set aside to function as endowment. Up until the early 1990s, these endowments were primarily invested in fixed income securities due to the theory that the institution's need for cash should come from dividends and interest. In 1991, a major shift in this investment strategy took place.[48]

The Uniform Management of Institutional Funds Act, as adopted by the state of Indiana in 1989, allowed not-for-profit institutions to appropriate the appreciation of their investment in excess of the historical value and not just the yield from dividends or interest.[49] Therefore, over a two-year period, the asset allocation was changed to about 65 percent stocks, 30 percent bonds and 5 percent cash investments. Wilson recalls, "This financial strategy was implemented during the biggest bull market in the history of the market...Saint Meinrad made a good decision, the market, the timing was beautiful." The actions enabled the Archabbey to change its investment philosophy.[50]

Analysis of Saint Meinrad's investments indicated that it would be more cost efficient for short-term borrowing to borrow from the bank rather than its investments, if it was assumed that the total return on the portfolio would be greater than the cost of the loan. Thus the institution stopped borrowing internally and used a local bank for short-term borrowing.

The Development Office and the First Capital Campaign

Abbot Timothy, early in his tenure, established an endowment committee. It had two subcommittees: one to focus on managing endowments and the other to focus on obtaining gifts. In 1979, Saint Meinrad was one of 15 seminaries in the United States to receive a grant from Lilly Endowment, Inc. to train development officers in the process of "planned giving" and "estate planning." Dan Conway was hired to undergo this training and to direct the planned giving program. Conway had been a work-study student with MacCauley, graduated from Saint Meinrad College, and received a master's in religious studies from Indiana University. He had taught religious studies in a high school and at John Carroll University and had been chair of the Theology Department at Walsh Jesuit High School, Stow, OH.[51] Schipp suggests that, "Dan was the communicator, the planner and the institutionalizer, if I may use that word, of [MacCauley's] vision. He's the one who really focused on making sure that the Saint Meinrad community—our boards, faculty and staff—paid due attention to communicating and communicating well. I think his particular gift was his writing."[52]

In 1980, under the guidance of MacCauley, Conway and Fr. Eric, the Development Office instituted the first capital campaign in the history of the institution, called "The Case for Saint Meinrad."[53] The purpose of the campaign was to raise $7.5 million to build a new monastery and a new library and to renovate older buildings based upon the master plan for the institution. Gregory G. Kempf, a member of the Board of Overseers and chairman of the Development Committee, became chairman of the campaign. When about half of the funds had been raised, groundbreaking began in the summer of 1980 for the new buildings.[54]

In 1982, the new monastery and library were completed and the capital campaign goals were met. In that same year, Lilly Endowment, Inc. invited the institution to participate in a matching grant program designed to strengthen educational institutions in Indiana. The terms of this grant required that Saint Meinrad raise a minimum of $1.5 million by February 1985 to receive a grant of $500,000 for renovation and energy conservation. The renovation project of refurbishing the old library and monastery (now faculty offices and St. Anselm Hall) would have a total cost of $5 million, so the building was accomplished in two phases. The first phase was for construction of faculty offices on the two floors of the old library wing. The funds were raised through a "mini-campaign," not a full-fledged capital campaign.[55]

The Development Office added more staff members and made several changes in leadership between 1981 and 1985. MacCauley was promoted in October 1981 to vice president for development and Conway became director of development. Dan Schipp joined the development staff in December 1982 as assistant to Fr. Eric. Schipp, a native of Ferdinand, IN, and a graduate of Notre Dame, had worked in several fields including teaching. In 1976, he came back to southern Indiana and started work with several development groups, including Lincoln Hills Development Corp. and Foresight Development Corp., where he wrote grants for small cities and towns in the area.[56]

In September 1983, MacCauley became senior consultant for planning and development. Conway assumed MacCauley's responsibilities as Saint Meinrad's chief development officer. Fr. Meinrad Brune, OSB, in 1984 was appointed associate director of development and was responsible for supervising the Development Office, including the recording and acknowledgment of gifts. The following year he became alumni director. In 1985 when MacCauley retired, Conway was promoted to vice president of planning and development and Schipp filled Conway's position as director of development.[57]

During the same time, the endowment was beginning to show some growth. The total endowment at Saint Meinrad grew from $1.3 million in 1979 to $3.9 million in 1984.

Some new programs emerged in the late 1980s. The Einsiedeln Society was established in 1987 as an organization to recognize people who have remembered Saint Meinrad in their wills, entered into a planned giving agreement, or who have made gifts totaling $5,000 or more for an endowment purpose.[58] In 1988, a mini-campaign called the "Challenge For Excellence," aimed at building an endowment for the homiletics program and renovating facilities for the communications curriculum in the College, was launched. This $1.5 million effort was in response to a challenge grant from a friend of Saint Meinrad, Virginia Marten, and the Lilly Endowment.[59]

In 1988, Conway left Saint Meinrad to become the director of development for the Archdiocese of Louisville and Schipp was promoted to vice president for development.[60] Schipp considered his role to be "the activator and facilitator of a total development process, team builder, bridge builder between Saint Meinrad and our various constituencies." Because long-range planning was now institutionalized, he focused his attention on inviting participation in the prayer and work of the community, especially the work of educating parish priests, and to "view development as a ministry and profession rather than a 'business' or 'sales.'"[61] The endowment was still growing; it had risen to $11.5 million in 1991.[62]

Into the Valley of the Shadow...The '60s-early '70s, the '90s

Financial stability of any institution has ups and downs. Saint Meinrad had two financial crises in the late 20th century. These resulted from several factors, including a decrease in young men interested in religious vocations, the building of diocesan schools and, in its wake, fewer students at Saint Meinrad High School, changes in governmental regulations for agriculture endeavors and not-for-profit organizations, and renovation and new building construction.

The 1950s through 1970s

The change to a fiscal business model in the 1950s pointed out not only the financial drain of the schools, but also the unprofitability of other traditional monastic businesses such as livestock and agriculture. Construction for a new science building, which became known as

St. Bede Hall, began in 1948.[63] However, the project, finished in 1952, led
to a debt of about $2 million. Due to increased visitors, student enroll-
ments and compliance with Vatican Council II directives for the training
of future priests, new construction and renovations of existing structures
needed to be accomplished. A guest house was built in 1961. In 1968,
Benet Hall, in 1969, the Archabbey Church, and in 1971, the fourth floor
of St. Bede Hall were renovated, which resulted in further financial strain
on the community.[64]

Due to this increased financial stress, around 1970, John Berry, a CPA
from Evansville who was described as having a "brusque personality,"
offered his assistance as a financial consultant.[65] He supposedly said that
"a monastery was not immune to bankruptcy" and recommended that to
decrease costs, the Archabbey should shut down the farming operation
and reduce the number of outside employees. Although his advice was
not popular, ultimately, his recommendations were reluctantly carried
out by the community in the mid-1970s.[66]

The High School

In 1861, Saint Meinrad opened a seminary for those considering the
priesthood.[67] By 1886, as mandated by national seminary reforms, Saint
Meinrad formed a Minor Seminary (four years of high school and first two
years of college) and Major Seminary (last two years of college and four
years of theology), which had various formats over the ensuing years. In
1933, the traditional American plan of four years of high school, four years
of college and four years of seminary were listed as departments within
the schools. The high school department was given permanent accreditation in 1939 under the guidance of Fr. Theodore Heck, OSB.[68]

In the 1950s, dioceses that previously sent students interested in the
priesthood to Saint Meinrad, had built, or were building, their own pre-
seminary schools. In the wake of Vatican II, higher standards were
required for those entering religious life. Some psychologists also suggested that it was better for boys to stay with their families during their

formative years than to go away to school. These considerations led some Saint Meinrad monks to feel that boarding schools, such as theirs, were not needed.[69]

By the early 1960s, Saint Meinrad's high school furnished few students who went on to study for the priesthood, although it had one of the highest enrollments in its history. On March 5, 1965, after much debate, the monks reluctantly voted to phase out the high school.[70] The closure of the school was traumatic, as it had been part of the monastery since its beginnings and was the life work of many monks.[71] Fr. Meinrad Brune notes that, after the vote, he found Fr. Herman Romoser, OSB, the rector, in tears. However, Fr. Herman told him, "I truly believe that the Holy Spirit was with the community as the monks decided to close the high school by the chapter vote."[72] Sadly, the rector died five months later from a pulmonary embolism after a simple hernia operation. The painful decision to close the school, in the long run, along with other difficult decisions such as selling its traditional agricultural businesses, helped the monastery to survive.

Farming, Livestock and Other Businesses

Details concerning agriculture and other natural resources businesses will be found in a separate chapter, "Land: Sustenance of the Abbey"; therefore, only a brief summary and its effect upon finances will be covered here. The farm had been one of the first efforts established by the community in 1854.[73] It expanded over the decades into a major operation. However, the new accounting methods of the 1950s showed that the farm was becoming less profitable. From 1955 through 1974, many agricultural operations were closed as they were losing money.

In the fall of 1955, all of the vineyards near the monastery were pulled up and transferred, along with the orchards, to Monte Cassino Hill. By December 1962, all of the gardens were closed due to lack of farm labor.[74] In March 1963, the barn and greenhouse associated with these gardens were torn down.[75] By 1967, it had become almost as cheap to buy eggs from area farmers as it was to produce them, so the chicken farm was closed. In 1966, the sandstone quarry was closed. In July 1971, the hog farm was shut down because state inspectors said it was polluting the Anderson River. It would be too expensive to upgrade the operation.[76]

Beginning in 1970, the tax exemption status for charitable organizations for income derived from unrelated businesses was removed. This meant that income produced from the farm, including livestock, produce or dairy, would now be taxed.[77] In 1971, the Department of Agriculture drew up stricter regulations for milk producers and distributors.[78] To meet compliance for Grade A milk, expensive new equipment and an upgraded dairy would be needed. Other farming operations such as crops were becoming more expensive as new equipment was also needed to upgrade these operations. Fewer brothers to work the farm also meant more costs, as farm workers needed to be hired.

On March 22, 1974, the monks reluctantly voted to close the farm to save money. On June 18 and 19, 1974, the Abbey auctioned its beef and dairy herds, some of which had been prized registered animals since 1900. The fields were rented out to bring in income, because lease payments weren't taxable.[79] The packing plant was transformed into a profitable custom butchering business. However, when it became unprofitable, it was closed in 1984. The winery was eliminated in 1998, as no monk was interested in being the winemaker and it was cheaper to buy wine than to make it.

The closings of the school, the farm, and eventually the winery, all traditional Benedictine "work," were difficult and painful decisions for the community. Wilson remarks, "So slowly, piece by piece, all the self-sufficient kinds of things dropped by the wayside and they started buying [produce] from the outside and started hiring lay people to do the work that had always been done by monks. The brothers had always been greatly involved in running the physical facilities for years and years and years. Now we only have a few brothers involved with physical facilities."[80]

The 1980s and 1990s

In the last two decades of the 20th century, the outside world considered Saint Meinrad a highly solvent institution. It paid its bills and shrewd investments greatly increased the worth of the endowment in the surging bull market of the 1990s. However, rising deficits caused by outside forces beyond the control of the institution led to increased borrowing and the brink of financial disaster. To remedy this situation, agonizing decisions were made, such as freezing wages and reducing benefits. As a last resort, the re-organization of the Abbey Press and the closing of the College were carried out for the very survival of the institution.

Abbey Press

Abbey Press, by the late 1980s, produced $700,000-$800,000 to $1.5 million a year in profits. Yet, Saint Meinrad had escalating debt. Wilson explains, "We were spending our bequest money to pay operations, but school enrollment was decreasing. Development theory suggests that it is best to set bequest money aside to function as an endowment. We were able to survive financially, although our borrowing would grow incrementally year by year. Banks were happy to give us loans because our equity was growing."[81]

Abbey Press had a special reduced rate for bulk mailing, allowing them to send mail and catalogs very inexpensively. However, because of a change in the United States Postal Service laws in 1991, inexpensive postal privileges for not-for-profits were taken away for material that promoted their products. This change added around a million dollars of additional expense per year in postage. The Press continued to make a profit. However, to pay the expenses for the whole institution, the amounts borrowed from the banks and interest on the loans kept increasing, along with the price of paper. To save money, retirement and health insurance benefits were reduced and an attractive early retirement package was offered to support staff and all the Abbey Press in 1992; few people took advantage of it.[82]

Wilson notes, "In 1995, we paid $600,000 in interest, where in the late 1970s and early 1980s, it was practically zero." The debt kept increasing and the very survival of the institution appeared threatened. To cut costs, it was decided that the Press needed to be downsized. Sixty-one workers were laid off, some fulltime and others part time, on Feb. 21, 1995.[83] However, the situation worsened. The fall of 1996 was the worst year in the history of the Press as no profit was going to be made for the year. "It was just devastating...I [Wilson] could see that our borrowing, which by then had reached a high point of $8 or $9 million, could be as high as $11 million in the late summer of '97." To save the Archabbey and its mission of educating priests, drastic measures had to be taken.[84]

The College or Minor Seminary

In 1959, Saint Meinrad College for young men considering the priesthood was separately incorporated. It was accredited in 1961 by the North Central Association. However, in the wake of Vatican II, fewer young men were interested in a religious vocation and enrollment declined in both the College and the School of Theology while costs of running the schools continued to climb. In an effort to increase enrollment in the College, several thousand dollars in financial aid as an enticement was given to each student, beginning in the late 1980s.

Young men were encouraged to attend and see if the priesthood might be of interest. If not, they could still get a good education. "Our enrollment expenses went from zero to a few hundred thousand, our financial aid went from almost nothing to several hundred thousand and our student revenues were dropping year by year."[85] However, enrollment continued to decline from about 106 in 1989 to 97 in 1996.[86]

The College and School of Theology's financial deficit over the 1990s had been an increasing concern of the Board of Overseers. Abbot Lambert Reilly, OSB, who was elected in 1995, "was aware that something was going to have to change, as the entire institution's financial stability was being threatened."[87]

On April 25, 1997, Wilson went to the meeting of the Board of Overseers with information of the grim budget picture for fiscal year 1997-98. If the College were to close, there would be a net cash saving of $800,000 to $1 million per year for the institution as a whole.[88] The next day, the Overseers recommended closing the College at the end of the 1997-98 school year. Fr. Simeon Daly, the librarian, an observer at an open meeting of the board, recalls that, "a layman on the Board of Overseers just said—and I was very angry when I first heard him say it—'Shut it down this year; you can't afford this operation.' To have someone from the outside come in and say you can't afford this operation was very hard to take. But it was the fact."[89]

On the afternoon of April 26, the Board of Trustees voted to close the College and to bring this recommendation to the monks to vote on it. The monks, with sadness, voted on April 28, 1997, to close the College. A few faculty and monks were re-assigned to the theology school.[90] Fr. Simeon summarizes this tragic time: "The whole history of the institution, the life of all the people involved, not just monks, but also lay people whose livelihoods were stopped in mid-life…what opportunities did they have and would they have to start all over someplace else? It was a very traumatic period."[91] Although it closed May 16, 1998, the College stayed in existence as a corporation during the 1998-99 school year so the few students who had transferred to other institutions to take courses could still get their degree from Saint Meinrad.[92]

Into Green Pastures

As a result of difficult and painful decisions, in a matter of two years Saint Meinrad had pulled itself out of it its financial valley. The Press was making a profit and the Development Office began a major capital campaign. The community celebrated its 150th anniversary in 2004.

Finances and Abbey Press

When Fr. Rupert was transferred to the Human Resources Department in 1991, Fr. Carl Deitchman, OSB, who was experienced in several aspects of management and publishing, was appointed general manager of Abbey Press. He introduced the Total Quality Management (TQM) style. Due to declining readership and increased expenses, the last monthly issue of *Marriage* magazine was published in August 1991. Gerald Wilhite, a layman who had previously worked at the Press, was asked by Fr. Carl to return as chief operating officer in 1994, dividing the duties of Fr. Carl. A year later, Fr. Carl left and Wilhite became general manager, a position he still holds today.

Under Wilhite's guidance, the Press was reorganized.[93] The marketing program was redesigned. Fewer catalogs were sent and less prospecting was done to save money. With the re-direction of the Press and the closing of the College, "by August 1998," Wilson states, "we had a borrowing of zero.... So the $600,000 that we were paying in interest has now been able to have been reinvested in many other things."[94] One Overseer, Robert Shine, who has a CPA firm in New Albany, IN, remarked that, in his 50- or 60-year career, he had never seen a turnaround like this before in an institution.[95]

In 1999, to be competitive with other businesses, the Press added an "online business." It was evolving from a "conventional catalog with an online element to an online business that also has a catalog."[96] The major product line for decades at Abbey Press had been Christmas cards. However, the use and, consequently, the sale of Christmas cards began to dramatically decline in the late 1990s. Fewer people were sending out cards, fewer were using regular mail and more were using e-mail cards. There was also increased competition from discount stores.

This decline affected the Press for the first time in 2005. Wilhite notes, "Between the years 1997 and 2003, the average annual income at Abbey Press was $2.75 million.... We had an unbroken string of seven years of profits. I think of that as a nice, little winning streak that we were on.

That felt pretty good while it was there…. We continually work to improve, though." Some items like the Precious Moments figurines, first marketed in the 1990s, along with personalized and memorial items, were still on the upswing. However, after two disappointing years, Abbey Press experienced improved financial results during the Holiday 2006 season.[97]

Like any good business, the evaluation of trends and changes in product lines is a continued process. However, there is a difference between the Press and other businesses. Wilhite explains, "We have gone to great lengths to define what products are appropriate for the Abbey Press to be selling consistent with the values of Saint Meinrad Archabbey." Product development is aimed at this philosophy. "We are not an upstart from somewhere wanting to play the inspirational-plotted game. We are the Abbey Press, and we're a part of Saint Meinrad Archabbey."[98]

The Development Office and the Second Capital Campaign

The Development Office increased its staffing in the late 1980s, especially in the "inviting support" area. Dan Schipp, vice president for development, notes, "The department is set up as an institutional advancement program, which means that we are responsible not just for fundraising, but also for all communications, alumni relations and special events. At one time in the mid-'80s, we were also responsible for recruitment and enrollment."[99]

The Development Office has two divisions: development and communications. The latter was called public relations until the early 1990s. The development division is in charge of annual giving, planned giving, alumni relations and major gifts. Annual giving includes the Saint Meinrad Sunday parish program, direct mail appeals, corporate matching gifts, personal contacts, gift recording and acknowledgment, and the Abbot Martin Marty Guild. This program, named after the first abbot, was established in 1993 to honor those who had given $1,000 or more per year to Saint Meinrad. Major and planned giving includes personal contacts with major donors, regional benefactor dinners, foundation proposals, and campaigns for special projects, along with The Einsiedeln Society.[100]

The Communications Division produces and/or reviews communications from the Archabbey. These include newsletters such as *On the Hill*, annual reports, advertisements, information for retreatants and guests, news media contacts, along with a Web site. In 2005, over 20 staff members were part of the Development Office. Some have been part of the office since the early years of the program, attesting to the Benedictine value of stability. After the retirement of Fr. Eric in 1994, various monks have been part of the development staff including Frs. Julian Peters, Brendan Moss and Jonathan Fassero. In 2006, Fr. Jonathan worked part-time in the development office and headed the enrollment program. Fr. Brendan was director of new donor initiatives. Fr. Simeon, after his retirement from the library in 2000, works part-time in the office interacting with donors and emeritus Abbot Bonaventure also works a few days a week in the office.[101]

The Development Office began a capital campaign to raise $40 million in five years under the direction of Abbot Lambert Reilly, President-Rector Fr. Mark O'Keefe, OSB, and Schipp. "The Call of Saint Meinrad: Seeking God and Serving the Church" was first introduced in 2001 and publicly announced in October 2003. Three major campaign goals were identified. The first, $21 million for new construction and renovation, included the renovation of St. Thomas Aquinas Chapel and Sherwood Hall and the building of a new guest house and a wellness-fitness center. The second goal, endowments of $9 million, included improving salaries for instructors, lifetime learning for parish workers, and support for the health care of older monks and the fitness center. The third goal, continued support for operations for $10 million, was aimed at annual giving to support the daily operations of the Archabbey. By its conclusion in June 2006, the campaign raised more than $42 million. The endowment had risen from $30.4 million in 2001 to about $60 million in 2006.[102]

Within a few months of the announcement of the campaign, two women, Virginia Basso and Bernice Davey, left bequests that totaled almost $27 million. Respecting the benefactors' interest, $7 million went to an endowment for financial aid to seminarians, another $6 million was allotted to an endowment for academic instruction, and $9.5 went for construction and operation of the guest house and hospitality.[103] The new guest house opened in November 2005.

In addition to endowments, grants were received to fund new programs. The School of Theology in December 2004 was awarded a $1.7 million grant from Lilly Endowment, Inc. of Indianapolis. The Saint Meinrad Institute for Priests and Presbyterates, supported by this grant, will provide programs to help priests during key transitional times in their lives. In March 2005, the School of Theology was awarded a $750,000 challenge grant from The Kresge Foundation. The money was earmarked for the renovation of Sherwood Hall, which houses seminarians and administrative offices. This award was included in the campaign that concluded on June 30, 2006.[104]

Saint Meinrad, primarily through its Abbey Press and Development Office, was financially sound by the early years of the first decade of the 21st century. Bequests as a percent of total gift income rose from 3.6% in 1968 to 45.4% in 2004.[105] Other business ventures were being tried, including Abbey Caskets, founded in 1999, to sell simple caskets inspired by those used by the monks.[106]

In summary, the finances of Saint Meinrad, like other monasteries and institutions, have waxed and waned during the past 50 years over the lifetime of the monks interviewed for this book. Without solid financial management, there has always been the danger of demise of any institution. Changes in the Catholic Church in the wake of Vatican II and other societal changes put serious financial strain on the Archabbey. However, due to wise, although sometimes painful, business decisions, and the efforts of its Development Office, Saint Meinrad became a model to other monastic communities of survival, adaptation and change.

Chapter Contributors

Fr. Rupert became Saint Meinrad's treasurer in 1948. He held this position, along with that of business manager, from 1972 to 1979, when he was appointed general manager of Abbey Press until his transfer from the Press in 1991 to human resources.

Fr. Eric, from 1958-67, was manager of publishing and then general manager, 1966-68, of Abbey Press. In 1968, he was appointed to the Development Office. He helped build its program and originated calligraphy as a trademark for the Archabbey. In later years, he did much of the artistic design for the department and retired in 1994.

Dan Schipp began work in the Development Office in 1982. He became director of development in 1985 and vice president for development in 1988, a position he still holds.

John Wilson was assistant business manager of Saint Meinrad from 1978 through 1989. He became the first lay treasurer/business manager in 1989, a position he still holds.

Endnotes

1. Patricia Wittberg, in *The Rise and Decline of Catholic Religious Orders* (1994, 3-4), contends that social movement cycles of growth and prosperity followed by decline and decay have always been part of monastic life.

Derek Edward Dawson Beales in *Prosperity and Plunder* (2003) details the rise and fall of monasteries from 1650-1815. C. H. Lawrence in *Medieval Monasticism* (2001) discussed early to late middle-ages socioeconomic trends. R. H. Snape in *English Monastic Finances in the Later Middle Ages* (1968) examines the finances of English monasteries from the 12th to the 16th centuries.

A synthesis of Beales (2003, 27-30), Lawrence, Snape and Wittberg suggests the following broad socioeconomic cycle in western European monastic communities, although details differ among these authors. In general, after their initial expansion in the sixth and seventh centuries, many monasteries were destroyed or declined in the eighth and ninth centuries. They revived in the tenth and 11th centuries, but disintegrated in the 13th and 14th centuries. Communities expanded again from the mid-17th to the early 18th centuries, but were suppressed or confiscated in the late 18th and early 19th centuries. They expanded in the late 19th century to the mid-20th and are now in decline in terms of financial resources and members in North America and Europe.

2. Lawrence (2001); Beales (2003); Snape (1968).
3. See Beales (2003) for post-Reformation information and also Wittberg (1994), Nygren, David J. and Miriam D. Ukeritis, *The Future of Religious Orders in the United States* (1993, xx-xxiii).
4. Kleber, Albert, *History of Saint Meinrad Archabbey* (1954, 57-58).
5. Kleber (1954, 172-173).
6. For information specific to Saint Meinrad, see Davis, Cyprian [Ed.], *To Prefer Nothing to Christ* (2004) and Kleber (1954).
7. See Nygren and Ukeritis (1993, 253-254) for details concerning the post-Vatican II era. Their research suggests that religious orders in the United States reached their greatest membership in the early 1960s. This included nearly 1,000 orders, with a membership of close to 200,000. These communities were "sustained in large measure by donations or support from works. For all intents and purposes, they labored for very little financial compensation," p. xxii. By the early 1990s, religious communities had lost 40 percent of their members. Due to increased costs and decreased enrollment, numerous schools, colleges and seminaries closed. See also Wittberg for post-Vatican II changes.
8. Fr. Rupert Ostdick to Prof. Ruth C. Engs, Aug. 24, 2005, interview transcription, Saint Meinrad Archives.
9. Kleber (1954, 506); Ostdick to Engs, 2005.
10. *Saint Meinrad Newsletter* 6:1, October 1962; Ostdick to Engs, 2005.
11. *Abbey Chronicles* April 3, 1963, 286.

12. *Saint Meinrad Newsletter* 23:3, September 1983.

13. For more information concerning the Press until 1951 see: Daly, Simeon, "St. Meinrad Abbey Press," in Boland, Paschal, [ed.] *From Monastic Scriptoriums to Contemporary Monastic Printing and Publishing* (1975).

14. Ibid.

15. Ibid.

16. *Saint Meinrad Newsletter* 3:2 January 1960.

17. *Saint Meinrad Newsletter* 6:2, January 1962.

18. *Community Bulletin*, July 17-23, 1966; Zoeller to Engs, 2005.

19. *Saint Meinrad Newsletter* 8:4, January 1966.

20. *Community Bulletin*, Aug. 22-Sept. 2, 1967.

21. *Community Bulletin*, Feb. 4-10, 1968.

22. Victor Christ-Janer & Associates, "Guide for Comprehensive Planning—St. Meinrad Archabbey," Report No. 2, June 1966.

23. Ibid.

24. *Saint Meinrad Newsletter* 9:4, August 1967.

24. For an ill-fated fundraising effort in the 1930s, see Davis, Cyprian, "Abbot Ignatius Esser, OSB: Builder and Visionary, 1930-1955." In Davis [ed.] (2004, 396-399). In the late 1950s, alumni were solicited for the construction of the "old" guest house finished in March 1960 at a total cost of $150,000. *Saint Meinrad Newsletter* 3:3, March 1960; Ibid. May 1960.

26. The initial committee, besides the abbot, included the following monks: Fathers Gabriel Verkamp, chairman; Marcellus Fisher, Fabian Frieders, Eric Lies, Basil Mattingly and Martin Dusseau. *Saint Meinrad Newsletter* 6:4, May 1963.

27. Daniel Schipp to Prof. Ruth C. Engs, Sept. 19, 2005, interview transcription, Saint Meinrad Archives.

28. Saint Meinrad Seminary, 1967-1968, Annual Report.

29. 1967 Annual Report, St. Meinrad Seminary, St. Meinrad, IN; *Saint Meinrad Newsletter* 8:4, January 1966.

30. *Saint Meinrad Newsletter* 9:3, Spring-Summer 1967.

31. Schipp to Engs, 2005.

32. Saint Meinrad Seminary, College and School of Theology, Annual Report 1969-1970; Schipp, Daniel, "Overview of Saint Meinrad Archabbey and School of Theology Development plan," paper presented August 2005, Saint Meinrad Archabbey; Schipp to Engs, 2005.

33. Schipp to Engs, 2005.

34. Fr. Marcellus was the former development director. He and several other monks served as part-time staff including Frs. Paschal, Gregory, Maurice, Adrian, Vincent, Daniel. *Community Bulletin*, Aug. 6-12, 1967.

35. Schipp, Daniel, "State of development: Report to the Monastic Community," paper presented Jan. 25, 1993, Saint Meinrad Archabbey.

36. Lies to Engs, 2005.

37. MacCauley, John S. "Draft Memo to: Development Committee of the Board of Overseers," June 19, 1973, Saint Meinrad Archabbey.

38. Ibid.

39. Ibid.

40. Lies, Eric, "Development at Saint Meinrad," white paper, April 19, 1990; *Saint Meinrad Newsletter* 10:1, Spring 1968.

41. *Saint Meinrad Newsletter*, Spring-Summer 1967; *Community Bulletin*, Aug. 13-19, 1967.

42. For further information on MacCauley's philosophy, see Lies (1990); Schipp (2005).

43. *Saint Meinrad Newsletter*, Special Edition, November 1968; Lies to Engs, 2005.

44. MacCauley (1973).

45. The first business manager listed for the Abbey was Fr. Benno Gerber in 1916. However, the position did not appear again until 1931 at the beginning of Abbot Ignatius Esser's long tenure. In 1916, Fr. Benno was also listed as treasurer, the first year for which this position was also listed. In 1973, the job of business manager and treasurer were combined and Fr. Rupert Ostdick held these positions until 1979. His successor was Br. Luke Hodde, the first brother to hold the position (Abbot's Office, "Book of lists" 1/15/04 based upon the ORDO).

46. "Five Year Plan for Abbey Press, Feb. 23, 1971," in Boland (1975).

47. Gerald Wilhite to Prof. Ruth C. Engs, Sept. 21, 2005, interview transcription, Saint Meinrad Archives.

48. John Wilson to Prof. Ruth C. Engs, July 12, 2004, interview transcription, Saint Meinrad Archives.

49. "Chapter 12. Uniform Management of Institutional Funds," downloaded from http://www.state.in.us/legislative/ic/code/title30/ar2/ch12.html, Oct. 30, 2005.

50. Ibid.

51. *Saint Meinrad Newsletter*, Theology Edition, September 1979; Schipp to Engs, 2005.

52. Schipp to Engs, 2005.

53. In the wake of capital campaigns, annual giving and gifts for endowments generally increase. Annual gifts from individuals, alumni and friends are ordinarily used for operation purposes. Gifts from alumni, friends, corporations and foundations contributed through special invitation are ordinarily used for building and renovation projects of an institution. Outright or deferred gifts, including bequests, are generally used for endowment and similar purposes. These often restrict the gift to specific projects. (The Case for Saint Meinrad: Saint Meinrad Capital Campaign. Saint Meinrad, IN, 1980).

54. Saint Meinrad Seminary, College and School of Theology, *Annual Report of our Stewardship* 1980; *Saint Meinrad Newsletter*, 21:4 December 1981; Ibid., 23:2, June 1983.

55. *Another Step Forward, the Case for Renovation of the Old Monastery & Library Buildings*, Saint Meinrad Archabbey and Seminary, n.d; Saint Meinrad Seminary, College and School of Theology, *Annual Report of our Stewardship* 1984; *Saint Meinrad Newsletter*, 24:4, January 1985.

56. *Saint Meinrad Newsletter*, 21:4, December 1981; Ibid., 23:1, April 1983.

57. *Saint Meinrad Newsletter*, 23:3, September 1983; Ibid., 24:3, September 1984; Ibid., 25:4, October 1985; *Community Bulletin*, Sept. 9-15, 1983.

58. Saint Meinrad Seminary, College and School of Theology, *Report of our Stewardship* 1987.

59. Saint Meinrad Seminary, College and School of Theology, *Annual Report of our Stewardship* 1988.

60. *Saint Meinrad Newsletter*, 27:3, Summer 1988.

61. Schipp, Daniel, "Report to the Monastic Community," paper presented, St. Meinrad, IN, Nov. 7, 1988.

62. Saint Meinrad Seminary, College and School of Theology, *Annual Report of our Stewardship* 1981; *A Journey of Faith Celebrating 150 Years*, Saint Meinrad Archabbey, 2004.

63. Kleber (1954, 481-482).

64. *Saint Meinrad Newsletter*, 6:2, January 1962; Ibid., 8:4, January 1966; Shaughnessy, Edward, "Construction of the Abbey Church of Saint Meinrad, 1898-1907," in Davis [Ed.] (2004, 437-484).

65. Berry was on the Board of Overseers for one year in 1972. Saint Meinrad Seminary, College and School of Theology, *Annual Report* 1972-1973.

66. Fr. Simeon Daly to Prof. Ruth C. Engs, June 9, 2005, interview transcription, Saint Meinrad archives; Wilson to Engs, 2005; Ostdick to Engs, 2005.

67. For the history of Saint Meinrad's seminaries see: White, Joseph, "The making of an American Seminary: Saint Meinrad before Vatican II," in Davis, [Ed.] 2004, 85-152.

68. See Fr. Theodore's profile for further information. Also see White (2004, 90, 100); Kleber, Albert (1974, 503).

69. Nygren and Ukeritis (1993, 254) report that, between 1962 and 1992, 39.6 percent of all Catholic boarding high schools closed in the United States. See also current *Official Catholic Directory*; Abbot Bonaventure Knaebel to Prof. Ruth C. Engs, June 15, 2005, interview transcription, Saint Meinrad Archives.

70. *Saint Meinrad Newsletter*, 8:4, January 1966; Ibid, 9:4, August 1967.

71. Fr. Theodore Heck to Prof. Ruth C. Engs, June 13, 2005, interview transcription, Saint Meinrad Archives.

72. Private communication, Fr. Meinrad Brune to Prof. Ruth C. Engs, July 2005.

73. See chapter, "Land: Sustenance of the Abbey," for more information about the wine making, farming, livestock, forestry, sandstone and similar businesses at Saint Meinrad.

74. *Saint Meinrad Newsletter*, 1:1, Dec. 6, 1962; Br. Jerome Croteau to Prof. Ruth C. Engs, July 2005, interview transcription, Saint Meinrad Archives.

75. *Frater Chronicles* xiii, March 1963.

76. Croteau to Engs, 2005.

77. "Sec.511. Imposition of tax on unrelated business income of charitable, etc., organizations." Title 26-Internal Revenue Code, Dec. 3, 1969. This tax was called Un-Related Business Income Tax (UBIT).

78. "Part 1000 General Provisions of Federal Milk Marketing Orders." Title 7-Agriculture, May 29, 1971.

79. *Saint Meinrad Newsletter*, Archabbey Edition, July 1974, 1; Croteau to Engs, 2005.

80. Wilson to Engs, 2005.

81. Ibid.

82. *Domestic Mail Manual*, Washington, DC: United States Postal Service 1992; Wilson to Engs, 2005.

83. Wilson to Engs, 2005; Powell, Bill, "Abbey Press lays off 61," *The Herald*, Wednesday, Feb. 22, 1995, p3.

84. Wilson to Engs, 2005.

85. Ibid.

86. Saint Meinrad registrar's office.

87. Wilson to Engs, 2005.

88. Ibid.

89. Daly to Engs, 2005.

90. Rasche, Martha, "Empty feeling is left as St. Meinrad closes," *The South Bend Tribune*, June 21, 1998; *Community Bulletin*, May 4, 1997.

91. Daly to Engs, 2005.

92. Rasche (1997); Wilson to Engs, 2005.

93. See "The Abbey Press: Illumination of the Abbey" for more details of the Press during the 1990s.

94. Wilson to Engs, 2005. In 2005, the Press had a dip in sales.

95. Wilson to Engs, 2005.

96. Wilhite to Engs, 2005.

97. Ibid.; Wilhite to Engs, e-mail: Nov. 30, 2006; Wilhite to Engs, e-mail: Jan. 5, 2007.

98. Ibid.

99. Schipp to Engs, 2005.

100. Ibid.

101. Ibid.

102. *The Call of Saint Meinrad: Seeking God and Serving the Church*, Saint Meinrad Archabbey, 2003; *On the Hill*, 44:3, Summer 2005. Schipp to Engs, private communication, October 2007.

103. Saint Meinrad Archabbey and School of Theology, 2004 Report of Stewardship, *A Journey of Faith Celebrating 150 Years*.

104. *On the Hill*, 44:3, Summer 2005.

105. Schipp (2005).

106. See the chapter "Land" for more details.

Chapter Thirteen

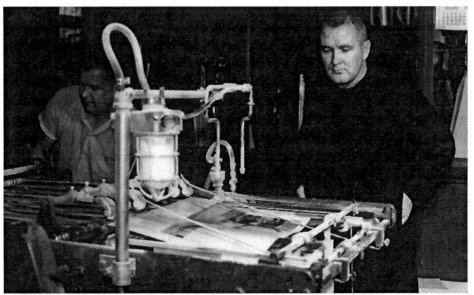

Br. Michael Kenealy watches a printing job at Abbey Press during the 1960s.

Abbey Press: Illumination of the Abbey

Simeon Daly, OSB, Rupert Ostdick, OSB, Maurus Zoeller, OSB, and Gerald Wilhite, with Ruth C. Engs

For centuries, many monastic communities carried on the tradition of the scriptorium, where religious manuscripts were transcribed onto new parchment. Rather than just copying words, in many cases the lettering was illuminated with detailed drawings. The *Book of Kells*, found at Trinity College in Dublin, Ireland, which was illustrated and scripted by Celtic monks in the ninth century, is an example of this tradition. In a sense, modern printing and publishing, such as accomplished by Abbey Press, is a continuation of this ancient monastic work.[1]

Several Saint Meinrad monks, whose interview profiles are found elsewhere in this book, have been involved with work at Abbey Press [2] and its divisions. These include Br. Benedict Barthel, Br. Terence Griffin, Fr. Eric Lies and Fr. Rupert Ostdick.

The chapter on "Finances and Fund Raising" discussed the financial ebb and flow of Abbey Press and how it is intertwined with the financial cycles of the Archabbey. The Press and its various divisions, since the last half of the 20th century, have been the major support of the Archabbey. This chapter discusses leadership changes and periods of reorganization, and outlines what the Press has printed, published, manufactured and marketed. It depicts *Marriage Magazine*, a major award-winning publication of its era, and the development of Abbey Press catalogs. Also mentioned are the book and pamphlet ventures, such as CareNotes, the sculpture operation and the gift shop.

Overview of Printing and Publishing at Abbey Press, 1867-2007

The Early Years

Abbey Press began in 1867 when Fr. Martin Marty, OSB, three years before he became the first abbot, bought a secondhand printing press for $450. Fr. Simeon Daly, in his early history of the Press, notes that, "Considering the poverty of the house at this time and the press of activities that burdened the understaffed community, such a purchase could only have been made with an eye to the future."[3] However, the press was not set up until 1869, when it was housed in a small room in the monastery. It is not known to what extent the press was used in its first decade of operation. Based upon scant evidence, it was likely used for two-page leaflets, programs for the colleges, death notices and printing on memorial cards for local families. Many of the early printings were in Latin or German.

Under Fr. Bede Maler, OSB, who was appointed the first publisher in 1889, articles of incorporation were drawn up on December 30, 1889. They suggest that the goals of Abbey Press were to further the religious, missionary and educational work of Saint Meinrad Archabbey by printing, publishing, manufacturing and distributing materials appropriate to that work. A goal was to provide employment for the monks, to provide employment to other people, and to provide printed materials for the monastery and the schools.[4]

In the spring of 1894, a utility building was built to the south of the monastery and college compound. About 12,000 square feet was allotted to Abbey Press. A German-language monthly, *Paradiesesfrüchte* (Fruits of Paradise), which Fr. Bede had started in 1892 but had been printed elsewhere, began to be printed by the Press in 1896. This magazine continued to be published until 1936, and had a circulation of 50,000 in the 1920s. It was the only magazine that lasted into the 20th century. Very few books for the public were issued in this era.[5]

This changed in 1914. Over the history of Abbey Press, reorganization and the appointment of new leadership have been accomplished a number of times. It often resulted in a new direction, new products, growth—and sometimes disaster. In 1914, Fr. Edward Berheide, OSB, ordained but a few weeks, was assigned to manage the Press. Fr. Simeon suggests, "To Father Edward must go much of the credit for the success of the Press today.... It is not because he left the office in any blaze of glory, but because he was the man who first envisioned its potential and showed in a practical way what could be done. From the very start he began thinking in growth and development." He was given $800 to start the business. He got rid of the old presses, purchased an intertype machine and, in 1916, a large automatic press.[6]

Until Fr. Edward was appointed manager, the work in the Press had been done by monks. He hired men and boys from the community, expanded the operations and built additional printing facilities. His philosophy was that the Press should concentrate on "job work," such as printing hospital forms, stationery and the like, and Catholic periodicals. He did not deviate from this over his years as manager. In 1930, the Press was printing five monthly magazines, three from the Abbey and two outside ones. It had "23 able and capable printers and binders" and it was turning a profit.[7]

Because of his success over his 16 years of management, Fr. Edward appealed to the monastery in 1930 to allow him to build a new facility for the Press. Fr. Simeon reports that Fr. Edward wrote, "Today, the Ship of the Abbey Press is serenely riding on the ocean of prosperity, surrounded by almost infinite opportunities." The building that now serves as the main office for the Press was begun in the fall of 1930 and completed in the spring of 1931. Alas, the Great Depression emerged. With decreasing sales and higher-than-expected building costs, the Press became mired in economic difficulties and debt and "the ship was temporarily on the rocks." In reflecting upon Fr. Edward's statement, Gerald Wilhite, the general manager since 1995, remarks, "Every time I start feeling like we're on top of the world here and doing a great job…, I go back and read this."[8]

Fr. Edward was removed from his position as manager in January 1934. Mr. August Ringeman took over management from 1935-40; however, Fr. Edward's policy of job printing with an occasional book on the side was followed, resulting in minimal success.[9] Fr. David Duessing, OSB, was manager from 1941-44. In 1945, Fr. Paschal Boland, OSB, was appointed manager of publishing. His greatest contribution was to expand the operation to include the publishing of books, to be discussed later.

The business was also divided into two divisions: Abbey Press, a print shop, and Grail Publications, a publisher and book dealer. By the early 1950s, 27 full-time workers were employed at the facility in addition to a few monks. A line of pamphlets and books developed under the title, Grail Publications, was printed by the Press. The printing division printed a variety of material that ranged from doctoral dissertations to reference books to the ORDO.[10]

Changes in management again took place in the mid- to late-1950s. In July 1955, Fr. Philip Mahin, OSB, was appointed head of Grail Publications succeeding Fr. Paschal. Books and pamphlets of Grail Publications were directed toward the Catholic reading public and clergy[11]. Fr. Eric Lies, OSB, who was art director for *The Grail*, became manager of the publishing division of Abbey Press in 1958. In that same year, Br. Maurus Zoeller, OSB, who had printing experience prior to entering the monastery, was appointed in August by Archabbot

Bonaventure Knaebel, OSB, to assist Fr. Robert Woerdeman, OSB, the manager of the printing division. Br. Maurus was manager of the printing division from 1960 to 1968.[12]

Reorganization of the 1960s

The 1960s were a time of change in society and in the monastic community, including the work of Abbey Press. These changes included reorganization, new equipment and facilities, a new mission, and increased employment of lay persons in management positions. By 1962, the Press was printing 14 periodicals. In that year, the management of Abbey Press and Grail Publications undertook a study to determine the future direction of the Press and the possibility of a major reorganization.[13]

In 1962, Br. Maurus purchased about 50 holy card designs from then-famous Clement Schmidt of Germany. Br. Maurus recalls, "I sent out catalogs to 40 seminaries around the United States to solicit printing of ordination invitations and holy cards. However, I awoke from sleep one night and realized that many of these holy card designs would make great notecards by adding some paper. Fr. Eric designed a brochure featuring these designs as note and holy cards. I mailed about 35,000 of these…and would you believe, I got better than a 30% mail order return!"[14] Due to this success, he enlarged the holy card designs to make scrolls, banners and posters. "The designs were also laminated onto particle board…. Plaques of different sizes were made."[15]

In the meantime, around 1960, Charles E. "Ned" Watts, an artist and marketer for an insurance agency in Louisville, KY, was hired part time to help with sales. Br. Maurus and Watts, with the support of Fr. Eric, formulated the concept of creating a catalog to sell Abbey goods and to develop new products. In 1962, Watts was hired full time to put out a catalog, which was first published in 1963.[16] Included in this catalog were the printing division's holy cards, posters and plaques. However, Br. Maurus explains, "Mr. Berlinger, an attorney of Berlinger & McGinnis, a religious card company, said that many of his designs, purchased from the same artist, were too similar to the ones we had. He insisted we should drop our designs or face legal action. Instead of agreeing, we offered to purchase his line of note cards, etc. At this point, the printing division was so heavily into publishing that it was decided that we should become one organization. That's why we went from printing to publishing."[17]

Abbey Press acquired the publishing rights of Berlinger & McGinnis in 1966.[18] In addition, "the responsibility of decision and policy making for the printing and publishing divisions of the Abbey Press will be assigned to Fr. Eric."[19] Fr. Eric thus became the first general manager for the entire Abbey Press operation on July 1, 1966. Br. Maurus remained as printing manager and Ned Watts, marketing manager.[20] Br. Maurus was not only manager of the printing division, but also headed the greeting card division. Fr. Eric, besides being general manager, was head of the publishing division and also oversaw *Marriage* magazine, marriage pamphlets and marriage paperbacks.[21]

To meet the demands of the expansion of the Press and its burgeoning catalog business, expensive equipment was acquired. This included, in December 1964, a new automatic letterpress, in 1965 a new stapling machine for folded magazines, and in 1966 a used 5/0 Meihle Perfector Press, which printed both sides of a 40"x 69" sheet in one pass through the press. It replaced a press that had been bought in 1916. The printing facility was also upgraded and expanded. A cooling system for the print shop was installed and part of the printing operation moved into buildings formerly used by the blacksmith and machine shops.[22]

Years of Dramatic Growth: Late 1960s through the 1970s

From the late 1960s through the late 1970s, major changes in the organizational structure, leadership, personnel and physical facilities reflected the Press' expansion and growth as a mail order business. As part of continued assessment, in the summer of 1967, the two divisions of the Press, the printing and publishing units, were combined into a single entity. In addition, an executive committee consisting of Fr. Eric, Ned Watts and Br. Maurus was formed. Watts also assumed marketing responsibility of the entire operation. Fr. Eric recalls, "During that period, Ned, Br. Maurus and I ran the show."[23]

On February 5, 1968, Fr. Paschal replaced Fr. Eric as general manager of the Press. Fr. Eric began working at the newly formed Development Office and Br. Maurus became new product development director. Additional reorganization in the summer of 1968 put Br. Maurus in charge of only new product development.[24] Br. Maurus recalls, "In '68, I was spending about 90 percent of my time developing products, or talking to artists and designers and putting things out in the catalog.... So I got out of the printing operation and turned it over to Mike Franchville, one of the lay people. New products started multiplying and multiplying and, at one point, I think about 48 of the 60 pages of Abbey Press-produced products (were in the catalog)."[25]

These changes led to increased sales and growth to the point where one year all monks were asked to volunteer to help out. The *Community Bulletin*, the newsletter for the monastic community, in November 1969 announced, "Happily the Abbey Press is booming with business and Christmas orders; so much so, that it has caused an immediate need for added help."[26] By 1972, the Bulletin mentioned, "Since the beginning of the fiscal year, July 1, 1972, 75,249 people have ordered items from the Abbey Press compared to 46,868 for the same period a year ago. This was a 25% increase."[27]

The number of personnel working at the Press also grew dramatically. By November 1969, Abbey Press employed 102 people, which included four monks, 41 men and 57 women.[28] Br. Maurus recalls, "When I went down there in '58, we had 26 people working in the Abbey Press printing division and there were eight only in publishing.... By '78, we had a big operation going.... There were about 150 full-time and maybe about 50 part-timers."[29]

In the early 1970s, new programs were launched and changes in personnel occurred. The Press had evolved into a direct-mail business to sell its, and others', products. In addition to printed materials, a religious sculpture operation began in 1972, leading to three divisions of the Press: printing, publishing and sundry products.[30]

In July 1971, the editor of Abbey Press Publications and *Marriage* magazine, Brian F. Daly, resigned. John J. McHale, the former editor-in-chief of Newman Press of Westminster, MD, was appointed the new editor and director of Abbey Press publications. McHale initiated an updated program of publications focusing on concern for home, community, church and world, along with an Abbey Press Book Catalog. The sales force that marketed Abbey Press products to gift shops, department stores and non-religious trade was also expanded.[31]

The Press gained a reputation as a publisher for whom authors liked to write. In 1972, Jean Laird, a writer for *Marriage* magazine, commented, "I have worked with them for the past five years and have sold more than two dozen article manuscripts and a paperback book to this publisher. I think they're great to work with."[32]

In 1974, under Fr. Paschal's guidance, the goals, structure and organization of the Press, which included more emphasis on a spiritual orientation, were laid out.[33] This resulted in a number of changes over the next few years. However, Fr. Paschal developed health problems, so on June 30, 1976, Peter Kaufman, who had served as controller of Abbey Press for five years, became general manager.

At the same time, Archabbot Gabriel Verkamp, OSB, established an Abbey Press board of directors, "to strengthen the relationship of the Archabbey with the Abbey Press." Its function was to make policy decisions and set policy standards for the Press. The archabbot served as chairman of this board and Fr. Rupert as executive secretary.[34] To achieve a closer legal link between the Abbey Press and the Archabbey, the archabbot appointed Fr. Rupert to be publisher of Abbey Press. His mission was to "[d]irect the conduct of the Press so that it will carry forward our apostolates and implement the goals and purposes of Saint Meinrad Archabbey."[35]

In the wake of the growth and expansion from the 1960s through the 1970s, the requisition of space and the construction of new buildings were in evidence. Abbey Press took over much of the shop building in August 1968. Two years later, the monks voted for further facilities expansion to complete a two-story connecting wing between the Abbey

Press building and this three-story shop building. This complex became known as Abbey Press Plant I.[36]

After the farm operations were closed in 1974, the Press expanded into the dairy barn, milking parlor and various small buildings.[37] In 1975, a new concrete-block, 11,000-square-foot building was constructed on the east side of the old dairy barn to handle the packaging and shipping of items ordered through the catalog.[38] This collection of buildings became known as Abbey Press Plant II. In later years, light manufacturing such as personalized items was also done here.

In 1977, a new 20,000-square-foot sculpture production facility was constructed as an addition to Plant II. Wilhite remarks, "Since 1970, I helped clean up the old files from the sandstone offices, scrubbed away the last remains of the cows in the dairy barn, and swept up the last of the feathers and other chicken signs from the chicken and brooder house."[39]

Some of the original building descriptions are still found in the daily language, especially for long-time co-workers. For example, customer service is in the "sculpture studio"; silkscreens are made and stored in the "bull pen"; the photo studio is in the "hayloft"; and Human Resources is housed in the "milking parlor." Br. Jacob Grisley, OSB, was appointed the computer programmer in 1976 for the only computer department for the Archabbey, which was at the Press. He continues there today as a consultant.[40]

The 1980s

As the 1970s were turning into the 1980s, more changes occurred. Long-range planning, goals, mission and a business plan emerged, along with extensive building. The general manager, Peter Kaufman, resigned in April 1979. This left a vacancy, so Fr. Rupert, who was the business manager/treasurer for the Archabbey, was asked to fill in temporarily as general manager. However, after a national search, the heads of the departments at the Press approached the archabbot and said they wanted Fr. Rupert on a permanent basis. Fr. Rupert became general manager in

November 1979 and the Press was on an upswing. The shipping department was getting out as many as 9,000 orders in a single day.[41]

Fr. Rupert was the first manager to draw up a comprehensive long-range plan. A revised mission statement and goals reflected the ecumenical nature of the times. The mission statement read, "Abbey Press provides the Archabbey with an opportunity to share reflections of its values and ideals directly with people of all faiths."[42]

Over Fr. Rupert's tenure, many new facilities were built to meet the needs of the growing business. In 1982, a new 45,000-square-foot warehouse was built and connected to the 20,000-square-foot addition of Plant II. The following year, an 18,000-square-foot freestanding building, across the parking lot on the west side of the Plant II complex, was built as a warehouse and storage. It is commonly referred to as Plant III. "We haven't built a significant new building since the Gift Shop in 1985, but we have remodeled many buildings," explains Wilhite.[43]

The Press also kept up with changing technology. In the summer of 1984, a room for computer equipment in Plant I was set up, along with a new phone room to handle up to 25 phones. About 3,500 orders a day were being processed.[44]

Over the 1980s, inspirational pamphlets and books became popular. A critical year was 1988, when a new direction for the publishing division began. Short inspirational pamphlets called CareNotes were first issued. These, to be discussed later, became best sellers.

In the 1980s, two individuals who worked at the Press, one a monk and the other a layman, were honing their skills, which led to both being appointed as general manager of the Press in the 1990s. Fr. Carl Dietchman, OSB, who had worked in product development during the early 1980s, returned to Saint Meinrad in 1989 after earning an MBA at Indiana University. He became director of product development and director of planning at Abbey Press. Gerald Wilhite, a new graduate of St. Benedict College in Ferdinand, IN, started to work with Br. Maurus in 1970 in the product development area. Wilhite left in the fall to teach, but came back to the Press in 1972 to become director of marketing and development. In 1985, Wilhite left the Press again, and went to St. Louis to work for the Brown Group, a woman's shoe company, and developed a successful catalog business.[45]

Reorganization of the 1990s

Fr. Rupert, after many years managing the Business Office and 12 years as general manager of Abbey Press, transferred to Human Resources in July 1991. Fr. Rupert notes in his farewell comments that he considered the greatest achievement over his tenure was, "Improved co-worker relations.... Co-workers now have a better sense of working together and have an improved understanding of how the entire Archabbey complex works together."[46] Fr. Rupert was replaced by Fr. Carl, who began a strategic planning process and tried new management techniques.

Under Fr. Carl's leadership, an organizational change method was initiated, which began to transform how Abbey Press did business. This was Total Quality Management (TQM). This concept is a "horizontal," as opposed to a "vertical," style of management. In other words, employees are encouraged to contribute to the work process. Managers are seen as facilitators, or coaches, and not bosses. When changes are proposed, they have to be measured to determine their impact and if they are effective. At this point, 245 full-time and 100 part-time employees worked at the Press.[47]

As a result of this strategic planning process, a revision of the Abbey Press mission statement reflected the views of the monks and the company employees. Besides the desire to satisfy the customer with quality products and services, it also emphasized that "these products and services show how God cares, saves and is near in our lives."[48] The Press was also an outreach ministry of the Archabbey. Revised goals were set including that, by 2000, the catalog was to market only products that were religious or inspirational.[49]

However, Fr. Carl began to be challenged by various financial and other problems—discussed in more detail in the "Financial and Fund Raising" chapter. These included increased postage and UPS rates, more competition from other catalogs, competition from less expensive sculptures and Christmas cards from the international markets, and declining sales.[50] In July 1994, Gerald Wilhite returned to the Abbey Press as chief operating officer to divide the duties of Fr. Carl. Wilhite remarks, "I've been searching for greener pastures twice, and I'm back here twice. In 1994, I was approached by Fr. Carl, who was wondering if I had any interest in returning to Abbey Press again. I took advantage of that instantly."[51]

In late 1994, more strategic planning and market assessment was carried out, leading to one of the most traumatic events the Press had ever experienced. Abbey Press laid off 38 full-time and 23 part-time employees on February 21, 1995. The sculpture operation was closed. Before the layoff, the Press employed 230 full-time and up to 200 part-time workers.[52] As part of the reorganization, changes for more cost and time effectiveness were recommended. These included drastically reducing new product development efforts, reducing the number of product lines sold through retail marketing, changes in direct marketing to focus mailings on the best customers and careful management of new titles.[53]

Within a few months after the layoff, Fr. Carl stepped down from his position. In May 1995, Wilhite was appointed general manager.[54] He instituted a five-year plan to save the Press and began to develop annual business plans. Wilhite explains, "It wasn't just a layoff of people with the reorganization. We very strongly revitalized our merchandise offer as a part of that reorganization. It defined very clearly what Abbey Press products are and are not."[55]

Before the reorganization of 1995, the Abbey Press mission was focused toward the nature of the business. The mission, after reorganization, focused on the products sold and the benefits they provide. The effort was to "build a brand that stands for the values of Saint Meinrad Archabbey."[56] This meant that some product lines were eliminated, including the company's Abbey Country Fare food products.[57] Even selling Abbey Press was considered, if the business could not be turned around.[58]

Fortunately, new business practices and cost-cutting changes led the Press, in 1998, to take off in an unprecedented earning cycle for the next seven years, mostly from the catalog operations. Personalized and memorial items became very popular. At Plant II, the manufacturing facility, a laser engraving machine and an additional computerized sewing machine were purchased to meet the needs of these items, which ranged from afghans to religious objects.[59]

Technological Challenges and New Strategic Plans in the First Decade of the 21st Century

Many challenges faced Abbey Press in the first decade of the 21st century. To be competitive, it adopted the technical advances of a rapidly changing business climate. Its catalog operation began an online business in 1999. Products from the catalog were offered at www.abbeypress.com. As the Christmas card market continued to decline in North America, new business ventures were explored, along with the creation of specialized catalogs. One of the most successful aspects of Abbey Press was the "Memorial, Grief, Caring" and personalized products side of the business.[60]

Making the transition from a catalog to online Web business was fraught with difficulties. New computer software had a large number of problems, so another system was installed in 2006.[61] Besides software glitches, Wilhite relates that, "Getting the online business up and operating was a big challenge. It's not only a different mentality of marketing and shopping, but the whole processing systems and material handling are different." Today a customer "places an order while she's at lunch, checks back at the end of the day to see if the order has been shipped, and if it hasn't, she'll call us up and wants to know why we're so slow!…. When it was just a mail order business, customers were happy if they got the order in a week or two."[62]

Reflecting the growing "Internet shopping age" and sluggish sales from increased competition, a revised strategic plan was introduced in February 2005. The product mission now stated that "Abbey Press is a marketer of inspirational, religious products that help and uplift people." Product lines were redefined to include "friends and family; care and self-help; seasons and celebrations; and church and community." The primary focus of Abbey Press was to be consumer direct marketing through catalogs and online. Other channels of distribution included trade marketing to stores, institutional marketing, printing of magazines and other materials, and the gift shop.[63]

In 2006, the workforce included 145 full-time and 139 seasonal or part-time people. Many of the co-workers had been at the Press for several decades. Wilhite notes, "The majority of them are in order processing, shipping, answering the phones, designing catalogs, designing and maintaining the Internet site, and computer techs who are keeping all of that up and running.... One of the big challenges in the not-so-distant future is how to manage the big turnover of co-workers who will be retiring soon. Probably more critically is how to replace those years of experience with new people."[64]

The monastic community took on an advisory role at the Press. The chairman of the board of the Abbey Press Board of Advisors is Archabbot Justin DuVall, OSB. Members of the monastic community include the prior, Fr. Tobias Colgan, OSB, and Fr. Warren Heitz, OSB. Other monks who worked as consultants to various aspects of the Press include Fr. Eric, Br. Maurus, Fr. Jeremy King, OSB, and Fr. Louis Mulcahy, OSB. Some young monks work there in the summer.

Although the bulk of the business of Abbey Press since the 1970s had been from the catalog operations, the printing side of the business was still active. Many Abbey Press products were printed on its presses, along with outside publications. Wilhite notes, "We specialize in printing for not-for-profits, because we know the rules of mailing as a non-for-profit and how to prepare the mailing. It gives us an advantage in that area." However, the Internet had a worldwide impact on printing. "It's a tough business to be in right now, and whether we can persevere for the long-term...I don't know."[65] Abbey Press, near the end of the first decade of the 21st century, over its almost 150-year history, had changed with the times and was a direct marketing, printing and publishing firm.

Marriage *Magazine, Other Serial Publications and Newsletters*

Abbey Press began as a publisher of periodicals near the end of the 19th century; most were short-lived and were generally in German. In December 1887, the *St. Meinrad's Raban*, a little newsletter, was circulated. Because of its success, Fr. Bede Maler, OSB, began the first major publication of the Abbey, *Sankt Benedikts Panier* (St. Benedict's Standard; 1889-94). Its aim was to be a Benedictine historical periodical. The *Raban* became a supplement to this publication. *Paradiesesfrüchte*, another German-language magazine, was started in 1892 by Fr. Bede. Its purpose was to foster devotion to the Holy Eucharist. In 1895, it subsumed the *Panier*, along with the *Raban*, which reported local news and contained current and past Benedictine history. In 1936, due to the Depression, the decrease of the German-speaking population in the country and an unscrupulous sales agency, it ceased being published.[66]

A short-lived English magazine was tried. The *Alma Mater*, begun in 1891, was aimed at alumni. In its first years, it was printed by students—most of the articles were by students or faculty. Later, scholars from other institutions contributed. In July 1895, it became *The Monthly Visitor*, "A Catholic magazine for the home circle and the fire side." It ceased publication at the end of 1896 due to publication expenses. It was not until Fr. Edward, the first manager of the Press, introduced a family magazine, *The Grail*, in 1919, that the publication and printing of magazines would become a major industry of Abbey Press.[67]

Marriage *Magazine*

The Grail, in English, aimed to be a Eucharistic family magazine. Fr. Simeon suggests Fr. Edward likely realized that a German magazine would not be successful, as English was the language of the country and anti-German feelings were still high due to World War I. Fr. Benedict Brown, OSB, who later became prior of Marmion Abbey, was its first editor. Under his guidance, it contained devotional articles along with science, history and literature. It also had Abbey and seminary news. The magazine proved to be highly popular, with 120,000 copies printed in 1920.[68]

After 15 years at the helm, a number of editors then followed Fr. Benedict in quick succession.[69] Fr. Cyril Gaul, OSB, was managing editor from 1937 to 1941 and, under his guidance, circulation greatly increased. He was followed by Fr. Paschal (1941-49).[70] Fr. Walter Sullivan, OSB, was appointed editor in 1949 and remained in this position until his death in January 1958. Under his leadership, "*The Grail* underwent a radical change in policy and format, formerly a Catholic monthly of general interest, it was redesigned to serve the family apostolate." It went from a standard-size magazine to a pocket-size version that looked similar to *Reader's Digest*. Like this popular general-interest magazine, it contained no advertisement. Fr. Raban Hathorn, OSB, associate editor, was named editor of *The Grail* in 1958 after Fr. Walter's death.[71]

In 1954, *The Grail* entered into an agreement with the Cana Conference of Chicago to change the magazine into one devoted exclusively to Catholic marriage and family life. This new editorial format was launched in the fall of 1955 and resulted in a steady growth of circulation. The magazine became highly regarded by Catholic Church leadership. The subtitle, "Magazine of Catholic Marriage," reflected this change. The contents included the four areas covered by the Cana Conferences: husband-wife, family-society, parent-child and family-God relationships. In December 1959, *The Grail* changed its name to *Marriage*. The magazine went international in 1963.[72]

However, by the mid-1960s, the circulation had declined to 82,770 copies. As part of the general reorganization of the Press in the mid-1960s, a number of changes were made in the *Marriage* magazine management staff. In the summer of 1966, lay men and women were appointed to important leadership positions for the first time. Charles Q. Mattingly was named editor, and Alice Zarrella, assistant editor. Brian F. Daly replaced Mattingly as editor in February 1969. In addition, a new advertising office was located in New York with a similar office at the Press under the direction of Ned Watts. Production was under the direction of Michael Franchville; Fr. Paschal remained as publisher.[73]

Brian Daly resigned at the end of July 1971. This resignation led to a discussion among members of the Press executive committee of whether *Marriage* magazine was financially viable. It decided to continue. John J. McHale was hired as the new editor of *Marriage* magazine and of Abbey Press publications.[74]

In the early 1970s, the magazine had become a prize-winning publication and had an excellent reputation. The Paulist Press, which distributed Catholic publications to parishes, reported, "that *Marriage* has been holding first or second place in sales for several months." The magazine was lauded for its ecumenical editorial board in 1972.[75]

Fr. Paschal, general manager of Abbey Press and publisher of the magazine, in the January 1974 issue, enlarged its format from a pocketbook size to a standard 8 1/2 by 11 inches format similar to the size of *Newsweek*. It was given a new title, *Marriage and Family Living*. The publication was awarded first place for general excellence in May 1975 at the Catholic Press Association convention. A 1982 survey of *Marriage* magazine readers found that the "typical reader has a median age of 34.5 with two or three children, a college degree, a median income of $28,300, is Roman Catholic, and the head of the household is involved in some sort of professional work."[76]

In 1988, the title changed again to *Marriage & Family*. After waning circulation, the magazine ceased to be published in 1991. Wilhite notes, "August 1991 was the last monthly publication of *Marriage* magazine. It was the end of an era. We got out of the magazine publication business." However, the Press continued to print a number of outside magazines.[77]

Other Serial Publications and Newsletters

From 1928 through 1964, St. Meinrad Seminary—later called the School of Theology—published a series of scholarly essays in a publication titled *St. Meinrad Historical Essays*, which went through a number of name changes.[78] This semi-annual publication was started by Fr. Cyril Gaul, OSB, Church history and Scripture instructor. He selected the best required research papers in his Church history class. Originally, it was duplicated on mimeograph, but it evolved into a scholarly journal. By 1965, when it was now called *Resonance*, authors included well-known theologians.

Besides publishing, the Press also printed Abbey-produced newsletters and outside magazines. Two newsletters concerning the activities of Abbey Press have been issued. In January 1972, Fr. Paschal, the general manager, began *Abbey Press Newsletter*, which discussed the operation of the Press and its personnel. It lasted only a few years. In the summer of 1982, *Abbey News*, which has been continuously published, served the same function.[79]

By 1951, two outside magazines, *Mary* and *Queen of All Hearts*, along with the Press' *Grail*, were printed. Outside magazines were often printed for only a few years because they ceased publication or went to other printers. By 1962, the printing division of the Press was printing 14 serials. Seven had been acquired during the previous year. In that year, periodicals printed by the Press had circulations between 5,000 and 150,000. To meet the expanding printing needs, new engraving equipment was acquired, including "a third large Miehle letterpress, a Baum folder, and a three-knife trimmer."[80]

Over the next decade, other magazines were acquired for printing by Abbey Press, which included *Ecology Today* and *Chicago Studies*. The *American Benedictine Review*, a scholarly journal, was printed from 1975 to the end of 1980. Beginning in 1975 and lasting through the 1980s, 16 magazines were printed at Abbey Press. Printing of outside publications continued to increase into the 21st century and, by 2007, 37 serial titles were printed. These ranged from secular to religious and included *Forum for Social Economics Journal*, an academic periodical; *Red and Black Newsletter*, for a college fraternity; and *Get Ready Newsletter*, for TD Jakes Ministries, a Protestant evangelical group. Some of the older serials that had been printed by the Press for a number of years ceased publication in the first decade of the 21st century.[81]

Books, Booklets and CareNotes

Very few books, or booklets, were published or printed by the Press before the third decade of the 20th century. In his review of the early years of the Press, Fr. Simeon found that the oldest booklet still in existence was printed by the Press in 1874. It was a small collection of rosary devotions, in German, for different seasons of the year. The next extant work is an edition of the holy *Rule* in English published in 1897. The first college catalog printed by the Press was in 1881. In 1889, a novice manual was printed in both a German and an English edition. It was re-edited in 1889, and again in 1912 and 1927, and was still used into the 1950s. Most imprints in the early years were largely for the monastic community or the seminary.[82]

During the early 20th century, in the wake of the condemnation of Modernism, "safe publications" that would not draw attention tended to be issued, including at Saint Meinrad.[83] The few books published beginning in 1919 and throughout the 1920s were aimed at clerics or for use in the seminary, such as the 414-page tome, *Introduction to the study of Sacred Scripture*, (1919) for the use of Saint Meinrad students. Seminary college catalogs were also published.

The first book aimed at the general reading public, in English, was a work of fiction, *Hills of Rest* (1926). Novels and books of short stories followed. In the 1930s, and into the early 1940s, biographies based on doctoral dissertations and histories of religious communities began to be published. These included *Simon Bruté de Rémur, First Bishop of Vincennes* (1931), *My brother, the Maryknoll Missionary* (1932), and *A Brief Historical Sketch of the Sisters of St. Benedict, Ferdinand, Indiana, 1867-1938* (1938).[84]

Fr. Paschal, after being appointed manager in 1944 of the newly created Grail Publications division of the Press, expanded book publications. Prior to this time, the publication division was termed "The Abbey Press," and after 1964, "Abbey Press." The first book issued under the Grail imprint was *Rome and the Study of Scripture* (1943); a reprint of this work was also one of the last to be published in 1964.[85]

Under the leadership of Fr. Philip Mahin, OSB, head of Grail Publications from 1955 to 1958, books and pamphlets were directed toward the Catholic reading public and clergy. Popular books on the lives of saints for children and Benedictine vocational material were published, printed or bound. These were sold to individuals, book stores, and pamphlet racks and represented the work of more than 100 authors.[86]

For example, most of the works of the noted children's author, Mary Fabyan Windeatt (1910-1979), who lived about two miles from the Abbey, were published by Grail. These included *Children of Fatima, The Lives of St. Paul* and *Our Lady of Guadalupe Color Book*. A major publication of the 1950s was the *History of Saint Meinrad Archabbey* (1954) by Fr. Albert Kleber, OSB, for the 100th anniversary of the foundation of Saint Meinrad.

Society began to change in the mid-1960s. In this decade, books published and printed by the Press reflected the beginning of the "self-help" era. Marriage paperback division was active. Books issued included such titles as *A Do-it-yourself Guide to Family Fun and Recreation* (1964) and *How to Be a Successful Mother* (1964). By 1967, 25 paperbacks were in print. These included *The Do-it-yourself Parent* and *Sex and Personal Growth*.[87]

The 1970s counter-culture era brought in both the questioning of religion and a renewed interest in spirituality, along with concerns about marriage. Reflecting this trend, a series of spiritual books was published by the Press under the general title of The Religious Experience Series. One of the ten best-selling Catholic press books in 1974 was *The God I Don't Believe In*. At the 1975 Catholic Press Association convention, *The Courage to Be Married* (1974) won first place in the Christian family category. Publications ranging from charismatic renewal to light fiction and women's liberation were also published in the mid-1970s.[88]

During the early 1980s, booklets and books were issued to help meet and solve life's challenges. A series of "When Books," under 100 pages in length, addressed concerns or crisis points of life. These included such titles as *When You Are Concerned with Homosexuality* (1980) and *When Pregnancy is a Problem* (1980). Inspirational novels such as *A Whisper in the Wind* (1987) were issued. These works led to one of the most successful product lines of Abbey Press in recent history, CareNotes, first published in 1988.

The CareNotes concept was developed by Linus Mundy, with the support of Fr. Keith McClellan, OSB. Soon after his ordination, Fr. Keith, in 1980, was assigned to work at Abbey Press. Two years later in January 1982, Archabbot Timothy Sweeney, OSB, appointed him manager of the publications division. In addition to developing new publications, he was also editor of *Marriage and Family Living*.

To further hone his publishing skills, Fr. Keith did graduate work in journalism at Ohio University, Athens, OH, in 1984-85.[89] Somewhat earlier, Linus Mundy graduated from Saint Meinrad High School (Minor Seminary) in one of its last classes in the late 1960s. After college, he worked for Abbey Press in publishing in the early 1970s for several years. He then left to become marketing director of *Saint Anthony Messenger* at Saint Anthony Press in Cincinnati, OH.

In the late 1980s, Mundy approached Fr. Keith with an idea for an inspirational publication product he wanted to do. Fr. Keith hired him in 1987 and *CareNotes* was born. Mundy described CareNotes as an alternative to a *Reader's Digest* story. It was quick and simple. Wilhite adds that, "The most successful of the CareNotes were in the 'Grief & Caring' area, as is the most successful part of Abbey Press products in the 'Memorial, Grief, Caring' side of the business.... This product brought a profitable new beginning to Abbey Press.... It has been our most important successful product and our most important product for quite a number of years."[90]

In 2001, Mundy, director of the CareNotes program, quoted in the *Saint Meinrad Newsletter*, explains that, "it's the understanding these booklets provide that people welcome so much. We don't provide answers; we provide understanding."[91] These little inspirational booklets had the publishing slogan of "Take one and take heart; give one and give hope." Wilhite explains, "CareNotes are serious reads in short-form." They have titles such as "Grieving in Your Own Way," "Finding Hope When Your Body Won't Heal" and "Sad Isn't Bad," aimed at children, and they were designed for hospitals, waiting rooms and religious organizations.

The typical customer is a hospital chaplain who buys a year's subscription of the CareNotes. By 2001, 65 million copies had been sold. Wilhite sums up the philosophy of CareNotes. "I'd like to think that this really is the heart of Abbey Press contributing to the monastic values. The ministry of Saint Meinrad is providing these kinds of materials... whenever there is a crisis or a particular need in [a person's] life that could be addressed."[92]

One Caring Place, a publishing imprint of Abbey Press, was created in 1994 for its inspirational "self-help" books and pamphlets. Its motto was: "Where there's health and healing for body, mind and spirit." Besides CareNotes, its product lines also include CareNotes for Teens, CareNotes for Kids, PrayerNotes, Care Cards and most Elf-help booklets.[93]

Elf-help booklets were conceived by a psychologist in the late 1980s. "Self-help" became "Elf help." Each booklet has 35 simple rules on a specific topic with illustrations of elf-like characters acting out the rule. In 1996, Abbey Press started to sell the proprietary rights of the Elf-help book line internationally. Licensing agreements included translations into languages of a number of countries. By 2006, 36 titles for the now-called Elf-help Therapy Book line were being offered.[94]

In the first decade of the 21st century, almost all of the Press' publications were the popular inspirational booklets. However, some more scholarly items were printed for different units of the Archabbey, including the *Benedictine Oblates of Saint Meinrad Archabbey* (2000), by Edward L. Shaughnessy, and *Prefer Nothing to Christ* (2004), edited by Fr. Cyprian Davis, OSB, on the occasion of the 150th anniversary of the founding of the Archabbey.

Abbey Press Catalogs

In the early years of the 20th century, various items were advertised in magazines published by the Press, such as *Paradiesesfrüchte*. These included a "cure all" for skin problems—wundpflaster—later called Rose Salve, "prepared with great care at the abbey." Calendars, art objects and Christmas cards were first introduced in 1920, and the first books, in English, in 1921. Grave memorials, "miraculous silver rings," boarding schools and tours were advertised in this, and the Abbey Press' *Grail*, until the mid-1930s. The catalog mail order business of Abbey Press did not begin until 1963. Since that time, the Press has developed a number of catalogs with a variety of products.

Direct Marketing Catalogs

The first catalog, *Abbey Press Catalogue: Everything for the Christian Family,* had a yellow cover with "pen and ink" lettering and featured a family reading together. This original catalog had 34 pages and its products ranged from Sacred Music by the Chancel Choir of St. Meinrad Archabbey on hi-fi records, to books, note cards and retreats. Fr. Eric recalls, "We blessed [the catalog] in the mail room. We were so excited. We had no idea what the results would be. The results were so good that even the abbot had to help us fill the orders!"[95]

By 1965, 250,000 copies of the 1966 catalog, now called *The Christian Family Catalog,* were mailed to oblates (lay members of the community) and *Marriage* magazine subscribers. The following year, the printing and publishing divisions combined their products for the catalog. Christmas cards, the most popular product, were featured in the catalog along with an "art in the home" line of religious sculptures, posters and art objects. By 1972, almost 4 million catalogs were being mailed. In the mid-1970s, special catalogs, such as a catalog devoted entirely to statues, were created.[96]

In 1983, the catalog developed a product line. Wilhite explains, "It had become more like what a specialty catalog is now defined as: a mixed group of products organized by theme." For the Christmas spread, for example, a variety of Christmas-related products, like a nativity set and art objects, were offered; it also offered many Christmas cards. *Abbey Holiday Edition* was introduced in 1984 and sent to a selected sample of customers. Sales from the catalogs were brisk. The most popular item was the "school bus" coffee mug designed by Abbey Press.[97]

The 1993 30th anniversary autumn/Christmas catalog featured a variety of personalized objects. Many of them were not particularly spiritual or religious, such as "tools to help you organize." These products could be found in many catalogs of the time. Wilhite states, "At this point in our life, we were making small, cheap (catalogs), and mailing millions in hoping for the best."[98]

However, by 1995, chronic losses in the catalog operations had come to the point where change was required. As part of the reorganization of 1995-96, discussed earlier, a long-range plan and re-evaluation of the mission of the Press resulted in several specialized catalogs being developed in the next few years. These included *You and Yours*, *Collections* and *Holidays*. Products that were not consistent with the Abbey Press product mission were discontinued. In October 1997, the not-for-profit mailing status for Abbey Press catalog was discontinued, leading to fewer catalogs being sent out. A marketing service was retained to help find the best customers.[99]

By 2003, most items in the catalog had a religious, spiritual or uplifting message. Personalized or memorial objects were popular. By 2006, the catalog was larger and printed on better paper. Products were organized by theme, and more variety of products was offered. *Abbey Blessings* was created in 2002 with a theme of "Celebrating the spirit in everyday." Items offered were religious, such as rosaries and crucifixes, or personalized plaques. In 2005, this catalog went to an exclusive online business, but it was not successful. It was found that catalogs needed both a mailed and an online presence.[100]

Trade Marketing Catalog

Dealer catalogs for retailers and dealers were also created to market items from the Press. These are the catalogs from which retailers order items for sale in their stores. In 1972, Abbey Press published a catalog of publications, *Abbey Press Book Catalog*. It was mailed to over 60,000 bookstores, schools and rectories. In 1984, 2,000 dealer catalogs were mailed prior to the Christian Booksellers Convention to acquaint potential buyers with products of Abbey Press and this proved to be successful. In the mid-1980s, dealer sales were seen as "a growing dimension of Abbey Press." They were generally a large quantity purchase of an entire line of a given product such as "Shadow Visions"—artwork in a framed box with glass on front—for a retail store or a chain of stores such as Hallmark.[101]

In 1989, all products sold through trade sales were developed in-house and were exclusive Abbey Press designs. Sales were brisk at trade shows into the early 1990s. Then the trade market slowed. This was reflected in trade shows, where attendance and sales were down by 1995. Beginning in the 1970s, trade shows were excellent avenues to display items sold by the Press. At the shows, thank you gifts to customers were sometimes given by the monks. For years, Fr. Eric signed or created calligraphy. The most amusing gift item given out was a "bobble head" toy of Br. Maurus in full habit. In 2004, it was created to commemorate the 40 years of the sales trade started by him in 1964. Br. Maurus relates, "I thought it was kind of silly. I didn't even know what a bobble head was. So anyway, I went and asked the Prior if I could be a bobble head. He looked me in the eye and said, 'As long as I can have one!'"[102]

As part of reorganization, new catalogs were developed for the trade market. By 2005, Wilhite remarked that the trade market "part of the business is alive and well, producing several catalogs for about 1,250 products we sell to stores."[103] In 2006, the *Abbey Press: the Message Company* catalog, marketed to retail organizations, was attractively printed on good quality paper and had 95 pages. Inspirational items were offered, such as coffee cups that said "don't quit," to rosary holders in Spanish and biblical quotations of artwork. Thirty product lines were now advertised, ranging from home blessings to words of wisdom. This area of the Press is strong and also has an online presence.

New Products and the Gift Shop

In the early 1960s, after the success of the first marketing of items by the Press in the brochure and catalog, many new products were developed. These items were sold in a small gift shop area in the guest house, in addition to the catalog. In the late 1970s, a separate gift shop was opened and later a new one was built that still does a brisk business.

New Products and the Sculpture Shop

In 1968, Br. Maurus was appointed manager of the new products department of the Press to oversee the creation of new merchandise. Many products were developed under his direction, including the use of silkscreening on wood, plastic, vinyl, brass, urethane and paper. Br. Maurus explained, "The products must all carry the message of God's desire that we have peace, love and joy. The art and text must be appropriate for that theme. If I cannot use the product or cannot think of anyone I would want to give the product to, then I feel it isn't worth developing."[104]

Calligraphy was a popular artform developed and marketed by the Press. In the first catalog of 1963, Fr. Eric, along with Fr. Gavin Barnes, OSB, and Fr. Colman Grabert, OSB, designed Christmas cards. Fr. Eric increased his output over the years. By 1984, ten of his products were in the retail catalog and many more in the dealers' catalog. Of Fr. Eric's products, the "Footprints in the Sand" ones were the best selling, both in "shadow vision" and in Christmas card forms.[105]

Some products developed in the mid-1960s, such as Fr. Eric's calligraphy works, were so successful that they were still selling in 2007 in different forms—for example, a "footprint garden stone." Not every item was popular. Some posters, pleated scrolls and rope hangers did not sell and were phased out and sold at discount at the Abbey Press Gift Shop yard sales.[106]

When Br. Maurus was appointed manager of the new gift shop in 1978, various individuals replaced him as manager of the new product development unit. Br. Maurus notes, "I would just choose what I wanted on every page." However, development of new products became a team effort, along with discussions of what items should be placed in the catalog.[107]

After products were developed, they needed to be produced. The Press initiated its own statue-making shop called the "sculpture shop" in August 1972. The operation began in "1,890 square feet of space in the east-side-of-the-road chicken house." Br. Benedict Barthel, OSB, was transferred from printing to work in this shop. Carl Mauck from

Cincinnati taught him the art of making molds and trained others in the various steps of producing sculpture.[108]

The shop was set up to handle plaster, plastic and metal statuary. During the first year of operation, the largest selling item was a 17-piece Christmas crib set that came in two sizes. The shop also made unusual items, such as a praying Buddhist monk and novelty statues called "Silly Sculps" with humorous captions beneath them.[109] These later were discontinued as they did not meet the mission of the Press.

In 1973, the sculpture shop was under the direction of Rose Mary Sitzman. During the Christmas rush for the last half of that year, 24 people were employed by the shop and nearly 35,000 pieces of sculpture were produced. Besides the crèches, nearly 50 other pieces of religious and family-related items comprised most of the shop production. The goods were sold through the *Abbey Press Christian Family Catalog* and the *Abbey Sculpture* catalog, a special 16-page catalog devoted entirely to sculpture.[110]

The sculpture business expanded rapidly and additional space for its operation was gradually added. By 1976, this also included renovation of the milking parlor after the dairy operation of the farm was discontinued in 1974. That same year, the Abbey Press board of directors recommended further expansion of the sculpture shop's facilities to enlarge its operations and to keep up with customer demand.[111]

A new 20,000-square-foot sculpture production facility was attached to Plant II in 1977, known as the "sculpture addition." The operation was moved from the chicken house to this new plant. However, Br. Benedict notes, "Later, because of the objectionable fumes produced in melting the mold material, this part of the operation was moved back to the chicken house, where we remained until 1995 when all production was sent to China."[112]

In February 1995, as part of the overall re-organization of the Press, the sculpture production division was closed. Foreign competition and decreased profitability led to this decision. Br. Maurus adds, "You have a life cycle for products. A lot of people (competitors) picked up Fr. Eric's footprints in the sand and other designs...and put them out in other forms…. The competition got pretty tough and you would have to move on to new things."[113]

However, sculptures and other objects were still sold by the Press after the manufacturing operation was closed. They were now made to specification in other countries, such as China, and then personalized back at the Press. Items made by other companies were also sold if they met the mission of the Press. Some collectibles were still very popular, including "Precious Moments" figurines, Thomas Kinkade's "Angels of Light" and "Seraphim Angels." These, along with personalized and memorial items, such as a Christmas tree ornament with the name of a deceased loved one, were still on the upswing in 2006.

Gift Shop

The St. Jude Guest House was built in 1962. Religious art was sold near the registration area. However, it was a small operation and mostly gathered dust. When guests stayed at the Guest House, they expected a regular gift shop. "They came here looking for it. They would drive around the monastery and ask, 'Where's your gift shop?'"[114] In the spring of 1968, Abbey Press assumed proprietorship of the gift shop in the Guest House and staffed it. In addition to the religious art previously sold by the shop, publications and items sold by the Press were displayed.[115]

As more items were created in the product development division and the sculpture shop, it was decided that a real gift shop was needed. In January 1978, the Abbey Gift Shoppe was opened in the old milk parlor. Products offered at the shop were developed at Abbey Press. They included holy cards, notes, mini-plaques, posters, greeting scrolls, gift banners, bookmarks and mini-posters. Br. Maurus was appointed the first manager of the gift shop and relates the philosophy of this store. "Any person coming to Saint Meinrad Archabbey and stopping in at the gift shop should be greeted according to the *Rule of St. Benedict*. Guests should be received as Christ. To the best of our ability, we try to take care of their needs."[116]

The gift shop began yard sales to get rid of extra items, discontinued lines and overstocks. Bargain hunters came from surrounding states to these sales. In the spring of 1985, for example, over 3,000 people came to the gift shop yard sale. It needs to be kept in mind that the gift shop, then and now, is on a very small road, state highway 545, near the town of St. Meinrad with a population of only about 600. These popular yard sales continued until about 2006. Discounted items are now sold in the outlet room of the gift shop.[117]

However, Br. Maurus notes, "We had a problem with the old gift shop because we had one toilet. You had to go through the furnace room to get to one toilet—one seat, one toilet. And buses would come there and it would take about two hours to get to the toilets."[118]

Because of the success of the gift shop—and its lack of bathroom facilities and other physical problems—the monastic community voted at the end of March 1985 to request a "new Gift Shoppe for the Abbey Press." A metal building was built north of the former dairy barn over the summer of 1985. It had air conditioning and freezers for cheese and sausage. The shop moved from the old dairy barn into the new building in late September 1985.[119]

The new gift shop had a display and storage area like a traditional kind of store. Wilhite notes, "It does remarkable business for a specialty gift shop located in a non-traffic area. Not many people just happen to wander here and stop in. They come because they want to come to the gift shop."[120] In December 1986, the *Community Bulletin* announced that the store, from now on, was to be called the "Abbey Press Gift Shop" and not Gift Shoppe. Besides the usual products, that year it also sold Christmas trees at $10 provided by the Abbey forester, Fr. Joseph Mort, OSB.[121]

In 1987, the gift shop offered two catalogs, *Abbey Country Fare* catalog, with gourmet food products, and *Abbey Press Gift Shop* catalog featuring religious books, music and gifts.[122] Br. Maurus left as manager of the gift shop in August 1990 and was appointed tour director and assistant guest house manager.

By the late 1990s, the gift shop began an online presence. It was remodeled in 2004 and again in 2006. As part of the remodeling, a display room for Abbey Caskets, a new business venture of the Archabbey started in 1999, was created. Wilhite notes, "I think the gift shop would be great for Abbey Press no matter what. People get Abbey Press catalogs, hunt us up and want to see our gift shop. They're delighted to find out that there's a monastery here. More likely, though, people will come to visit the monastery and part of their experience visiting here is to go to the gift shop. That's what Br. Maurus had in mind to begin with. When people come to visit Saint Meinrad, they should be able to see what we do and what we sell."[123]

In summary, many monastic communities, since the early Middle Ages, have illuminated and transcribed manuscripts, and later adopted printing to enlighten society with literature and Christian concepts. Abbey Press began as a small venture to supply the monastic community and its schools with printed materials.

Over the past century and a half, the Press has grown into a major marketer of products that promote Christian values and beliefs. Abbey Press now has five channels of distribution: printing, the oldest business; trade marketing, selling to stores; direct marketing, selling direct to consumers at home; institutional marketing, which primarily has been CareNotes sold to churches, schools and hospitals; and the gift shop, which offers merchandise. Collectively, those make up Abbey Press. The essence of the Press today is found in an introductory paragraph on its trade Web site, which states, "It has become our mission to develop products that inspire, encourage, hearten, help, cheer, assist, and support through prayer and meditation for all Christian faiths."[124]

Chapter Contributors

Fr. Simeon, head of the Saint Meinrad Archabbey Library for his whole career, wrote, "St. Meinrad Abbey Press," (1975) an essay of the early history of the Press.

Fr. Rupert, in November 1979, was appointed general manager of Abbey Press until his transfer to Human Resources in 1991.

Br. Maurus was head of the printing division, sundry products and manager of the gift shop. He shaped the direction of the Press into a catalog business.

Gerald Wilhite became general manager in 1995. His leadership decisions pointed the Press in new directions as a catalog Internet business in a rapidly changing and competitive environment of the turn of the 21st century.

Endnotes

1. For further information on the scriptoria of the early Middle Ages see: McKitterick, Rosamond, *Books, Scribes, and Learning in the Frankish Kingdoms, 6th-9th Centuries* (1994); Henderson, George, *From Durrow to Kells* (1987).

2. The printing and publishing business of Saint Meinrad Archabbey is sometimes called The Abbey Press by older monastic community members; it is inscribed this way on the original press facility built in 1930-31 and is used in writings of the Abbey until the early 1960s. It was called Abbey Press in its first catalog of 1963 and subsequent publications of the Archabbey.

3. The early history of the Press is based upon a paper presented in 1954 at the American Benedictine Academy by Fr. Simeon Daly, OSB, "St. Meinrad Abbey Press," (1975); Fr. Albert Kleber's *History of Saint Meinrad Archabbey, 1854-1954* (1954) and material gleaned by the editor from the rare book room of the Saint Meinrad Archabbey Library.

4. Gerald Wilhite to Prof. Ruth C. Engs, September 21, 2005, interview transcription, Saint Meinrad Archabbey Archives; Wilhite, Gerald, "Abbey Press Recent History," unpublished paper, Saint Meinrad Archabbey, 2005.

5. Daly, S., 1975, 9.

6. Daly, S., 1975, 10-11.

7. Daly, S., 1975, 18.

8. Daly, S., 1975, 18; Wilhite to Engs, September 2005.

9. The yearly ORDO, which lists the liturgical calendar along with the occupation of living monks of various communities of the Swiss-American Congregation of the Benedictine Confederation, shows that after Fr. Edward's removal, no monk was listed as manager of the Press from 1935-40. Daly, S. (1975, 19), however, suggests that a lay worker, Mr. August Ringeman, may have served as manager during this period as does the *Abbey News*, Summer 1995 issue.

10. See footnote 9 for definition of ORDO. Daly, S., 1975, 20; *Saint Meinrad Newsletter*, 6:2, January 1962.

11. *Saint Meinrad Newsletter*, 1:4, Spring 1958.

12. Br. Maurus Zoeller to Prof. Ruth C. Engs, e-mail: Jan. 2, 2006.

13. *Saint Meinrad Newsletter*, 6:2, January 1962.

14. Br. Maurus Zoeller to Prof. Ruth C. Engs, interview transcription, Sept. 20, 2005, Saint Meinrad Archabbey Archives.

15. Zoeller to Engs, private communication, Jan. 22, 2007.

16. Zoeller to Engs, 2005; Fr. Eric Lies to Prof. Ruth C. Engs, interview transcription, Aug. 22-23, 2005, Saint Meinrad Archabbey Archives.

17. Zoeller to Engs, Jan. 22, 2007.

18. *Saint Meinrad Newsletter*, 8:4, January 1966; *Community Bulletin*, Nov. 5-11, 1967.

19. *Community Bulletin*, June 26-July 2, 1966.

20 *Community Bulletin*, July 17-23, 1966; Zoeller to Engs, 2005.

21. *Community Bulletin*, July 17-23, 1966.

22. *Community Bulletin*, Jan. 3-9, 1965; *Community Bulletin*, Dec. 5-11, 1965; *Community Bulletin*, March 27-April 2, 1966; *Community Bulletin*, April 17-23, 1966; *Community Bulletin*, April 24-30, 1966.

23. *Community Bulletin*, Aug. 27-Sept. 2, 1967; Lies to Engs, 2005.

24. *Community Bulletin*, Feb. 4-10, 1968; *Community Bulletin*, July 28-Aug. 3, 1968.

25. Zoeller to Engs, 2005.

26. *Community Bulletin*, Nov. 23-29, 1969.

27. *Community Bulletin*, Nov. 12-18, 1972.

28. *Community Bulletin*, Nov. 16-22, 1969.

29. Zoeller to Engs, 2005.

30. "Five Year Plan for Abbey Press, Feb. 23, 1971," in Boland (1975).

31. *Community Bulletin*, March 28-April 3, 1971; *Community Bulletin*, June 20-26, 1971; *Saint Meinrad Newsletter*, 14:1, 1973; *Abbey Press Newsletter* 1:1, January 1972.

32. *Community Bulletin*, Nov. 12-18, 1972.

33. *Community Bulletin*, July 7-14, 1974.

34. Other members included Fr. Columba Kelly, OSB, Fr. Eric and Fr. Hilary Ottensmeyer, OSB; *Community Bulletin*, April 25-May 1, 1976.

35. *Community Bulletin*, Aug. 22-28, 1976.

36. *Community Bulletin*, July 7-13, 1968; *Community Bulletin*, April 26-May 2, 1970; *Saint Meinrad Newsletter*, 11:5, 1970; Gerald Wilhite to Prof. Ruth C. Engs, e-mail: Dec. 12, 2006.

37. See the "Land" chapter for information concerning the farming operation.

38. *Saint Meinrad Newsletter*, 16:6, July 1975.

39. Wilhite to Engs, September 2005.

40. Wilhite to Engs, Dec. 12, 2006.

41. *Community Bulletin*, Nov. 16-22, 1979.

42. "Abbey Press Five Year Plan," white paper, Saint Meinrad, July 1980; *Community Bulletin*, March 22-28, 1985.

43. Wilhite to Engs, Dec. 12, 2006.

44. *Community Bulletin*, Aug. 30-Sept. 6, 1984.

45. *Saint Meinrad Newsletter*, 28:3, Fall 1989; Wilhite to Engs, September 2005.

46. Quote from *Saint Meinrad Newsletter*, 30:3, Summer 1991.

47. *Saint Meinrad Newsletter*, 32:1, Winter 1993.

48. *Saint Meinrad Newsletter*, 32:2, Spring 1993.

49. *Saint Meinrad Newsletter*, 32:1, Winter 1993; *Saint Meinrad Newsletter*, 32:2, Spring 1993.

50. *Saint Meinrad Newsletter*, 32:1, Winter 1993.

51. Wilhite to Engs, September 2005.

52. Powell, Bill, "Abbey Press lays off 61," *The Herald*, Wednesday, Feb. 22, 1995, 3.

53. "Reduction in Work Force at Abbey Press," Feb. 21, 1995, white paper, Saint Meinrad Archabbey.

54. *Saint Meinrad Newsletter*, 34:3, Summer 1995.

55. Wilhite to Engs, September 2005.

56. Wilhite, 2005.

57. Luecke, Vince, *The Ferdinand News*, Feb. 23, 1995.

58. "Abbey Press Business Plan Fiscal Year 1997-78" in the *Community Bulletin*, May 18, 1997.

59. *Community Bulletin*, Sept. 6, 1998.

60. Wilhite to Engs, September 2005.

61. *Community Bulletin*, Jan. 22, 2006.

62. Wilhite to Engs, September 2005.

63. Gramelspacher, M., et al. Abbey Press Strategic Plan Fye 2006-10, unpublished paper, Saint Meinrad, January 2005.

64. Wilhite to Engs, September 2005; Wilhite to Engs, Dec. 12, 2006.

65. Wilhite to Engs, September 2005.

66 Kleber, 1954, 389-391.

67. Daly, S., 1975, 7.

68. Ibid., 12.

69. Fr. Hilary De Jean, OSB (1934-37), Fr. Jerome Palmer, OSB (1937-38), and Fr. Paschal Boland, OSB (1938-41) appeared to have served as editors in these time periods, although there is ambiguity concerning this; Daly, 1975, 20; ORDO.

70. Daly, S., 1975, 20.

71. *Saint Meinrad Newsletter*, 1:4, Spring 1958.

72. *Saint Meinrad Newsletter*, 3:2, January 1960; *Saint Meinrad Newsletter*, 6:1, October 1963.

73. *Community Bulletin*, Dec. 25-31, 1966; *Community Bulletin*, Sept. 18-24, 1966; *Marriage*, June 1969.

74. *Community Bulletin*, March 28-April 3, 1971; *Community Bulletin*, June 20-26, 1971.

75. *Community Bulletin*, Dec. 6-12, 1970; *Community Bulletin*, Oct. 1-7, 1972.

76. *Saint Meinrad Newsletter*, 15:1, January 1974; *Community Bulletin*, May 18-24, 1975; *Community Bulletin*, Oct. 22-28, 1982.

77. Wilhite to Engs, September 2005; Worldcat, the academic online library catalog, indicated Jan. 1, 2007, that 230 libraries worldwide have it in their collection.

78 It was titled *Historical Essays* (1928), *St. Meinrad Historical Essays* (1929-1946), *St. Meinrad Essays* (1946-1963) and *Resonance* (1965-1975).

79. See the "Finances and Fund Raising" chapter for information about newsletters, in particular the ones published by the Development Office. *Community Bulletin*, Jan. 25-29, 1972; Wilhite to Engs, Dec. 12, 2006.

80. Daly, S., 1975, 16; *Saint Meinrad Newsletter*, 6:2, January 1962.

81. *Community Bulletin*, March 21-27, 1971; *Community Bulletin*, April 6-12, 1975; *Community Bulletin*, Sept. 6-12, 1984; *Community Bulletin*, May 16-23, 1985; Wilhite to Engs, Dec. 12, 2006.

82. Daly, S., 1975, 2-4.

83. For more information on the campaign against Modernism see: Appleby, Scott R., *Church and Age Unite* (1992).

84. This information gleaned from books examined in the Saint Meinrad Library and Worldcat.

85. Ibid.

86. *Saint Meinrad Newsletter*, 1:4, Spring 1958.

87. *Community Bulletin*, Sept. 8-14, 1968.

88. *Community Bulletin*, Feb. 6-12, 1972; *Community Bulletin*, Feb. 15-22, 1974; *Community Bulletin*, March 2-8, 1975; *Saint Meinrad Newsletter*, 16:6, July 1975.

89. Community Bulletin, Jan. 15-21, 1982; Community Bulletin, Sept. 6-12, 1984.

90. Wilhite to Engs, e-mail: Jan. 5, 2007; Wilhite to Engs, September 2005; *Saint Meinrad Newsletter*, 40:2, Spring 2001.

91. *Saint Meinrad Newsletter*, 40:2, Spring 2001.

92. *Saint Meinrad Newsletter*, 40:2, Spring 2001; Wilhite to Engs, September 2005.

93. *Saint Meinrad Newsletter*, 35:1, Winter 1996; Wilhite to Engs, Dec. 12, 2006.

94. *Community Bulletin*, Oct. 20, 1996; *Saint Meinrad Newsletter*, 35:1, Winter 1996.

95. Lies to Engs, 2005.

96. *Community Bulletin*, Oct. 24-30, 1965; *Community Bulletin*, Oct. 30-Nov. 5, 1966; *Community Bulletin*, Feb. 1-7, 1970; *Community Bulletin*, Oct. 15-21, 1972; *Saint Meinrad Newsletter*, 15:1, January 1974.

97. Wilhite to Engs, September 2005; *Community Bulletin*, Oct. 11-18, 1984; *Community Bulletin*, Nov. 1-8, 1984.

98. Wilhite to Engs, September 2005.

99. *Community Bulletin*, May 18, 1997.

100. *Community Bulletin*, Aug. 11, 2002; Wilhite to Engs, September 2005; Wilhite to Engs, Dec. 12, 2006.

101. *Community Bulletin*, Nov. 12-18, 1972; *Saint Meinrad Newsletter*, 14:1, 1973; *Community Bulletin*, July 5-12, 1984.

102. *Saint Meinrad Newsletter*, 28:3, Fall 1989; *Community Bulletin*, Aug. 7, 1996; Zoeller to Engs, 2005.

103. Wilhite to Engs, September 2005.

104. *Community Bulletin*, July 28-Aug. 3, 1968; Br. Maurus quoted in *Abbey News*, July 1983.

105. *Community Bulletin*, Nov. 15-29, 1984. "Footprints in the Sand" is a poem of ambiguous origins.

106. Zoeller to Engs, 2005.

107. Zoeller to Engs, 2005.

108. *Saint Meinrad Newsletter*, 28:2, Summer 1989; *Community Bulletin*, Oct. 15-21, 1972.

109. *Saint Meinrad Newsletter*, 14:1, 1973.

110. *Saint Meinrad Newsletter*, 15:1, January 1974.

111. *Community Bulletin*, June 13-19, 1976.

112. Wilhite to Engs, Dec.12, 2006; Wilhite to Engs, e-mail: Jan. 5, 2007; Br. Benedict Barthel to Ruth C. Engs, interview transcription, Nov. 16, 2005, Saint Meinrad Archives.

113. Zoeller to Engs, 2005.

114. Wilhite to Engs, September 2005.

115. *Community Bulletin*, May 5-11, 1968.

116. Br. Maurus quoted in *Abbey News*, July 1983.

117. *Community Bulletin*, Nov. 1-8, 1984; *Community Bulletin*, April 4-11, 1985.

118. *Community Bulletin*, Dec. 4-10, 1981. See the "Land" chapter about Br. Vincent Brunette's operation along with other farm information; Zoeller to Engs, 2005.

119. *Community Bulletin*, Sept. 27-Oct. 4, 1985; *Saint Meinrad Newsletter*, 25:4, October 1985.

120. Wilhite to Engs, September 2005.

121. *Community Bulletin*, Dec. 5-12, 1986. See the "Land" chapter for more information concerning the forestry operation at Saint Meinrad.

122. *Community Bulletin*, Oct. 9-16, 1987.

123. Wilhite to Engs, September 2005.

124. www.abbeytrade.com.

Chapter Fourteen

Baling hay was a familiar summer chore, as seen in this 1947 photo.

Land: The Sustenance of the Abbey
Ruth C. Engs

In Europe, monastic communities have lived off their lands in a variety of ways, depending upon the resources in their region. Crops, orchards, timber, stone, livestock and other agricultural endeavors sustained the monastery. However, most communities were not completely self-sufficient or entirely operated as closed subsistence economies. They bartered, traded or sold products, and used the cash to buy necessities from markets close to home. Monastic lands were also rented out for cash, and in many cases tenants were responsible for supplying produce for the maintenance of the community for a part of the year.[1]

Benedictine monasticism, since its very beginnings, has been based on an agrarian model. Historian James Bond suggests that Benedictine communities, in particular, have had a tradition from the Middle Ages of being "concentrated in anciently-settled, fertile, low-lying countryside where there was a strong emphasis on arable farming."[2] The tradition of monastic communities, both male and female, of the Order of St. Benedict owning land that could supply sustenance to the community continued into the late 20th century.

In 1853, two monks, Fr. Ulrich Christen, OSB, and Fr. Bede O'Connor, OSB, from the Benedictine monastery of the Blessed Virgin Mary in Einsiedeln, Switzerland, were sent to southern Indiana. They were to investigate the possibility of founding a mission in the Diocese of Vincennes as a safe haven from anti-Catholic political forces that threatened to confiscate Church and monastic holdings in Switzerland, and to minister to the growing German-speaking population in the region. Arable land was sought that could be the sustenance of a new foundation.[3]

Fr. Albert Kleber, OSB, in his 100-year history of Saint Meinrad in 1954, reports that Fr. Ulrich "found a place of his liking—he called it 'simply a paradise'—in Spencer County, in the southern part of the Parish of St. Ferdinand, and about six miles south of the town; it consisted of a number of tracts situated on the western bank of the Anderson River."[4] Fr. Ulrich negotiated the purchase of 2,400 acres that had been broken into various tracts. He reported, "that besides fertile soil, there were majestic forests, and underneath the ground, coal, sandstone of excellent quality…limestone from which lime could be burnt, and even a little iron."[5] In addition, there were two farms with a log house and barns, springs, gristmill and sawmill.

Of the two farms he bought, Fr. Ulrich particularly liked the 160-acre one owned by Catherine and Heinrich (Henry) Denning. Half of it was cleared and it was on a hill overlooking the Anderson Valley. Although the price was high—$2,700—Fr. Ulrich bought it in February 1854, along with other properties. His abbot, Henry IV Schmid von Baar, at Einsiedeln, was not pleased with his hasty and expensive purchases.[6] The community, with four Swiss monks, was officially founded as a mission on the feast of St. Benedict, March 21, 1854, on the Denning farm property. It was named after the martyred saint of hospitality, St. Meinrad.

Thus began the Saint Meinrad mission in the wilderness of southern Indiana. It was made a conventual priory on May 1, 1864, and elevated to an independent abbey on September 30, 1870, with Fr. Martin Marty, OSB, as its first abbot. The monastic lands were used for the sustenance of the abbey for over 100 years. In this chapter, a brief history of the early activities will be sketched along with information concerning land management, livestock, viticulture, sandstone and forest operations in the last half of the 20th century. This time period is contemporary with the lives of the monks interviewed for this book. It is also during this period that most of the traditional monastic agricultural, livestock and other operations were discontinued.

Acquisition and Sale of Land

Over the years, Saint Meinrad has bought and sold, or has been given, land. Various land management conservation programs of the times were also implemented. In the first decade of the foundation's existence, multiple problems plagued the community, including rising debt, illness and death, and personal conflicts among the brethren. Because of these problems, in 1858, the four monks of the community petitioned the abbot to partially liquidate the land holdings to reduce the debt.[7] Fr. Martin and Fr. Fintan Mundwiler, OSB, were sent from Einsiedeln to sort out the situation; they arrived at the community in September 1860.

Under Fr. Martin's leadership, various legal arrangements were made in the ensuing years to solve the debt problem. These included, but were not limited to, the creation of a parish and town of St. Meinrad on monastic property near the priory for which parcels were auctioned off and the sale of a number of acres of land. Common land management practices of the day, such as draining the swampy area near the community, clearing the forests and digging a well, greatly reduced diseases such as malaria, typhoid fever and others.[8]

In the 20th century, land was acquired near the monastery, or agreements were made, with governmental agencies for conservation programs. For example, in 1937, the abbey purchased from George Denning and his wife, and a few years later from other neighbors, a large tract of land to the northeast in the Anderson Valley for a water reservoir. The Works Progress Administration built a dam for "checking soil erosion, conserving water, effecting flood control, and propagating and protecting fish and other aquatic life."[9]

Thirty years later, in 1968, a governmental land conservancy agreement was established called the Anderson River Watershed Conservancy District Plan. Its purpose was to prevent floods, the loss of top soil by erosion and the control of water. Ten years later, in 1978, funding for the project finally became available.[10] In 2006, another governmental conservation program was undertaken, to be discussed later, in connection with the Archabbey's forests.

In July 1967, three small tracts of land east of the Archabbey were sold to the town of St. Meinrad as a recreation area.[11] The Archabbey was forced to sell land under eminent domain laws. Ten acres of the beef farm pasture were sold to the state in 1968 for Interstate 64.[12] Camp Benedict, the monastic recreation area, discussed below, was sold for a state park.

The Archabbey bought, or donated, some of its properties for churches or new foundations. In 1938, the little town of Siberia was laid out on Archabbey property; one block for the church was donated by the Archabbey.[13] The Archabbey acquired land for new foundations in other states. For instance, in 1949, 400 acres of neglected farmland was bought in Marvin, SD. This was for the new foundation of Blue Cloud, which was made an abbey in 1954.[14] Land donated to Saint Meinrad by benefactors, outside of the St. Meinrad region, was sold, including farms located in Bloomington, Terre Haute and other areas in the late 1970s.[15]

Camp Benedict

William Rice, of Louisville, KY, owned 3.6 acres on the Blue River about halfway between St. Meinrad and Louisville. He sold it to the Archabbey in May 1932, "lest the camp fall into wrong hands," for $2,500. The Archabbey promptly named it Camp Benedict. It had a large house and a playhouse, which was turned into St. William's Chapel.[16] In 1954, an additional 19 acres was bought from a "Mr. Kenneth Harper."[17] This camp was used for decades as a summer vacation spot for the monastic community. Many monks interviewed for this book reminisced about their experiences at "camp" when they were youths. The camp afforded swimming, caving, hiking and fun. In June 1969, for example, the *Community Bulletin* (newsletter for the monastic community) announced a new item for camp that year. "The Holland Dairy will stop each week to replenish the supply of milk and ice cream," likely to the delight of the campers.[18] Each monk was generally allowed one week during the summer for his vacation at the camp.

Alas, in the late 1960s, the state decided that the acreage was ideal for a park in the Wyandotte Cave area as part of its expanding recreation and park system. The Archabbey was forced to sell the property in 1972. The state offered about $42,000 for the land. The *Community Bulletin* reports, "if we accept this offer (and it seems we have little choice) we have until January 1, 1973 to vacate the premises."[19] In November, it was announced, "Camp Benedict has been stripped of all movable furnishings and is now, to all intents and purposes, abandoned to the State of Indiana."[20]

However, the following month, the monks approved the purchase of about three acres of property on the northwest side of Troy, IN, for Camp Benedict II. It adjoined the Anderson River and had three cabins. A mortgage was negotiated for the property and cabins.[21] Besides being used in the summer, fall outings were also held at the camp.[22] However, in the last decade of the 20th century, as the size of the monastic community decreased and more monks took vacations with family and friends, the camp was used to a lesser extent. Some of the older monks did not like it, and it was also subjected to vandalism.[23] With these changes and the general financial concerns of the mid-1990s, the camp was sold to Bob Tuggle and family in February 1997.[24]

General Agriculture

In the spring of 1854, Fr. Jerome Bachmann, OSB, who was sent to the new foundation as its first, but contentious, prior, began to cultivate a small section for growing crops. Since the fields were newly cleared forests, plowing was difficult. He also rented three other farms to settlers. In July 1854, seven young brother candidates from Germany came to the mission to join three candidates, already there, to help with the physical labor. However, during this first year, death, malaria, intestinal disorders and other illnesses incapacitated many connected to the community.[25]

During this first year, the agriculture endeavors were not very successful. A disastrous drought struck the Midwest during that year, resulting in little produce from the orchards and fields. In 1855, three new missionary monks were sent, including Fr. Athanasius Tschopp, OSB, as the second prior, to deal with the many problems of the mission. Liquidating the property was considered by the abbot at Einsiedeln, but the monks, led by the new prior, preferred to persevere.[26]

Fortunately, 1855 had a bountiful harvest "in the field, meadow, and orchard."[27] By 1856, 16 hired hands were employed. They, plus the members of the community, all lived together in the small log cabin on the property. This crowding, lack of screens and poor sanitation contributed to illnesses among the men. In the fall of that year, a two-story frame building was completed. The following spring, separate quarters were built for the hired hands.[28]

Fr. Wolfgang Schlumpf, OSB, volunteered to come to Saint Meinrad from Einsiedeln in 1862. In 1864, he became procurator (business manager). In this position, he took over management of the farm and building activities.[29] By 1867, the farm was making an income. Kleber notes, "an orchard and a vineyard were planted and cared for; an extensive tract of land was cultivated; the largely swampy Anderson Valley was drained; the forest was cleared; buildings erected."[30] However, there were only a few brothers to work the land. Most of the work was being done by hired farmhands, and they consumed a large part of the farm income. During that year, two brothers made their profession, including Br. Bernardine Olinger, OSB, who was put in charge of the farm and the farmhands under the authority of Fr. Wolfgang.[31]

Farm operations continued to expand into the 20th century, along with land management practices. In the first few decades of the century, many young men from Germany came to the community to work. Fr. Simeon Daly, OSB, discusses the farm operation in the mid-1930s. "These older German Brothers were primarily farm workers and craftsmen.... We had a hog and a beef farm. The community reaped much from these industries. All through the depression our table was fed by our own industry—primarily farming.... In the post-World War II years, 1,000 people, including students, monks, faculty and co-workers, were being fed by the farm operations."[32]

Who was in charge of agricultural, livestock and other aspects of farm life is often unclear. The overseer of all agricultural and related operations was often the administrative position called the "oeconomo" or "econome." However, the procurator (business manager) sometimes acted as general manager. A day-to-day manager of the farm, or a particular operation, was also appointed. Various monks assisted, and laymen were hired for many of the jobs. The oeconomo in the 20th century included Fr. Louis Fuchs, OSB (1910-1943), Fr. Dominic Metzler, OSB (1943-57), and Fr. Joseph Mort, OSB (1958-64). Br. Damian Schlepers, OSB, was in charge of the Archabbey Farms in the late 1960s and 1970s.[33]

Other monks who supervised various farm operations included Br. Dominic Warnecke, OSB (1966-1973), and Br. Benjamin Brown, OSB, and Br. Luke Hodde, OSB, from 1973 to 1974.[34] In 1971, Fr. John Thuis, OSB, was head of sandstone, farm, dairy, chickens and the coal mine; he was procurator two times (1935-56; 1959-62).[35] Novices and students often worked on the farm. Br. Terence Griffin, OSB, for example, notes that, as a novice, he helped with the chickens and gathered eggs under the direction of "an elderly brother called Br. Donald Delbeke from Belgium."[36]

By the late 1960s, Saint Meinrad Archabbey Farms had flowered into an award-winning enterprise, both in terms of production and conservation. In 1968, the *Community Bulletin* reports, "Judges have awarded top honors to the Abbey Farms in the Spencer County Greener Pastures Program. This is a county program to encourage country farmers to promote better conservation of their farmland."[37] The Archabbey had won the county's top honors for three successive years.

The award was based upon a number of factors. These included the variety of grasses grown on pasture and hay land, production per acres in terms of tons of hay and corn silage, and the pasture rotation system. Production of beef and dairy cattle, soil conservation practices and land use to its fullest potential were also examined. Br. Damian accepted the outstanding farmer award for the monastic community. The following July, the Archabbey hosted the event, and Saint Meinrad Archabbey Farms was at the peak of its reputation and production.[38]

Livestock

From the very first year of the community, livestock was kept. By the end of May 1854, "the stables and the yard were stocked with two horses, a foal, a team of oxen, a cow and a calf, a ewe with a young one, two young sheep, twenty chickens, four geese, one beehive…and one dog, and one cat."[39] From the viewpoint of the turn of the 21st century, this little farm, with the exception of the oxen, would be typical of a Hoosier hobby farm. Money would be spent, but little, if any, income would be gained from the operation.

Due to a number of factors, to be discussed later, the last of Saint Meinrad's livestock were sold in 1974. Rabbits were raised as a hobby by one monk for about ten years into the mid-1990s. In 2007, the only creatures raised were honey bees, for which there are six colonies cared for by Fr. Anthony Vinson, OSB.[40] Since little information is readily available concerning the livestock operations at the Archabbey, only the briefest description of this aspect of the farm operation will be discussed.

Chickens and Hogs

Both chickens and hogs were raised as food for the community from its very beginnings. In the early years, "hogs were usually let run free to forage in the woods."[41] Later they were moved further away from the monastery complex. Chickens also likely roamed the grounds, as grubs were a ready supply of food. Kleber reports that until 1931 "the old chicken yard with its many unsightly sheds [was located] just south of the road leading down to the Abbey cemetery.... In January, 1931, a long and neat poultry house was erected south east of the vineyard. In December, 1939, a duplicate was built just west of it."[42]

In the years of the mid-20th century, Br. Dominic Warnecke reports that, "Br. Donald Delbeke took care of the chickens for years and when he died in 1963, Br. Casimir [Wisniewski, OSB] took care of them."[43] The poultry business was one of the first major farm businesses to be closed. In 1967, a study was conducted by Archabbey personnel, in conjunction with members of the agricultural department of Purdue University. Results of the study suggested it would be best to "specialize in dairy, swine, beef, and grain crops" as part of the overall development plan for the farm. A lack of monastic manpower, and because it had become almost as cheap to buy eggs from area farmers as it was to produce them, led to this decision. The operation was closed in the summer of 1967.[44] The chicken houses were then used for storage, enterprises of Abbey Press such as sculpture making, and later as art and woodworking work-shops for the monks. The red-painted chicken houses remain today to the northwest of the gift shop.

The hog farm was the next livestock business to go. Br. Terence notes, "They raised the hogs; fattened them until they got a certain weight, then they slaughtered them. They were for our consumption."[45] By 1969, the "swine herd produced about 850 pigs for market each year."[46] However, the hog farm was closed in July 1971. The state had determined that the operation, where it was located, had improper drainage into the Anderson River. To comply with the new state regulations, the hog pens and houses would have to be relocated and a holding tank for wastes built. The lack of space, available capital, and monks to construct and operate a renovated enterprise did not justify the expense. After its closure, the large buildings were used for storage and small ones torn down.[47]

Dairy Cows and Beef Cattle

Kleber reports that, in 1869, a 300-foot-long stable for cattle and horses was built.[48] A dairy and beef cattle operation was built up over the years. Abbot Ignatius Esser, OSB, considered the dairy enterprise essential. His first building project "was the construction of a dairy barn south of the garden land. The old, unsightly stable off the east front of the monastery was torn down. The cows were transferred to the new building in January, 1931. The word 'stable' no longer befitted the new building; it was a modern dairy barn—'The Abbey Dell Dairy Barn'— clean, well-lighted, and with modern equipment. Apart from the 'nursery,' and 'the kindergarten,' and enclosures for two bulls, there are stanchions for fifty cows."[49]

Br. Terence recalls that when he first came in the 1950s, "they had dairy cows, but we did not have anything to do with that." A popular pastime for guests would be tours of the milking parlor and watching the cows being milked.[50] In 1965, however, this popular attraction was closed to visitors and monks alike. The monastic community was told to stay out of the buildings in which the farm animals were housed, because of the possibility of spreading diseases to the livestock.[51]

Beginning around 1965, due to an expanding dairy operation and new health department requirements, updated equipment was installed and new construction at the Abbey Dell Dairy was carried out. In 1965, a "bulk tank," which chilled the milk, was established in the dairy for the storage of milk. Two new silos were completed by the summer of 1967, and a new milking parlor, "located between the loafing shed" and the main barn, was completed in the summer of 1968. Adhering to these regulations allowed the farm to get top prices for the sale of excess milk.[52]

In 1969, the dairy herd consisted of 65 milking cows and 30 bred heifers. In addition, there were 90 head of young dairy calves.

Br. Damian, superintendent of the farm, in consultation with Purdue University, began an expansion "toward a goal of 100 milking cows."[53]

By the mid-1960s, the dairy was an award-winning operation. The herd received a silver medal for excellence at Purdue University and a "meritorious sire award" for its Holstein dairy cattle. The dairy was accepted by the American Breeder Service of Deforest, WI, for "progeny testing of bulls." This meant that the herd was "now on a computerized genetic mating service."[54]

The beef cattle business has waxed and waned for decades. In the mid-1960s, the price of beef went up. This led to a decision "to get back into the beef business." The *Community Bulletin* reports, "Br. Damian will begin buying feeders and fattening them up for the packing plant."[55] By 1969, the farm had 73 head of beef on a "feeder program" with 88 head of beef having been marketed. Br. Damian notes, "It is hoped that this will be increased to 300 head annually."[56]

Most of the beef cattle were Black Angus. In 1971, Saint Meinrad Archabbey was elected to the Aberdeen Angus Association as a breeder of registered Angus cattle. Some experimental breeding was also accomplished in 1971. Cattle were bred that could gain more weight on improved pasture lands in terms of pounds of beef per acre. Under the direction of Br. Damian, a new experimental cross of a Holstein dam and Simmental bull was produced. This heifer was to be bred to a Charolais bull so that this cross would increase the weight of the animal for market.[57] By 1973, the beef herds consisted of around 136 head of registered Black Angus and Holstein-Simmental cattle, and about 340 acres of corn, silage and soybeans were under cultivation for livestock feed.[58]

However, at the peak of the farm's success, stricter governmental regulations mandated even more expensive equipment to continue the farm operation. In 1971, the Department of Agriculture drew up stricter regulations for milk producers and distributors.[59] To meet compliance for Grade A milk, expensive new equipment and upgrading the dairy would be needed. Without changes, the dairy would be able to sell Grade C milk for cheese making, but there was little profit in it. Changes in tax laws related to charitable organizations deemed that income derived from "unrelated businesses," such as the farm, would now be taxed. See the "Finance and Fund Raising" chapter for more detail.

Fr. Simeon adds, "Farming got to a point where a small farmer couldn't sell produce for the cost it took to raise it.... Even though we had made money before, we were losing money and our equipment was beginning to wear out. If we wanted to do a decent job we would have to have more tractors and build another silo. These things would cost a hundred thousand dollars and we didn't have a hundred thousand dollars to spend. So we had to sell off our farming operation."[60] In 1972, there were only a couple of monks working on the farm. This meant high wages were being paid to outside help.

On March 22, 1974, the *Community Bulletin* reports, "The community decided to liquidate our agricultural assets with the exception of real estate."[61] The fields were leased to a neighbor to bring in income, because lease payments weren't taxable. The farm buildings were converted into space for the growing Abbey Press. The registered Holstein dairy herd was sold. On June 18 and 19, an auction was held. The Archabbey sold its registered Angus beef cattle, including the 5-year-old sire "Clank Jr. of Ennis, one of the best Angus bulls you have seen anywhere."[62]

The majority of farm implements, dairy equipment and agricultural machinery were also sold. Even the sawmill and truck scales from the no-longer-used quarry were auctioned. The farm crew, assisted by a wide assortment of community volunteers, harvested the remaining wheat crop and baling straw. It was sold to the highway department for the new I-64 interstate that was being constructed.[63] However, a custom butchering operation at the packing plant continued until 1985, when it was no longer profitable.

Marian Mission and Cattle Ranch in Tennessee

Although the farm operations at the Archabbey were soon to be closed, a few monks still had the opportunity to be in the farming and cattle business, even though it was away from the Archabbey. As part of the "back to the land movement" of the late 1960s and early 1970s, a primitive subsistence existence and a new foundation were attempted under the authority of Archabbot Gabriel Verkamp, OSB. In the spring of 1970, the archabbot was asked by the Diocese of Nashville if he would like to start a new foundation, and to minister to the few families in the parish, at South Pittsburgh, TN. For this purpose, the Nashville Diocese was willing to donate 600 acres of land on the Tennessee River.

The archabbot agreed, and Fr. Basil Mattingly, OSB, and Fr. Joseph Mort—who had been the farm manager—were appointed in May 1970 to start the Marian Mission.[64] However, this new mission did not receive support from Saint Meinrad. The *Community Bulletin* reports that the land, "Besides furnishing subsistence for the monks,…will provide an experimental project in development of land and timber."[65] Three months after they had arrived, a trailer with water and electricity and another trailer, which served as chapel and library, had been established.

To buy fertilizers, seed, fencing and other farm needs, donations were accepted and fundraisers were held to support this experimental community. Fr. Joseph, however, soon left and went back to the Archabbey.[66] Fr. Basil began to rehabilitate the despoiled woodlands and to clear land for pasture and hay, mostly on his own, and with occasional volunteer help from local people and Saint Meinrad monks. He bought pigs, cattle and farm machinery.[67]

In the meantime, Fr. Paschal Boland, OSB, had seen the Virgin of the Poor shrine in Banneux, Belgium. He thought a hill on the mission property would be a good place for a replica of the shrine. Several brothers from Saint Meinrad worked for short periods of time in the late 1970s on the chapel, including Br. Terence, Br. Vincent Brunette, OSB, and Br. Anselm Clark, OSB, who stayed for a few years. Fr. Donald Walpole, OSB, decorated the chapel with a mosaic. The sandstone flagstones were from the Saint Meinrad quarry. In 1983, the shrine was dedicated.[68] Later, when Fr. Augustine Davis, OSB, headed the mission, a "Walk Around Rosary" was created. Tiles representing each rosary bead were imbedded in the concrete sidewalk surrounding the shrine.[69]

By the mid-1980s, Fr. Basil had a cattle operation of about 40 head of red "white-face cattle." After working there for 16 years, Fr. Basil asked for permission to teach in Africa.[70] Fr. Richard Hindel, OSB, replaced him for a few months. Then Fr. Augustine took over the mission in December 1988. He recalls, "I was sent to the mission to close it down."[71]

However, rather than closing it, Fr. Augustine expanded the farm operation. He reports that, over the ten years he managed the farm, "the herd of cattle doubled to about 100, and the forty families in the parish also grew to about a hundred." Besides taking care of the cattle, each year he put up about 200 bales of hay for the winter. Two years before he left the mission, the farming operation was closed. The pasture and hay field were rented and the cattle sold to neighboring farmers. Fr. Augustine returned to the Archabbey in June 1996.

Gardens, Orchards and Vineyards

The pioneer monks of Saint Meinrad cleared the land to obtain arable land in which they could grow crops for their own survival. During the first year of its foundation in 1854, wheat was sown, and apple trees and grapevines were planted. The gardens, orchards and vineyards served the community for a little over a hundred years. They had all been shut down by the end of the 20th century.

Orchards and Gardens

Kleber, in his history, reports, "By April 15, 1854, 150 apple trees… had been planted."[74] How much of this original planting survived the drought that summer or where they were planted is not readily known. Tradition suggests that an apple orchard was planted below the vineyard along the south and east side of the hill below the monastery in 1868.[75] Fr. Theodore Heck, OSB, recalls that a second orchard was later planted on the north side of the monastic hill and another one near the current Guest House.[76]

The orchards, over the years, produced many apples. Fr. Eric Lies, OSB, recalls as a young monk, "When apples were in season, at each meal we would get three kinds of apples. Fresh apples, stewed apples or apple pancakes."[77] In 1946, the monastery purchased some land in back of the Monte Cassino Chapel. Br. Jerome Croteau, OSB, writes that, "Brother Nicholas Orth planted an orchard and constructed a lake on the property."[78] Br. Ambrose Kaschmitter, OSB, was in charge of orchards from 1954 to 1961.[79] One problem with the orchards, and especially the one near Monte Cassino, was that it was difficult to keep the deer from eating the apples.[80]

The monastery, since its beginnings, had a vegetable garden. The garden in the 1930s was planted on the flat area to the east of the monastery. Fr. Fintan Baltz, OSB, expanded the garden during World War II. He was also instrumental in building a small lake, named after him, near the garden. A sandstone pumping station distributed water from the lake to the garden through a network of buried pipes.

Br. Benedict Barthel, OSB, recalls that the garden, "at its peak, extended—more or less—from Lake Fintan eastward to highway 545; southward to the entrance road running past the former Gessner residence; westward to the present road running north and south past the lake.... In the garden spinach, potatoes, tomatoes and corn were grown."[81] "Eating corn," as opposed to corn for livestock, was used for making "nonsense." This was a crumbled type of cornbread served with syrup and butter, which was eaten for breakfast (See Appendix A for recipe).

During its most productive years, Fr. Fintan's "Victory Garden" ranged from ten to 20 acres. Students from the high school and seminary worked in it. The garden fed the monastic community and its students, and excess produce was sold. Novices were put to work taking the eyes out of the potatoes harvested from the garden. The potatoes were stored for the winter in a potato cellar. In 1940, a new cellar was built into the slope east of the vineyard to replace one previously constructed around 1928, which was deficient.[82]

Upon Fr. Fintan's death in 1960, the large vegetable gardens were closed. They were reopened a year later and produced record yields, but were soon closed again the following year when it became evident that there was not enough available manpower to make it economical. By

December 1962, all of the Archabbey gardens had been closed down, and the gardening equipment and supplies had been relocated or sold to outside concerns.[83] In March 1963, the barn and greenhouse, associated with the gardens, were torn down. By 1964, a catering company was hired to cook the meals; they were required to purchase their own produce.[84] Some community members were not happy that the brothers no longer controlled the kitchen.[85]

However, in 1966, Br. Anselm was appointed kitchen manager, after the current manager of the catering firm, Crotty Brothers, left. He was considered part of their organization.[86] In the 1980s, the catering service was discontinued and the Archabbey hired its own chefs and co-workers in the kitchen.[87]

From the mid- to the late-1980s, Br. Flavian Schwenk, OSB, Br. Angelo Vitale, OSB, and Br. Dominic resurrected the vegetable garden near Lake Fintan for a few years. The large harvest supplied the kitchen, thus saving money. The brothers grew tomatoes, green peppers, squash, corn, green beans, cucumbers, cantaloupe, eggplants, cabbage and other vegetables over this period.[88]

This garden was again discontinued due to the lack of manpower. However, Fr. Harry Hagan, OSB, notes, "We still have a little garden. Mainly 50 tomato plants, some green beans for novices to pick, and some cucumbers to make icebox dills."[89] By the late 1990s, other than this little garden, the farming traditions of the Archabbey had disappeared.

John Wilson, the treasurer/business manager, notes with some sadness that the monastery went from "being almost totally self-sufficient to one of the few things that's left...the garden."[90] This feeling is also expressed by Br. Terence. He remembers, "We had at one time a farm, a dairy, beef cattle. To feed the cattle, we had hay and corn. We had a vineyard, hogs and a packing plant, which was our own food. That's an example of what's come and gone."[91]

Vineyards and Wine Making

Vineyards and wine making have been associated with monastic communities since the Middle Ages. However, conflicting opinions exist as to whether monks, or wealthy laity, saved the secrets of viticulture from antiquity. Seward (1975) suggests that monastic communities had the resources and security to patiently improve the quality of their vines over generations. Younger (1966), on the other hand, suggests that the laity gifted their vineyards to the Church. Either way, by the end of the high Middle Ages (1300 c.e.), the Church had numerous vineyards on the Continent. Wine was used, not only for the Mass, but also for daily consumption in climatic regions where the grape was easily cultivated.

The Saint Meinrad monastic community, in the warmer southern region of Indiana near the Ohio River, was one of the first winemakers in the state. Kleber, in his history, reports that in 1857, Fr. Athanasius, the second prior, described the abundance and qualities of wild grapes that could be, and were used, for making Mass wine.[93] Kleber notes, "By April 15, 1854...more than 1000 grapevine cuttings had been planted."[31] The traditional date for planting the vineyard that was used until the mid-1950s, was 1868. This vineyard was located on the south and east hillside at the base of the monastery-seminary complex.[95]

Who was the vintner, the wine maker, or even the individual in charge of the wine cellar, and the dates they served in these capacities, is not always clear. In the early years in the community of the monks interviewed for this book, Br. Wendelen Rust, OSB (1936-39), Br. Wolfgang Mieslinger, OSB (1940-44), and Br. Bartholomew Enright, OSB (1945-52), had major responsibilities for viticulture or wine making.[96]

Since the early 1950s, the landscaping and grounds crew also took care of the orchards and vines. Br. Jerome, for example, worked in both the vineyard and wine cellar (1952-85). By the early 1950s, Br. Herman Zwerger, OSB, was supervisor of the wine cellar and the winemaker. Other monks who worked in the vineyard in the 1950s included Br. Charles DeSutter, OSB, and sometimes Br. Ambrose Kaschmitter, OSB, who was in charge of the orchards.[97] Br. Kim Malloy, OSB, served as winery manager (1966-71), and Br. Mario Ibison, OSB, worked in the vineyards from around 1971 to the early 1990s.[98]

The most noted vintner and winemaker was Br. David Petry, OSB, who spent over 20 years (1965-86) in the enterprise. Br. Dominic recalls that, "During the time when Br. David Petry was in charge of the grounds and vineyard, the vineyard was expanded from the 5 acres to 10 acres."[99] In July 1971, the Abbey Wine Cellar and the Vineyard and Orchard Departments were combined into one unit, called the "Vineyard & Wine Cellar Department." Br. David was appointed head of this department. Under his guidance, the wine operation reached its zenith and waned after his death in 1986.[100]

Br. Dominic, who had been an assistant in the landscaping and vineyard department (1971-81) and the wine cellar, replaced Br. David as manager of the vineyard in 1985. In 1991, Br. Dominic acted primarily as vintner. Br. Benjamin Brown became winemaker in 1991 until the operation was closed in 1998. Trina Paulin (an employee) became supervisor of landscaping and vintner around 1995.[101]

In his essay, "The Vineyard Remembered," Br. Jerome recalls that when he arrived as a candidate at Saint Meinrad in September 1947, the vineyard was located on a three-acre section of land behind the carpenter shop (on the southeast side of the monastic complex hill) and that Br. Bartholomew Enright, OSB, was in charge of it.[102] He writes that the "vines were about seventy-five years old, and each year were producing less and less grapes, requiring us to purchase about half of the grapes needed for wine making."[103]

"In 1953," he explains, "I went to St. Stanislaus seminary, St. Louis, Missouri, which was operated by the Society of Jesus. The community operated a forty-acre vineyard and produced Mass wine for sale to the public. The purpose of this trip was to get some information on how to operate a similar vineyard and winery here at St. Meinrad."[104]

In the fall of 1954, five acres of land on Monte Cassino were prepared for the spring planting of a new vineyard. Br. Jerome, in his essay, discusses the planting in some detail. The crew made concrete posts weighing over 300 pounds, similar to ones they had seen at the St. Stanislaus vineyard. The rows for the vines were about 210 feet long and two posts were placed at each end with ten posts between the ends. In February 1955, Br. Charles was also assigned to work in the vineyard. He and Br. Jerome were the primary planters of the new vineyard.[105]

In the late spring of 1955, "Concord grapes, which do not make the best type of wine, but they grow well in this area [were planted]," notes Br. Jerome.[106] The old vineyard near the monastery complex was destroyed. During the second year, the first crop of ten tons was harvested. "The third year crop amounted to forty tons, and we were unsure what to do with such a large crop...only later were we able to dispose of the surplus crop by selling it to the Meyer winery in Cincinnati, Ohio."[107]

Picking the ripened grapes was generally the job of younger members of the community. Br. Terence remembers, "It took a week. The novices and anyone else who volunteered would do this. I volunteered a few times…. We used a clipper that almost looks like a wire snipper. You would use those to clip a bunch of grapes."[108] Working in the vineyard was very hard work. Wilson recalled that, when he first came to work at the Archabbey, "Because it had been their history and tradition, we always took the juniors and novices up there [to the vineyard] at Monte Cassino in August in the terrible heat. The great big hornets hollowed the core out of the grape. So [the novices] would go up there to do some physical work for a week or so and haul the grapes here."[109]

In 1958, the St. Stanislaus winery closed down. Their wine making equipment, including vats, was bought to improve wine making at Saint Meinrad. However, the wine was not always the best. Br. Jerome reports, "Abbot Bonaventure had been receiving complaints regarding the bitter/sour taste of the Mass wine, and I was told to give Father [Tom Leibold, who operated a winery for his community] samples of our Mass wine to be tested…. it showed that [it] had almost reached the point of turning into vinegar." Because of this problem, in 1965 Mass wine was bought until Br. David began to make good wine around 1974.[110]

In the fall of 1972, soon after Br. David was made head of both the vineyard and wine making, he and Brs. Mario, Dominic and Jerome took a tour of the vine-growing areas of northeastern United States. This resulted in the first wine-tasting party ever at the Archabbey, which continued almost annually until the winery was closed. In January 1973, Br. David was sent for a year to Hammonds Port, NY, in the Finger Lakes Region, to study the operations of the vineyards and wine making in the region.[112] It was hoped that Saint Meinrad's Abbey Wine might eventually develop into a commercial venture.

Under Br. David's guidance, several varieties of grapes were added to the Archabbey's vineyard, including European vinifera such as Chardonnay, Merlot and Cabernet Sauvignon. Several did not survive because of the differences in climate and soil. The De Charnac grape was most frequently fermented for Mass wine. The Concord grape was used to make everyday table wine for the monastery.[113] Wilson notes that the vineyard and wine making was Br. David's "love and his passion, and he made really good wine.... Saint Meinrad was a dry red wine."[114]

The wine cellar was in the basement archway between what is now St. Anselm and Sherwood halls near the current Development Office. Several large fermenting vats and barrels were located there. Grapes would be brought in boxes into what is called the "Holly Courtyard." The grapes would be dumped through a chute into the cellar for fermentation and processing. In the spring of 1987, the wine cellar moved to the old packing plant, headed by Br. Dominic and his ground crew. Since it was above ground, it was now called a winery. The old cellar was turned into offices.[115]

The grape harvest, like most other harvests, waxed and waned due to weather and other factors. From 1965 to 1973, large harvests from 20 to 30 tons of grapes were picked and about 3,000 gallons of wine were processed. In 1967, no grapes were picked for use by the community as they had an ample supply.[116] In September 1972, another bumper crop was described.[117] Br. Jerome recalls that, "In the olden days we were probably getting around 6 to 8 tons near here."[118]

However, the following year, the *Community Bulletin* reports, "This past spring the vineyards suffered considerable damage from two late frosts. Due to this fact, the crop of grapes this year will be about half the take as last year. Therefore, your brother vineyard keepers will have to reserve the whole crop this year for the monastic community, and sales of grapes to the outside will have to be curtailed completely for this season."[119] Again in 1976, the grape harvest failed and wine was rationed to only Sundays and feast days.[120]

However, through the early and mid-1980s, large harvests were reported. The *Community Bulletin* reports, in 1984 for example, "It seems that it was a good year. We had plenty of grapes for our needs and we also sold a good amount of grapes.... The grapes are picked, the firewood is stacked outside the calefactory, the air is cool in the morning, can fall be far away?"[121]

The year after Br. David's death, the harvest declined. The monastic community was told that wine would not be served in the refectory during Lent except on Sundays and feast days because there was only 25 gallons on hand.[122] Although there was a good crop in 1989, after 1991 the grape production and enthusiasm for the operation waned. By 1995, the grape harvest consisted of only seven tons of Concord grapes, three tons of a French hybrid and only a few pounds of white grapes.[123]

In January 1997, Archabbot Lambert Reilly, OSB, announced that, in consultation with Br. Benjamin, the current winemaker, and business management, the vineyard would be closed and wine making would cease. He noted, "We have enough table wine to last for about 18 months to 2 years. The Mass wine will be depleted in approximately 6-8 months.[124] Wilson recalls, "We did a little search and found we could buy it cheaper and with better quality. So we ripped the five acres of grapes out. I hated it personally because of my personal interest in it."[125] At Thanksgiving 1998, the first purchased wine was served to the community.[126]

The closing of the winery, the orchards, the garden and vineyard brought disappointment and sadness to several monks. For example, Br. Terence notes, "I was disappointed that they were closing the wine cellar. Ideally, a hundred years ago, the monks were supposed to be independent and do everything themselves. In this day and age, you buy from a company in large economy size."[127]

Fr. Theodore (who came to the community in 1918) recollects, "These old grapes—years ago, we would have large vineyards, large orchards, and had plenty of vegetables and fruits. But the restrictions became so great in so many ways, especially when we had to do so much spraying that it became as costly to spray as it was to buy the food. So we [gave these up] because of the problems.... We raised most of the things we grew, we grew what we needed. We had a large herd of cattle and a herd of steer cattle for butchering and we had our own milk cows. We had our own butcher shop...three-fourths of the food we raised right here on the grounds; if we could do that again, that would be a big help to us."[128]

Sandstone

Kleber, in his history of Saint Meinrad, writes, "A great asset to the building activity of the Abbey were its stone quarry and its forests."[129] Sandstone useful for building construction was noted by pioneer members of the community. The first prior, Fr. Athanasius, quoted by Kleber, points out the many outcroppings of a "solid, yellowish sandstone," which Fr. Bede thought, if one had the money, beautiful churches could be built.[130] The monks, in the late 1860s, opened their first quarry close to the current Monte Cassino Shrine, about a mile from the monastery. It provided stone for the buildings of the original monastery, the seminary and church, and small outbuildings. Years later, the Archabbey opened another quarry north of this location as a successful commercial business.[131]

From the late 1860s and throughout the next ten years, the Saint Meinrad community constructed new buildings using sandstone from the quarry. The first stones quarried were used for a shrine to Mary on the Monte Cassino hill. The foundation stone for this shrine was laid September 20, 1868, and the sanctuary completed in April 1870.[132]

Preparations for construction of a new monastery were made in 1869 with Fr. Wolfgang Schlumpf, OSB, the procurator, in charge of the building activity for the new structure. On the afternoon of May 2, 1872, the first stone for the monastery was laid. The largest ones were hauled from the quarry to the building site by teams of oxen. In addition to hired workers, brothers, novices, candidates and students helped with the construction. In September 1874, the first and second floors were occupied and the seminary students moved into the old wooden monastery. In 1878-79, the sandstone building for students, attached to the monastery, was built.[133]

Alas, the monastery and seminary buildings were destroyed in the great fire of October 5, 1887. After the fire, Saint Meinrad sandstone was used again to rebuild the buildings. Fr. Benno Gerber, OSB, the new procurator, directed the reconstruction. The monks moved into the restored monastery on October 6, 1889. Further construction then expanded the original structure beyond its original footprint in 1892 and 1893. In 1896, a northward extension on the monastery was completed.[134]

Abbot Athanasius Schmitt, OSB, elected in 1898, constructed a number of buildings throughout his reign. Most, but not all, used the Archabbey's sandstone. The most ambitious project was the Abbey Church. This massive Romanesque structure dominates the hill on which it still stands. Fr. Benno supervised the construction. The sandstone was dressed with chisel and mallet, as no saws or compressed air hammers were available. On June 16, 1899, the first stone was laid, and on the feast of St. Benedict, March 21, 1907, the community entered the church for the first time.[135]

Within a few years of the completion of the church, Saint Meinrad sandstone was used for a new east-west wing of the monastic-seminary complex near the church to house the library, chapter room and brothers oratory. Fr. Benno was too old, so Fr. Augustine Haberkorn, OSB, took over as building master. The first stone was laid July 19, 1911, and the building was finished at the end of 1914. In 1922, a new major seminary (last two years of college and four years of theology) wing, which reached to near the southwest corner of the church, was built. Finely dressed sandstone was also used for the interior of this building.[136]

A new minor seminary (high school and two years of college) wing, completed in 1932, was attached to the southwest of the monastery-seminary complex. Although some small outbuildings used sandstone blocks, larger projects such as the Abbey Press (1930), for example, used buff-colored brick. St. Bede Hall (1950) was constructed of concrete with a sandstone veneer from the new quarry. The "new library" (1982) was constructed of concrete and the "new monastery" (1982) was faced with Bedford, Indiana, sandstone.[137]

Saint Meinrad sandstone was sold for the construction of a number of churches, post offices, houses and government buildings in Indiana and neighboring states. For example, in 1934, the state used Saint Meinrad sandstone for the interior of the new Indiana State Library and Historical Building. By the 1940s, the Monte Cassino sandstone operation was closed. However, the sandstone enterprise continued on a 24-acre quarry located northeast of Monte Cassino on the Edwin Weyer farm (near the I-64 interstate). The Archabbey paid a royalty to Weyer on the per cubic foot of sandstone quarried. Fr. Rupert Ostdick, OSB, explains that the stone was cut out of the ground on the Weyer farm and transported "to the quarry-shop located just off the Ferdinand East road where it was dressed, either for our own use, or for sale to outside customers." In 1969, the Archabbey purchased the Weyer farm on which the sandstone quarry was located.[138]

During the height of its operation, from the 1950s through the mid-1960s, the St. Meinrad Sandstone Co. supplied stone for buildings in the state, region and around the country. In 1950, Saint Meinrad donated sandstone veneer for its daughter house at Blue Cloud Abbey, Marvin, SD.[139] Saint Meinrad sandstone was used for the facing of several churches, including St. Michael's, Greenfield, IN, and both the interior and exterior of Christ the King Church in Wichita, KS, and a church in Cincinnati, OH. The National Parks Service, in 1965, approved the use of Saint Meinrad sandstone in its parks. This included the Lincoln Boyhood National Memorial, Lincoln City, IN. Another large building project that used this sandstone in the mid-1960s was the Park Avenue Bridge in Long Island, NY.[140]

However, problems plagued the sandstone operation. A decreased use in sandstone and an increased use of limestone for building facings caused a decline in business in the 1960s. Problems with antiquated equipment and key personnel leaving, or becoming sick, slowed down production. By the end of the decade, declining income and increased competition from five new sandstone businesses in southern Indiana led to concern about the continuation of the enterprise.[141]

Fr. Rupert notes, "I'd say that we saw the handwriting on the wall."[142] Therefore, in the late summer of 1969, the monastic community decided to close the sandstone quarry. The *Community Bulletin* reports the decision to close the operation was "due to the 'tight money' situation, a cutback in construction generally, and the fact that some of our key employees at the quarry have decided to seek employment elsewhere." A skeleton crew was kept to fulfill current orders.[143]

Fr. Rupert recollects that, "The only piece of decent updated equipment I could remember, from that era, was a stone splitter that…made the back-breaking work of dressing the stone so much simpler and so much more efficient."[144] To keep the business competitive, a substantial investment in new equipment and paid labor would have been necessary. At this point, no monks, except the manager, Fr. John Thuis, worked in the quarry. He had been superintendent of the St. Meinrad Sandstone Co. for a number of years.[145] Br. Vincent Brunette carved tombstones from the sandstone for the Archabbey cemetery.[146] Fr. Rupert notes that "[the sandstone business] had been a part of the monastic tradition in this house since the eighteen-seventies when the first stone was quarried at Monte Cassino…. It was with a good deal of regret that we were unable to continue that."[147]

The quarry lay dormant for almost 40 years until it was reactivated in 2004 for a couple of years. In May 2003, a lease agreement was signed with Mansfield Stone, Inc. to operate "the abbey's old quarry." As part of the agreement, conservation measures were stipulated. The stone was to be cut with a diamond belt saw that had little environmental impact. The company was not allowed to blast and had to remove the stone by mechanical means. Once the stone was cut, it was hauled to Mansfield's facility in Brazil, IN, about 120 miles away, where it was cut to specification. The first stone cut, in July 2004, went for the new guest house completed in October 2005. However, at the end of June 2006, the Archabbey ended the lease agreement.[148]

Forest

Timber management, trees as a crop, and conservation measures are recent concepts arising out of the early 20th century. Prior to that time, the land was quickly, and painstakingly, cleared of forests to create tillable ground. The timber and lumber were sold and used to construct buildings and make household goods, and the scraps were used as firewood. There was little concept of forest management. "Taming the wilderness," as illustrated on the Indiana state seal, meant clearing as much forest as possible. During the early days of Saint Meinrad, the wilderness was also tamed, arable land was created and buildings were erected. Kleber, for example, reports that, "More than 1000 saw logs were cut from the monastery woods."[149]

Little information is readily available concerning the Archabbey's forest and timber operation in its earliest years. Who managed the forest, and how, is not clear. This duty was likely under the broad responsibilities of the econome, or the procurator. Since the last half of the 20th century, Fr. Joseph Mort served as econome (1958-64), and was listed as forester in 1972, as assistant forester in 1975, and again as forester in the mid-1980s until he became sick in 1988. Fr. Kevin Ryan, OSB, spent a total of about ten years as forester. He was forester in 1975, and also in the late 1980s to 1996. Fr. Guy Mansini, OSB, has served as forester since 1996, and remains in this position today. Since the mid-1970s, the forester, in addition to this position, also had other jobs including teaching or being pastor of a parish.[150]

In the latter part of the 20th century, forestry management became an important activity of the Archabbey. It remains the only land-related activity still under control of the community today.

In 1967, the Archabbey cooperated with Purdue University in "a provenance study" on rapid growth of timber for use as pulp, saw timber and veneer backing. "A half-acre plot, located below Monte Cassino on the Anderson River was planted with hybrid poplars on April 1."[151] A thinning harvest was expected in 20 years with the remaining trees being allowed to grow to maturity for saw wood. The experiment would also determine the environmental range for such tree farms.[152]

A decade later, in 1976, 1,100 acres of timberland, owned by the community, were being managed by the Archabbey forestry department. This acreage was divided into eight separate forests in the vicinity of the Archabbey; the largest consisted of 650 acres. Ongoing timber stand improvement measures included eliminating wild grape vines and cutting down "trash trees," such as sassafras, to make sure small hardwood trees got enough light. The Archabbey forest department also grew Christmas trees, cut posts for use in the vineyard and provided firewood for general use at Camp Benedict. Other management projects consisted of constructing and repairing forest roads and fire breaks, logging pines, planting trees, and measuring and marketing trees for harvest.[153]

In the late 1970s, a government grant for timber stand improvement was submitted. In July 1977, the *Community Bulletin* announced that "Archabbey forest was given a 'share-fund' grant for timber-standing improvement for areas that have been logged out lately, and also funds for the improvement of fire lanes, which will allow easier access to work areas.... The funds are being used in the largest of our eight holdings, the so-called Dotterweich Forest, which covers one square mile in Perry County."[154]

Twenty years later, the Archabbey's good forestry management and tree planting brought an abundant timber harvest. In 1997, around 160,000; in 1999, 94,000; and in 2000, 84,000 board feet of timber were sold. In 2002, the Archabbey sold 786 trees on 63 acres in Perry County. In 2004, it sold to Leibering & Sons of Lamar, IN, over 452,000 board feet of white pine, 36,000 feet of yellow pine, about 30,000 board feet of hardwood, plus approximately 45 acres of red and Virginia pine to be used as pulp wood.[155]

Tree planting to replace the harvested trees also took place in the first few years of the 21st century. By 2005, about nine acres of hardwood had been planted during the previous six years, three acres near the sandstone quarry and six acres of oak, ash and walnut on a property called the Miller farm. This, and other acreage near the farm, was to be turned into classified forest. Timber stand improvement on 60 acres in Dotterweich Woods in Perry County was also accomplished. The Department of Natural Resources, in 2005, also approved a proposed schedule of harvest for the next 15 years.[156]

A governmental and an industrial program resulted in still more trees being planted and further conservation measures being implemented for the Archabbey forests. Although conservation tillage practices had been used for years with the Archabbey cropland along the Anderson River, the soil was subject to extensive erosion by annual flooding of the river. In addition, the majority of the drain tile under the ground was old and barely functional. Replacing the tile would be extremely expensive. Jeff and Jim Ebert, who rented this cropland from the Archabbey, brought the Wetland Reserve Program, a federal conservation program, to Saint Meinrad's attention.[157]

In this program, "the government seeks to restore or preserve wetlands, especially for the sake of wildlife preservation, soil conservation, and water purity, but not excluding timber production."[158] This plan stipulated, that "the majority of our cropland would be planted with trees as part of a thirty-year lease with the government. As part of the lease, the government would pay roughly $1,500 per acre up front along with a payment of up to approximately $400 per acre for the cost of buying and planting the trees and maintenance for the first two years after planting."[159]

Entry into the program would end all tilling of the ground, but after the end of the lease the Archabbey could do whatever it wished with the property. In 2005, about 375 acres that was presently being tilled, or used for pasture, were accepted for the forest program.[160] The Wetland Reserve Program contracts were awarded to Richard Harvey of Leavenworth, IN. Planting of mixed hardwood seedlings began in early spring 2007. Pat Clark, head of Saint Meinrad's Physical Facilities, notes, "We will be planting in excess of 345 acres. Some of the Wetland Reserve acres already have trees growing on them. The total amount of acres to be in trees is 382+ acres."[161]

John Wilson, the business manager, reports that this program is "a turning point in our history. It is also a turning point in our economic relations with the local community.... This conversion means that the Archabbey will be more involved in the local timber and wood products industry than ever, which is another important component of the economies of Perry, Spencer, and Dubois counties."[162] Furniture making, for example, had been a traditional business of these counties for decades.

The Abbey participated in another tree planting arrangement. In February 2006, Saint Meinrad entered into an agreement with Indiana & Michigan Power, owners of the nearby Rockport power plant near the Ohio River, which is part of American Electric Power (AEP). This agreement was an aspect of the "carbon bank" conservation program. It allowed industries that burn coal, or produce a large "carbon footprint," to plant trees as an effort to stabilize the level of greenhouse gases in the atmosphere. The planted trees, when mature, would be used for building construction or furniture that kept the carbon bound in the wood.

AEP planted over 80,000 trees of mixed hardwoods on 160+ acres in late spring of 2006.[163] They were planted on the old Weyer farm (near the quarry) and Moeller farm, and "also on Monte Cassino (21 ac.) and along the Monte Cassino Road to Ferdinand (23 ac.)."[164] The forest, as a crop and renewable resource, had replaced the traditional agricultural activities of the monastery by the first decade of the 21st century, but had the potential of offering sustenance from the land, in terms of its timber crop, for many years to come.

In summary, the old traditional Benedictine monastic land activities had disappeared by the late 1990s due to stringent governmental regulations, lack of passion for this type of work among younger monks, and the fact that most products were cheaper to buy than to grow or raise. Gone were the orchards, the vineyards, the dairy and cattle businesses, the hogs and chickens, and the large garden that produced enough vegetables to feed the community along with its students for much of the year. However, a forestry industry began to emerge by turn of the 21st century. Saint Meinrad Archabbey evolved from a small mid-19th century, semi-subsistence community to a 21st-century market economy in order to survive and continue its mission of educating priests and lay leaders of the Church, along with seeking God through the ancient tradition of *ora et labora*.

Author's note: The monks of the mid- to late-20th century who held leadership positions in agriculture and similar ventures are, for the most part, deceased or do not clearly remember their earlier days. Most enterprises related to the land, with the exception of forestry, have either ceased operations or are no longer under the direct control of the Archabbey; therefore, this chapter is based upon recollections of various monastic members and information from the *Community Bulletin*.

Endnotes

1. Bond, James, *Monastic Landscapes*, 2004, 36-37; see this work for extensive information concerning all aspects of the use of monastic lands by various communities in Britain.

2. Bond, 2004, 34.

3. See Davis, Cyprian, *To Prefer Nothing to Christ* (2004) and Kleber, Albert, *History of Saint Meinrad Archabbey* (1954) for information on the early history of the foundation of Saint Meinrad Archabbey.

4. Kleber, 1954, 49.

5. Kleber, 1954, 49.

6. Kleber, 1954, 49-51; Gollar, C. Walker, "The Good People of Indiana," In Davis, 2004, 38.

7. Kleber, 1954, 122.

8. Kleber, 1954, 132, 138-140.

9. Kleber, 1954, 489-90.

10. *Community Bulletin*, July 4-20, 1968; Nov. 26-Dec. 9, 1978.

11. *Community Bulletin*, July 23-29, 1967.

12. *Community Bulletin*, Nov. 3-9, 1968.

13. Kleber, 1954, 502.

14. Ibid., 499-500.

15. *Community Bulletin*, Jan. 11-18, 1974; *Community Bulletin*, March 20-26, 1977.

16. Kleber, 1954, 475.

17. *Community Bulletin*, Sept. 10-16, 1972.

18. *Community Bulletin*, June 1-7, 1969.

19. *Community Bulletin*, Sept. 10-16, 1972.

20. *Community Bulletin*, Nov. 5-11, 1972.

21. *Community Bulletin*, Dec. 10-16; *Community Bulletin*, Dec. 17-23, 1972.

22. *Community Bulletin*, Sept. 17-23, 1978.

23. *Community Bulletin*, June 30, 1996.

24. *Community Bulletin*, Feb. 23, 1997.

25. Kleber, 1954, 69, 86-88, 90. In European monasteries, the "lay" brothers did the physical work of the community.

26. Kleber, 1954, 71, 91, 105-108.

27. Ibid., 109.

28. Kleber, 1954, 110, 180, 453. In 1927, the original frame monastery building was torn down and a new frame building, St. Placid Hall, was erected on its old foundation. St. Placid Hall, in turn, was torn down in 1991.

29. Kleber, 1954, 158, 173.

30. Ibid., 140.

31. Ibid., 173-74.

32. Fr. Simeon Daly to Prof. Ruth C. Engs, June 9, 2005, interview transcription, Saint Meinrad Archabbey Archives.

33. *Community Bulletin*, June 13-19, 1971; *Community Bulletin*, Aug. 29-Sept. 4, 1971. See Abbot's Office, "Book of lists," unpublished paper, Jan. 15, 2004, Saint Meinrad Archabbey. Br. Damian is no longer a member of the community.

34. Br. Benjamin Brown to Prof. Ruth C. Engs, e-mail: Feb. 27, 2007. Br. Luke is no longer a member of the community.

35. Abbot's Office, "Book of lists," (2004).

36. Br. Terence Griffin to Prof. Ruth C. Engs, interview transcription, Nov. 19, 2005, Saint Meinrad Archabbey Archives.

37. *Community Bulletin*, July 14-20, 1968.

38. *Community Bulletin*, Jan. 26-Feb. 1, 1969; *Community Bulletin*, July 13-19, 1969.

39. Kleber, 1954, 71.

40. Mathews, Garret, "Monk learns that even when beekeeping stings, it's still sweet as honey." *Courier & Press*, Sunday, May 14, 2006.

41. Kleber, 1954, 70.

42. Ibid., 473.

43. Br. Dominic Warnecke to Prof. Ruth C. Engs, e-mail: Feb. 4-5, 2007.

44. *Community Bulletin*, June 4-10, 1967.

45. Griffin to Engs, 2005.

46. *Saint Meinrad Newsletter*, 11:1, 1969.

47. *Community Bulletin*, June 20-26, 1971.

48. Kleber, 1954, 221.

49. Ibid., 473.

50. Griffin to Engs, 2005.

51. *Community Bulletin*, Oct. 17-23, 1965.

52. *Community Bulletin*, June 27-July 3, 1965; *Community Bulletin*, July 23-29, 1967; *Community Bulletin*, Jan. 21-27, 1968; *Community Bulletin*, April 14-20, 1968.

53. *Saint Meinrad Newsletter*, 11:1, 1969.

54. *Community Bulletin*, Dec. 4-10, 1966; *Community Bulletin*, Sept. 7-13, 1969.

55. *Community Bulletin*, July 11-17, 1965.

56. *Saint Meinrad Newsletter*, 11:1, 1969.

57. *Community Bulletin*, April 25-May 1, 1971; May 23-29, 1971.

58. Richard Endress, *The Enduring Vision* (1974, 360-363).

59. "Part 1000 General provisions of federal milk marketing orders." *Title 7-Agriculture*, May 29, 1971.

60. Daly to Engs, 2005.

61. *Community Bulletin*, June 7-14, 1974.

62. Auction notice in *Community Bulletin*, June 7-14, 1974.

63. *Saint Meinrad Newsletter*, Archabbey Edition, July 1974; *Community Bulletin*, June 29-July 7, 1974.

64. *Community Bulletin*, May 31-June 6, 1970.

65. *Community Bulletin*, May 31-June 6, 1970; private communication, Fr. Augustine Davis to Prof. Ruth C. Engs, Dec. 20, 2006.

66. Unidentified newspaper clipping in *Community Bulletin*, Oct. 11-17, 1970; *Community Bulletin*, Oct. 31-Nov. 6, 1971; Davis (Augustine) to Engs, 2006.

67. *Community Bulletin*, Feb. 18-24, 1979; Davis (Augustine) to Engs, 2006.

68. *Community Bulletin*, May 1-7, 1977; *Community Bulletin*, Jan. 8-14, 1978; Davis (Augustine) to Engs, 2006.

69. Davis (Augustine) to Engs, e-mail: Feb. 3, 2007.

70. Davis (Augustine) to Engs, 2006. Fr. Basil and Br. Anselm later transferred to Prince of Peace Abbey, Oceanside, CA.

71. Davis (Augustine) to Engs, 2006; *Community Bulletin*, Dec. 19-21, 1988.

72. Davis (Augustine) to Engs, 2006.

73. *Community Bulletin*, June 2, 1996.

74. Kleber, 1954, 71.

75. See photo of Fr. Cyrinthomas, the econome, on the east side of the monastery with vines and apple trees in the mid-1890s, in Kleber, 1954, 388.

76. Fr. Theodore Heck to Prof. Ruth C. Engs, personal communication, Jan. 22, 2007.

77. Fr. Eric Lies to Prof. Ruth C. Engs, interview transcription, Aug. 22-23, 2005, Saint Meinrad Archabbey Archives.

78. Croteau, Jerome, "The Vineyard Remembered," unpublished paper, Saint Meinrad Archabbey (1991, 2).

79. Croteau, 1991, 8.

80. Fr. Theodore Heck to Prof. Ruth C. Engs, interview transcription, June 13, 2005, Saint Meinrad Archabbey Archives.

81. Br. Benedict Barthel to Prof. Ruth Engs, interview transcription, Saint Meinrad Archabbey Archives, Nov. 16, 2005; Barthel to Engs, personal communication, Feb. 27, 2007.

82. Kleber, 1954, 477.

83. *Community Bulletin*, Dec. 6, 1962; Endress, 1974, 360.

84. Endress, 1974, 360.

85. Heck to Engs, 2005.

86. *Community Bulletin*, July 31-Aug. 6, 1966.

87. Br. Terence Griffin to Prof. Ruth Engs, e-mail: Feb. 7, 2007.

88. *Community Bulletin*, Oct. 4-11, 1985; *Community Bulletin*, July 29-Aug. 5, 1988; Br. Dominic Warnecke to Prof. Ruth Engs, e-mail: Feb. 2007.

89. Fr. Harry Hagan to Prof. Ruth C. Engs, e-mail: Jan. 10, 2007.

90. Wilson to Engs, 2004.

91. Griffin to Engs, 2005.

92. Seward, *Monks and Wine* (1979, 15) and Younger, W. *Gods, Men, and Wine* (233-234) 1966. See also Engs, Ruth, "Do traditional western European drinking practices have origins in antiquity?" *Addiction Research* 2:3 (1995, 227-239).

93. Kleber, 1974, 109.

94. Ibid., 71.

95. Croteau, 1991, 1; Bridenbaugh, Russ, "Vines Age with Abbey," *Indianapolis News*, June 12, 1991, d-8.

96. See "Book of lists," 2004.

97. Croteau, 1991, 4.

98. "Book of lists;" 2004; *Community Bulletin*, Sept. 22-27, 1974.

99. Br. Dominic Warnecke to Prof. Ruth C. Engs, e-mail: Feb. 6, 2007.

100. *Community Bulletin*, July 11-17, 1971; *Saint Meinrad Newsletter*, 25:2a January 1986.

101. ORDO, "Book of Lists," 2004; *Community Bulletin*, Sept. 22-27, 1974; Warnecke to Engs, Feb, 4, 2007; Br. Benjamin Brown to Ruth C. Engs, e-mail: Feb. 27, 2007.

102. Croteau, 1991, 1.

103. Ibid., 2.

104. Ibid., 3.

105. Ibid., 4, 8.

106. Ibid., 6.

107. Ibid., 6.

108. Griffin to Engs, 2005.

109. Wilson to Engs, 2004.

110. Croteau, 1991, 7, 8.

111. *Community Bulletin*, Nov. 19-25, 1972.

112. *Community Bulletin*, Jan. 7-13, 1973.

113. *Saint Meinrad Newsletter* 29:4, Fall 1990; Bridenbaugh, 1991.

114. Wilson to Engs, 2005.

115. *Community Bulletin*, Dec. 5-12, 1986; *Community Bulletin*, March 6-13, 1987.

116. *Community Bulletin*, Aug. 29-Sept. 4, 1965; *Community Bulletin*, Oct. 2-8, 1966; *Community Bulletin*, Aug. 6-12, 1967.

117. *Community Bulletin*, Sept. 10-16, 1972.

118. Br. Jerome Croteau to Prof. Ruth C. Engs, interview transcription, July 13, 2005, Saint Meinrad Archabbey Archives.

119. *Community Bulletin*, Aug. 17-24, 1973.

120. *Community Bulletin*, Jan. 9-15, 1977; *Community Bulletin*, Feb. 20-26, 1977.

121. *Community Bulletin*, Sept. 6-12, 1984.

122. *Community Bulletin*, Feb. 7-8, 1986.

123. *Community Bulletin*, Aug. 6, 1995.

124. *Community Bulletin*, Jan. 2, 1997.

125. Wilson to Engs, 2005.

126. *Community Bulletin*, Nov. 25, 1998.

127. Griffin to Engs, 2005.

128. Heck to Engs, 2005.

129. Kleber, 1954, 429.

130. Ibid., 109.

131. In addition to the sandstone, a coal mine was run for several decades, but was closed in 1964. The coal was used by the power plant for heating and backup generation of electricity. After the mine closed, coal was bought for the steam plant (*Community Bulletin*, Dec. 13-19, 1964). In 1971, the power plant switched to natural gas to curtail air pollution (*Community Bulletin*, July 11-17, 1971).

132. Kleber, 1954, 199-202.

133. Ibid., 221, 225-229.

134. Ibid., 384, 386-387, 389.

135. Ibid., 430-32. For details of this construction, see Shaughnessy, Edward, "Construction of the Abbey Church of Saint Meinrad, 1898-1907," (2004, 438-84).

136. Kleber, 1954, 436, 438-440, 442.

137. Ibid., 477-478; Janet Braunecker, Saint Meinrad Archabbey, Physical Plant, to Prof. Ruth C. Engs, e-mail: Feb. 5, 2007.

138. Ostdick to Engs, e-mail: Feb. 1, 2007; *Community Bulletin*, May 11, 2003.

139. *Community Bulletin*, April 20-26, 1969; Kleber, 1954, 499-500.

140. *Community Bulletin*, June 27-July 3, 1965.

141. *Community Bulletin*, Nov. 21-26, 1965.

142. Rupert to Engs, 2006.

143. *Community Bulletin*, Sept. 7-13, 1969.

144. Rupert to Engs, 2006.

145. Community Bulletin, Aug. 29-Sept. 4, 1971.

146. *Saint Meinrad Newsletter*, 34:3, Summer 1995.

147. Rupert to Engs, 2006.

148. *Community Bulletin*, May 11, 2003; *Community Bulletin*, July 18, 2004; Pat Clark, head of Physical Facilities, to Prof. Ruth C. Engs, e-mail: Feb. 12, 2007.

149. Kleber, 1954, 221.

150. *Community Bulletin*, Oct. 31-Nov. 6, 1971; *Community Bulletin*, Aug. 31-Sept. 6, 1975; *Saint Meinrad Newsletter*, Archabbey Edition 17:3, January 1976; *Community Bulletin*, July 14, 1996; "Book of lists," 2004, and ORDO.

151. *Community Bulletin*, Aug. 20-26, 1967.

152. *Community Bulletin*, Aug. 20-26, 1967.

153. *Saint Meinrad Newsletter*, 17:3, January 1976.

154. *Community Bulletin*, July 10-16, 1977.

155. *Community Bulletin*, Nov. 12, 2000; *Community Bulletin*, May 5, 2002; *Community Bulletin*, Sept. 12, 2004.

156. *Community Bulletin*, Feb. 27, 2005; *Community Bulletin*, April 28, 2002.

157. *Community Bulletin*, Aug. 17, 2003.

158. *Community Bulletin*, May 1, 2005.

159. *Community Bulletin*, Aug. 17, 2003.

160. *Community Bulletin*, Aug. 17, 2003; *Community Bulletin*, May 1, 2005.

161. Clark to Engs, e-mail: Feb. 12, 2007.

162. Wilson quoted in *Community Bulletin*, April 3, 2005.

163. *Community Bulletin*, Nov. 20, 2005; *Community Bulletin*, April 30, 2006; "Saint Meinrad: News," www.saintmeinrad.edu, release date, 5/1/06, downloaded June 21, 2006; Clark to Engs, e-mail: Feb. 12, 2007.

164. Clark to Engs, e-mail: Feb. 12, 2007.

Appendix A

Recipe for "Nonsense"

The breakfast dish "nonsense" is fondly remembered by most of the older monks of Saint Meinrad Archabbey. It is also remembered by monks at Saint Meinrad's daughter houses. Although the date is not certain, it likely ceased being regularly served at the Archabbey around 1970.

The brothers, who originally made nonsense, generally used a recipe of "a handful of this and a bagful of that." Some monks thought that nonsense was fried and others thought it was baked. Therefore, it could have been based upon Germanic *Schmarren* (scrambled pancake in a skillet) or cornbread (baked) of the Yankee pioneer farmers.

During the mid-19th century, Europeans generally did not consume corn (maize); it was food for livestock only. However, Fr. Albert Kleber, OSB, historian of Saint Meinrad through 1954, mentions that in the pioneer monastic community, "ordinary bread was corn bread." Since wheat is sometimes more difficult to grow than corn in the humid Ohio Valley, perhaps the brother cooks "stretched the wheat" by adding ground corn to make their bread and nonsense.

The following recipe was re-created by the editor (Ruth C. Engs) based upon descriptions of the monks. Several versions were made and then taste-tested by the monks. The following is the one most similar to what they remembered. This recipe will serve eight adults, or four hungry young Benedictine monks.

Nonsense
> 2 cups flour
> 1 cup corn meal
> 1/2 cup sugar
> 2 teaspoons baking powder
> 1/2 teaspoon salt
> 3 large eggs
> 1/3 cup corn oil
> 3/4 cup of milk

Mix dry ingredients together in a large bowl. Mix eggs and corn oil separately and add to dry ingredients. Slowly add milk and stir. If too thick, add more milk. Spoon into a 9" x 12" heavily greased baking pan. Bake at 350 degrees for 20-25 minutes. Cool. Cut into 8 squares. Crumble a square into a cereal bowl. Serve with maple or other syrup, or molasses or apple sauce, and butter.

Printed in the United States
116867LV00004B/246/A

9 780870 294112